G000160486

Just as important is the ability to produce excellent cooking time and again. We make as many visits as we need to be sure of quality and consistency.

Our company's two founders, Édouard and André Michelin, published, in France, the first Michelin Guide in 1900 to provide motorists with practical information about where they could service and repair their cars and find quality accommodation or a good meal.
The star rating system for outstanding restaurants was introduced in 1926. These awards have become over the years, the benchmark of reliability and excellence in over twenty European countries, since 2005 in the United States and since last year in Tokyo.

We sincerely hope that the Michelin Guide Tokyo 2009 will become your favourite guide to the restaurants and hotels in Tokyo.
On behalf of all Michelin employees, we wish you the very best enjoyment in your Tokyo hotel and dining experience.

Bon appétit.

# THE MICHELIN GUIDE'S COMMITMENTS

"This volume was created at the turn of the century and will last at least as long".

**This foreword to the very first edition of the MICHELIN Guide, written in 1900, has become famous over the years and the Guide has lived up to the prediction. It is read across the world and the key to its popularity is the consistency of its commitment to its readers, which is based on the following promises.**

## Anonymous inspections:

Our inspectors make regular and anonymous visits to restaurants and hotels to gauge the quality of products and services offered to an ordinary customer. They settle their own bill and may then introduce themselves and ask for more information about the establishment. Our readers' comments are also a valuable source of information, which we can then follow up with another visit of our own.

## Independence:

Our choice of establishments is a completely independent one, made for the benefit of our readers alone. The decisions to be taken are discussed around the table by the inspectors and the editor. Inclusion in the Guide is completely free of charge.

**Selection and choice:**

The Guide offers a selection of the best restaurants and hotels.

This is only possible because all the inspectors rigorously apply the same methods.

**Annual updates:**

All the practical information, the classifications and awards are revised and updated every single year to give the most reliable information possible.

Consistency: The criteria for the classifications are the same in every country covered by the Michelin Guide.

**...And our aim:**

To do everything possible to make travel, holidays and eating out a pleasure, as part of Michelin's ongoing commitment to improving travel and mobility.

# CONTENTS

# THE MICHELIN GUIDE OVER THE YEARS

**Today the Michelin Guide and its famous red cover are known around the world. But who really knows the story behind this «travellers' bible» that has served people in many countries for many years? After winning over Europe and the United States, Bibendum – «The Michelin Man» – is now in Japan, and will relate the fantastic adventure that started in France, a long time ago...**

## The first steps

Everything began one fine day in 1900, when André and Édouard Michelin published a guide to be offered free of charge to motorists. It included information to help these pioneers (barely 3,500 automobiles were on the road) to travel around France: garages, town plans, sights to see, lodgings and restaurants, and so forth. The guide was an instant success and became the indispensable companion of all drivers and travellers, bar none.

On the strength of this success and driven on by the development of the motor car, *the Manufacture française* extended the scope of «the little book with the red cover» to other European countries beginning in 1904, and a few years later (1908) published an adaptation of the *Guide France* in English.

## A star is born

As of 1920, the guide was no longer free, but marketed for sale. Little by little, the practical information gave way to a wider selection of hotels and restaurants. The mysterious, daunting «Michelin inspector» was not in the picture at first. Rather, it was touring clubs and readers that contributed to the discerning selection of establishments.

The goal of officially identifying places «where one dines well» was materialized in 1926 by the *Étoile de Bonne Table* – the first Michelin star – soon to be followed by two and three-star establishments (1931 for the provinces and 1933 for Paris). The guide thus clearly focused on

gastronomy and the quest for good restaurants became its real driving force.

## In step with the times

During the Second World War, the guide did not appear. The post-war edition of 1945 did not use star ratings, which were applied again as of 1951, when conditions were more settled. Ever more successful, the Guide was to cover all of Western Europe as of the 1960s. In 1982, *Main Cities of Europe* was published in English, marking Michelin's decidedly European dimension.

## 100 years young...

2000 was a winning year for Michelin: the Guide celebrated its 100th anniversary and Bibendum was voted

best corporate logo of the century!

More dynamic than ever, the «little red guide» took on new challenges and set off for the United States. The guide New York not only lived up to expectations, but the first edition was awarded the prize for «Best Restaurant Guide in the World». Next off the presses: San Francisco in 2006, Los Angeles and Las Vegas in 2007.

The newest challenge: discovering the best restaurants in Asia. In autumn 2007, Michelin Tokyo guide was published with a great response. Tokyo is well known as one of the world's famous capitals of fine cuisine. With this first edition, Asia joins the collection with a brilliant start: the restaurants in the 2009 edition are all starred as well as 2008 edition.

Twenty countries covered in Europe, four guides to US cities and one guide to Japan: as the third millennium begins, the Michelin Guide confirms its international dimension. Just a gleam in the eyes of the founders more than a century ago, Bibendum is now an international star to be proud of, carrying the Michelin tradition into the 21st century.

# HOW TO USE THIS GUIDE – RESTAURANT

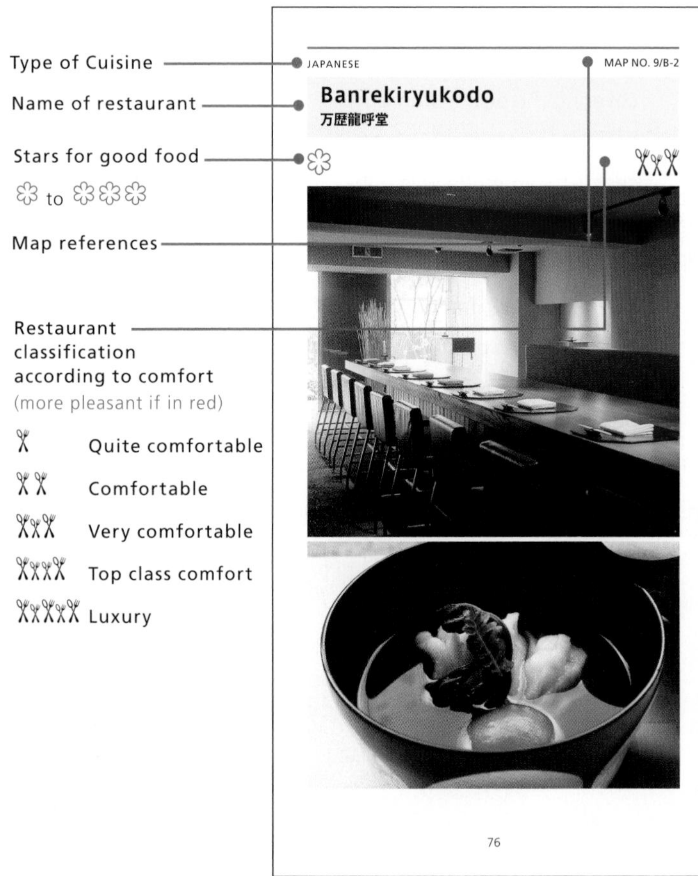

10

The striking wooden door of this Japanese restaurant in Higashi-Azabu is framed by a wall of glass and the interior is simple and modern. A large counter is positioned in the centre of the first floor and at the back you will find a private room with a high ceiling that seats up to 10 guests. The cavern-like basement has a low ceiling and secluded semi-private table seating. The head chef worked in Kyoto and offers appealing cuisine. *Suppon-jiru* (soft-shelled turtle soup) is sealed with a buckwheat pastry to lock in the aroma. Here, even *sashimi* is unique: sea bream from Naruto is served with a dipping sauce made of *karami-daikon* (piquant Japanese radish) and white *ponzu*. The smooth-textured *chawanmushi* (savoury egg custard) is made with *konoko* (salted sea cucumber ovaries), shark fin and lily roots. Four set menus are available, which change every month. The restaurant's unique flair is displayed in its food as well as in its use of tableware. Banrekiryukodo offers a new style of Japanese cuisine while respecting tradition. It is popular with couples and foreign nationals and also used for business occasions.

■ Opening hours, last orders
Lunch=11:30-14:00 (L.O.)
Dinner=18:00-21:00 (L.O.) Bank Holidays 17:00-20:30 (L.O.)

■ Annual and weekly closing
Closed mid-August, late December-early January and Sunday

■ Price
Lunch= menu ¥ 8,400-15,750
Dinner= menu ¥ 10,500-26,250
Service charge= 10%

TEL. 03-3505-5686
FAX. 03-3505-5693
2-33-5 Higashi-Azabu, Minato-ku
www.banreki.com

77

Restaurant symbols

- Cash only
- Wheelchair access
- Shoes must be removed
- Terrace dinning
- No smoking area
- Completely no smoking restaurant
- Interesting view
- Valet parking
- Car park
- 25 Private room with maximum capacity
- Counter restaurant
- Reservation required
- Interesting wine list
- Interesting sake list

# HOW TO USE THIS GUIDE – HOTEL

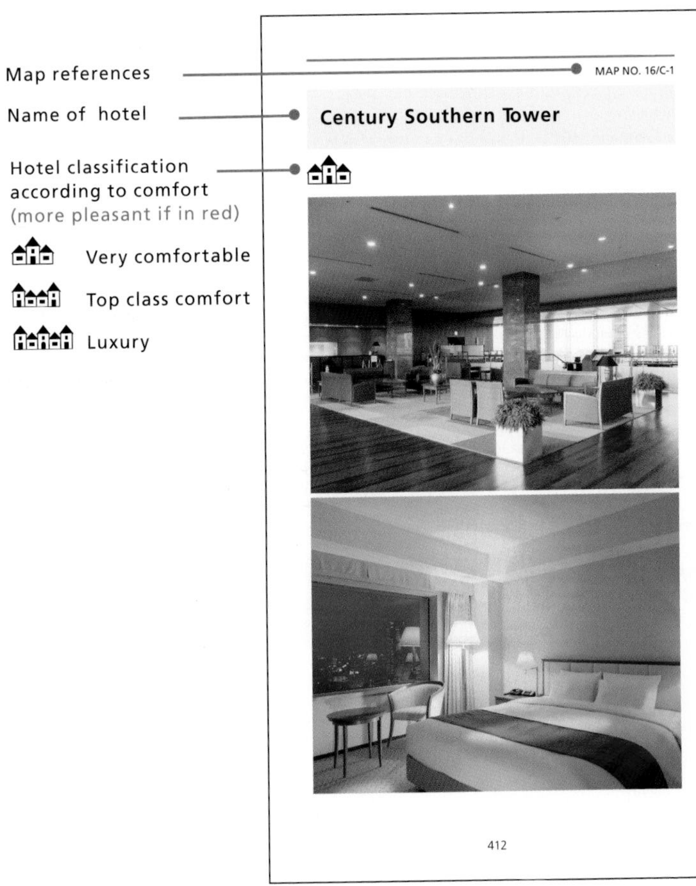

This hotel occupies the 19th to 35th floors of the Odakyu Southern Tower. There are two entrances: the one on the second floor is accessible from the Southern Terrace pedestrian mall near the South Exit of Shinjuku Station; the other, on the first floor, is just a short walk towards Shinjuku from the West Exit of Yoyogi Station. The main lobby is on the 20th floor; the neighbouring lounge and bar offer fine views across Tokyo. Although the hotel is next to a busy railway, the guest rooms are soundproofed with double-glazed windows and are quite comfortable. Standard rooms range in size from 19 to 34m² and all rooms are suitable for business or leisure guests. Those on the eastern side command views of Shinjuku Gyoen, giving guests a sense of the season; guest rooms on the west look onto the Shinjuku skyscraper district and Yoyogi Park - each room is equipped with a panoramic map so guests can place the important landmarks. Despite cutting out conventional hotel services, such as bell and room services, the hotel manages to cater to guest needs through luggage carts, vending machines and a small convenience store.

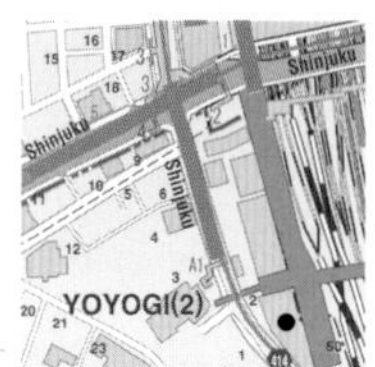

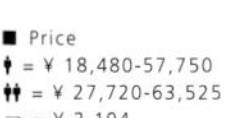

■ Price
single = ¥ 18,480-57,750
double = ¥ 27,720-63,525
breakfast = ¥ 2,194

Rooms=375
Restaurants=3

TEL. 03-5354-0111
FAX. 03-5354-0100
2-2-1 Yoyogi, Shibuya-ku
www.southerntower.co.jp

413

## Hotel symbols

| | |
|---|---|
| ♿ | Wheelchair access |
| | Interesting view from bedrooms |
| | Valet parking |
| P | Car park |
| | No smoking bedrooms |
| | Conference rooms |
| | Indoor swimming pool |
| | Outdoor swimming pool |
| Spa | Spa |
| | Fitness |

# RESTAURANTS

# STARRED RESTAURANTS

All the restaurants within the Tokyo Guide have one, two or three Michelin Stars and are our way of highlighting restaurants that offer particularly good food.

When awarding stars there are a number of factors we consider: the quality and freshness of the ingredients, the technical skill and flair that goes into their preparation, the clarity of the flavours, the value for money and, ultimately, the taste. Of equal importance is the ability to produce excellent food not once but time and time again. Our inspectors make as many visits as necessary so that you can be sure of this quality and consistency.

A two or three star restaurant has to offer something very special in its cooking that separates it from the rest. Three stars – our highest award – are given to the very best. Cuisines in any style of restaurant and of any nationality are eligible for a star. The decoration, service and comfort levels have no bearing on the award.

## Exceptional cuisine, worth a special journey.

**One always eats here extremely well, sometimes superbly. Distinctive dishes are precisely executed, using superlative ingredients.**

| | | | |
|---|---|---|---|
| Hamadaya | XXXX | 116 | MAP NO. 5/B-1 |
| Ishikawa | XX | 140 | MAP NO. 20/D-1 |
| Joël Robuchon | XXXXX | 142 | MAP NO. 7/C-2 |
| Kanda | XX | 148 | MAP NO. 10/A-4 |
| Koju | X | 162 | MAP NO. 6/C-2 |
| L'Osier | XXXX | 202 | MAP NO. 6/C-2 |
| Quintessence | XXX | 248 | MAP NO. 10/A-3 |
| Sukiyabashi Jiro | X | 288 | MAP NO. 6/C-1 |
| Sushi Mizutani | X | 304 | MAP NO. 6/C-2 |

## Excellent cuisine, worth a detour.

**Skillfully and carefully crafted dishes of outstanding quality.**

| | | | |
|---|---|---|---|
| Aimée Vibert | XXXX | 54 | MAP NO. 3/A-2 |
| Argento Aso | XXXX | 60 | MAP NO. 6/D-1 |
| Crescent | XXXX | 92 | MAP NO. 9/B-2 |
| Cuisine[s] Michel Troisgros | XXXX | 94 | MAP NO. 19/A,B-3 |
| Daigo | XXXX | 96 | MAP NO. 9/B-2 |
| Édition Koji Shimomura | XXX | 100 | MAP NO. 9/B-2 |
| Esaki | XX | 102 | MAP NO. 16/D-2 |
| Fukudaya | XXXXX | 110 | MAP NO. 3/A-2 |
| Hatsunezushi | X | 120 | MAP NO. 11/B-2 |
| Hishinuma | XX | 132 | MAP NO. 10/A-4 |
| Horikane | X | 134 | MAP NO. 10/A-3 |

## A very good restaurant in its category.

**A place offering cuisine prepared to a consistently high standard.**

| | | | |
|---|---|---|---|
| Abe | X | 52 | MAP NO. 9/B-2 |
| Ajiman | X | 56 | MAP NO. 10/A-4 |
| Aragawa | XXX | 58 | MAP NO. 9/C-1 |
| Aroma-Frèsca | XXX | 62 | MAP NO. 10/B-3 |
| Asagi | X | 64 | MAP NO. 6/C-1 |
| Au Goût du Jour Nouvelle Ère | XX | 66 | MAP NO. 4/C-2 |
| Ayumasa | X | 68 | MAP NO. 9/C-1 |
| Banrekiryukodo | XXX | 70 | MAP NO. 9/B-2 |
| Beige Alain Ducasse | XXX | 72 | MAP NO. 6/D-1 |
| Bice | XXX | 74 | MAP NO. 9/C-1 |
| Chemins | XXX | 76 | MAP NO. 9/B-1 |
| Chez Matsuo | XXX | 78 | MAP NO. 16/C-2 |
| Chez Tomo | XX | 80 | MAP NO. 10/A-3 |
| Chikuyo-tei Honten | XX | 82 | MAP NO. 6/C-2 |
| China Blue | XXX | 84 | MAP NO. 9/C-1 |
| Chugoku Hanten Fureika | XX | 86 | MAP NO. 10/A-4 |
| Cogito | X | 88 | MAP NO. 10/A-4 |
| Coucagno | XXX | 90 | MAP NO. 16/C-3 |
| Dons de la Nature | XXX | 98 | MAP NO. 6/D-1 |
| Faro | XXX | 104 | MAP NO. 6/C-2 |
| Fugu Fukuji | X | 106 | MAP NO. 6/D-2 |
| Fukamachi | X | 108 | MAP NO. 6/D-1 |
| Fukuju | X | 112 | MAP NO. 6/C-2 |
| Gordon Ramsay | XXX | 114 | MAP NO. 9/C-1 |
| Harutaka | X | 118 | MAP NO. 6/C-2 |

# RESTAURANTS BY AREA

## CHUO-KU

### KIOICHO

| | | | | |
|---|---|---|---|---|
| Fukudaya | ✿✿ | XXXXX | 110 | MAP NO. 3/A-2 |
| La Tour d'Argent | ✿ | XXXXX | 182 | MAP NO. 3/A-2 |
| Nadaman Honten Sazanka-so | ✿ | XXXX | 226 | MAP NO. 3/A-2 |

### MARUNOUCHI

| | | | | |
|---|---|---|---|---|
| Au Goût du Jour Nouvelle Ère | ✿ | XX | 66 | MAP NO. 4/C-2 |
| Monnalisa Marunouchi | ✿ | XXX | 220 | MAP NO. 4/C-2 |

### NAGATACHO

| | | | | |
|---|---|---|---|---|
| Yamanochaya | ✿ | XX | 372 | MAP NO. 3/A-3 |

### NIBANCHO

| | | | | |
|---|---|---|---|---|
| Aimée Vibert | ✿✿ | XXXX | 54 | MAP NO. 3/A-2 |

### UCHISAIWAICHO

| | | | | |
|---|---|---|---|---|
| Les Saisons | ✿ | XXXXX | 200 | MAP NO. 4/C-3 |

### YURAKUCHO

| | | | | |
|---|---|---|---|---|
| Hei Fung Terrace | ✿ | XXX | 122 | MAP NO. 4/C-3 |

## CHUO-KU

### GINZA

| | | | | |
|---|---|---|---|---|
| Argento Aso | ✿✿ | XXXX | 60 | MAP NO. 6/D-1 |
| Asagi | ✿ | X | 64 | MAP NO. 6/C-1 |
| Beige Alain Ducasse | ✿ | XXX | 72 | MAP NO. 6/D-1 |
| Chikuyo-tei Honten | ✿ | XX | 82 | MAP NO. 6/C-2 |
| Dons de la Nature | ✿ | XXX | 98 | MAP NO. 6/D-1 |
| Faro | ✿ | XXX | 104 | MAP NO. 6/C-2 |

## KYOBASHI, NIHONBASHI, NIHONBASHI-MUROMACHI

| | | | | |
|---|---|---|---|---|
| Fukamachi | ✿ | X | 108 | MAP NO. 6/D-1 |
| Sant Pau | ✿✿ | XXXX | 268 | MAP NO. 5/B-1 |
| Sakuragawa | ✿ | XX | 264 | MAP NO. 5/A-1 |
| Sense | ✿ | XXX | 276 | MAP NO. 5/A-1 |
| Signature | ✿ | XXXX | 284 | MAP NO. 5/A-1 |
| Tapas Molecular Bar | ✿ | XX | 326 | MAP NO. 5/A-1 |

## NIHONBASHI-NINGYOCHO

| | | | | |
|---|---|---|---|---|
| Hamadaya | ✿✿✿ | XXXX | 116 | MAP NO. 5/B-1 |

## TSUKIJI

| | | | | |
|---|---|---|---|---|
| Mitsuta | ✿ | XX | 214 | MAP NO. 6/D-2 |
| Uemura Honten | ✿ | XXX | 350 | MAP NO. 6/D-2 |
| Yamamoto | ✿✿ | XXX | 368 | MAP NO. 6/D-2 |

# MEGURO-KU

## KOMABA

| | | | | |
|---|---|---|---|---|
| Miravile | ✿ | XX | 212 | MAP NO. 7/B-1 |

## MITA

| | | | | |
|---|---|---|---|---|
| Joël Robuchon | ✿✿✿ | XXXXX | 142 | MAP NO. 7/C-2 |
| La Table de Joël Robuchon | ✿✿ | XXX | 176 | MAP NO. 7/C-2 |
| Yebisu | ✿ | XXX | 376 | MAP NO. 7/C-2 |

## TAKABAN

| | | | | |
|---|---|---|---|---|
| Suzuki | ✿ | X | 316 | MAP NO. 8/B-3 |

# MINATO-KU

## AKASAKA

| | | | | |
|---|---|---|---|---|
| Abe | ✿ | X | 52 | MAP NO. 9/B-2 |

## ATAGO, MITA, SHIBA-KOEN, TORANOMON



## AZABU-JUBAN, HIGASHI-AZABU, MINAMI-AZABU, MOTO-AZABU, NISHI-AZABU, ROPPONGI

## HIGASHI-SHINBASHI, NISHI-SHINBASHI, SHINBASHI


| | | | | |
|---|---|---|---|---|
| Aragawa | ✿ | XXX | 58 | MAP NO. 9/C-1 |
| Ayumasa | ✿ | X | 68 | MAP NO. 9/C-1 |
| Bice | ✿ | XXX | 74 | MAP NO. 9/C-1 |
| China Blue | ✿ | XXX | 84 | MAP NO. 9/C-1 |
| Gordon Ramsay | ✿ | XXX | 114 | MAP NO. 9/C-1 |
| Hirosaku | ✿ | X | 130 | MAP NO. 9/C-1 |
| Sasada | ✿ | X | 270 | MAP NO. 9/C-1 |
| Tateru Yoshino Shiodome | ✿ | XXX | 330 | MAP NO. 9/C-1 |


## KITA-AOYAMA, MINAMI-AOYAMA


| | | | | |
|---|---|---|---|---|
| L'Embellir | ✿ | XXX | 192 | MAP NO. 9/A-2 |
| Les Créations de Narisawa | ✿ | XXX | 194 | MAP NO. 9/A-1 |
| Pierre Gagnaire | ✿✿ | XXXX | 246 | MAP NO. 9/A-2 |
| Ristorante Honda | ✿ | XX | 256 | MAP NO. 9/A-2 |
| Sushi Musashi | ✿ | X | 306 | MAP NO. 9/A-2 |
| Tensei | ✿ | X | 334 | MAP NO. 9/A-2 |
| Umi | ✿✿ | X | 356 | MAP NO. 9/A-2 |


## MOTO-AKASAKA


| | | | | |
|---|---|---|---|---|
| Tsujitome | ✿ | XXX | 346 | MAP NO. 9/B-1 |
| Yoshihashi | ✿ | XX | 386 | MAP NO. 9/B-1 |


## SHIROKANE, SHIROKANEDAI


| | | | | |
|---|---|---|---|---|
| Chez Tomo | ✿ | XX | 80 | MAP NO. 10/A-3 |
| Horikane | ✿✿ | X | 134 | MAP NO. 10/A-3 |
| Quintessence | ✿✿✿ | XXX | 248 | MAP NO. 10/A-3 |


# OTA-KU

## NISHI-KAMATA


| | | | | |
|---|---|---|---|---|
| Hatsunezushi | ✿✿ | X | 120 | MAP NO. 11/B-2 |

## SETAGAYA-KU

### DAIZAWA

| | | | | |
|---|---|---|---|---|
| Sushi Fukumoto | ✿ | X | 294 | MAP NO. 14/C-1 |

## SHIBUYA-KU

### EBISU, EBISU-MINAMI, EBISU-NISHI, SARUGAKUCHO

| | | | | |
|---|---|---|---|---|
| Le Jeu de l’Assiette | ✿ | XX | 188 | MAP NO. 16/C-3 |
| Les Enfants Gâtés | ✿ | XXX | 196 | MAP NO. 16/C-3 |
| Maison Paul Bocuse | ✿ | XXX | 206 | MAP NO. 16/C-3 |
| Monnalisa Ebisu | ✿ | XXX | 218 | MAP NO. 16/C-3 |
| Nasubi-tei | ✿ | X | 232 | MAP NO. 16/D-3 |
| Okina | ✿ | XX | 240 | MAP NO. 16/C-3 |
| Ristorante Aso | ✿✿ | XXXX | 254 | MAP NO. 16/C-3 |
| Sugawara | ✿ | X | 286 | MAP NO. 16/C-3 |

### JINGUMAE

| | | | | |
|---|---|---|---|---|
| Esaki | ✿✿ | XX | 102 | MAP NO. 16/D-2 |
| Higuchi | ✿ | X | 124 | MAP NO. 16/C-2 |
| Kogetsu | ✿✿ | X | 160 | MAP NO. 16/C-2 |
| Sekiho-tei | ✿ | XX | 274 | MAP NO. 16/D-2 |
| Shigeyoshi | ✿ | X | 280 | MAP NO. 16/C-2 |
| Ukai-tei Omotesando | ✿ | XXXX | 354 | MAP NO. 16/C-2 |

### SAKURAGAOKACHO

| | | | | |
|---|---|---|---|---|
| Coucagno | ✿ | XXX | 90 | MAP NO. 16/C-3 |

### SHOTO

| | | | | |
|---|---|---|---|---|
| Chez Matsuo | ✿ | XXX | 78 | MAP NO. 16/C-2 |

## SHINAGAWA-KU

### MINAMI-OI


| | | | | |
|---|---|---|---|---|
| Makimura | ✿ | X | 208 | MAP NO. 17/B-3 |


### OSAKI


| | | | | |
|---|---|---|---|---|
| Ohara's | ✿ | XXX | 236 | MAP NO. 17/B-1,2 |


## SHINJUKU-KU

### ARAKICHO, YOTSUYA


| | | | | |
|---|---|---|---|---|
| L'Anneau d'Or | ✿ | XX | 174 | MAP NO. 20/C-3 |
| Yoneyama | ✿ | X | 384 | MAP NO. 20/C-3 |


### KAGURAZAKA, NANDOMACHI, WAKAMIYACHO


| | | | | |
|---|---|---|---|---|
| Ichimonji | ✿✿ | XX | 138 | MAP NO. 20/D-1 |
| Ishikawa | ✿✿✿ | XX | 140 | MAP NO. 20/D-1 |
| Komuro | ✿ | X | 164 | MAP NO. 20/D-1 |
| L'Alliance | ✿ | XXXX | 172 | MAP NO. 20/D-1 |
| Le Mange-Tout | ✿✿ | XX | 190 | MAP NO. 20/C-2 |
| Uotoku | ✿ | XXX | 358 | MAP NO. 20/D-1 |
| Yamasaki | ✿ | X | 374 | MAP NO. 20/D-1 |


### KAWADACHO


| | | | | |
|---|---|---|---|---|
| Ogasawara Hakushaku-tei | ✿ | XXXX | 234 | MAP NO. 20/C-2 |


### NISHI-SHINJUKU


| | | | | |
|---|---|---|---|---|
| Cuisine[s] Michel Troisgros | ✿✿ | XXXX | 94 | MAP NO. 19/A,B-3 |


### SHINJUKU


| | | | | |
|---|---|---|---|---|
| Nakajima | ✿ | X | 228 | MAP NO. 19/B-3 |

## SUGINAMI-KU

### KAMIOGI

| Yotsuha | ✿ | 🍴 | 390 | MAP NO. 21/B-2 |
|---|---|---|---|---|

## SUMIDA-KU

### KAMEZAWA

| Hosokawa | ✿ | 🍴 | 136 | MAP NO. 24/A-4 |
|---|---|---|---|---|

### KOTOBASHI

| Yokoyama | ✿ | 🍴 | 380 | MAP NO. 24/B-4 |
|---|---|---|---|---|

## TAITO-KU

### ASAKUSA

| Sushi Isshin Asakusa | ✿ | 🍴 | 296 | MAP NO. 26/C-2 |
|---|---|---|---|---|

## TOSHIMA-KU

### MEJIRO

| Wako | ✿✿ | 🍴🍴 | 364 | MAP NO. 27/B-2 |
|---|---|---|---|---|

# RESTAURANTS BY CUISINE TYPE

## JAPANESE

| | | | | |
|---|---|---|---|---|
| Abe | ✿ | X | 52 | MAP NO. 9/B-2 |
| Ayumasa | ✿ | X | 68 | MAP NO. 9/C-1 |
| Banrekiryukodo | ✿ | XXX | 70 | MAP NO. 9/B-2 |
| Daigo | ✿✿ | XXXX | 96 | MAP NO. 9/B-2 |
| Esaki | ✿✿ | XX | 102 | MAP NO. 16/D-2 |
| Fukudaya | ✿✿ | XXXXX | 110 | MAP NO. 3/A-2 |
| Fukuju | ✿ | X | 112 | MAP NO. 6/C-2 |
| Hamadaya | ✿✿✿ | XXXX | 116 | MAP NO. 5/B-1 |
| Higuchi | ✿ | X | 124 | MAP NO. 16/C-2 |
| Hinokizaka | ✿ | XXX | 126 | MAP NO. 9/A,B-2 |
| Hirosaku | ✿ | X | 130 | MAP NO. 9/C-1 |
| Hishinuma | ✿✿ | XX | 132 | MAP NO. 10/A-4 |
| Horikane | ✿✿ | X | 134 | MAP NO. 10/A-3 |
| Ichimonji | ✿✿ | XX | 138 | MAP NO. 20/D-1 |
| Ishikawa | ✿✿✿ | XX | 140 | MAP NO. 20/D-1 |
| Kadowaki | ✿✿ | X | 144 | MAP NO. 10/A-4 |
| Kamiya Nogizaka | ✿ | XX | 146 | MAP NO. 9/A-2 |
| Kanda | ✿✿✿ | XX | 148 | MAP NO. 10/A-4 |
| Kikuchi | ✿ | X | 152 | MAP NO. 9/A-2 |
| Kikumi | ✿ | XX | 154 | MAP NO. 9/B-2 |
| Kikunoi | ✿✿ | XXXX | 156 | MAP NO. 9/B-2 |
| Kogetsu | ✿✿ | X | 160 | MAP NO. 16/C-2 |
| Koju | ✿✿✿ | X | 162 | MAP NO. 6/C-2 |
| Komuro | ✿ | X | 164 | MAP NO. 20/D-1 |
| Makimura | ✿ | X | 208 | MAP NO. 17/B-3 |
| Minoichi | ✿ | X | 210 | MAP NO. 6/C-2 |

| | | | | |
|---|---|---|---|---|
| Yoneyama | ✿ | X | 384 | MAP NO. 20/C-3 |
| Yotsuha | ✿ | X | 390 | MAP NO. 21/B-2 |
| Yukicho | ✿ | XX | 392 | MAP NO. 6/C-2 |
| Yukimura | ✿✿ | XX | 394 | MAP NO. 10/A-4 |

## JAPANESE CONTEMPORARY

| | | | | |
|---|---|---|---|---|
| Kodama | ✿✿ | XX | 158 | MAP NO. 9/A-2 |
| La Bombance | ✿ | X | 170 | MAP NO. 9/A-2 |
| Ryugin | ✿✿ | XXX | 260 | MAP NO. 10/A-4 |

## JAPANESE FUGU

| | | | | |
|---|---|---|---|---|
| Ajiman | ✿ | X | 56 | MAP NO. 10/A-4 |
| Fugu Fukuji | ✿ | X | 106 | MAP NO. 6/D-2 |
| Usukifugu Yamadaya | ✿✿ | XXX | 360 | MAP NO. 9/A-2 |
| Yamamoto | ✿✿ | XXX | 368 | MAP NO. 6/D-2 |
| Yamane | ✿ | XXX | 370 | MAP NO. 6/C-2 |

## JAPANESE SOBA

| | | | | |
|---|---|---|---|---|
| Hosokawa | ✿ | X | 136 | MAP NO. 24/A-4 |
| Kosetsu | ✿ | XX | 168 | MAP NO. 6/D-1 |
| Okina | ✿ | XX | 240 | MAP NO. 16/C-3 |
| Takeyabu | ✿ | XX | 320 | MAP NO. 10/A-4 |

## JAPANESE SUKIYAKI

| | | | | |
|---|---|---|---|---|
| Yoshihashi | ✿ | XX | 386 | MAP NO. 9/B-1 |

## JAPANESE SUSHI

| | | | | |
|---|---|---|---|---|
| Harutaka | ✿ | X | 118 | MAP NO. 6/C-2 |
| Hatsunezushi | ✿✿ | X | 120 | MAP NO. 11/B-2 |
| Sawada | ✿✿ | X | 272 | MAP NO. 6/D-2 |
| Shin | ✿ | X | 282 | MAP NO. 9/A-2 |
| Sukiyabashi Jiro | ✿✿✿ | X | 288 | MAP NO. 6/C-1 |

| | | | | |
|---|---|---|---|---|
| Sushi Aoki Ginza | ✿ | ✕ | 290 | MAP NO. 6/C-1 |
| Sushi Aoki Nishiazabu | ✿ | ✕ | 292 | MAP NO. 9/A-2 |
| Sushi Fukumoto | ✿ | ✕ | 294 | MAP NO. 14/C-1 |
| Sushi Isshin Asakusa | ✿ | ✕ | 296 | MAP NO. 26/C-2 |
| Sushi Iwa | ✿ | ✕ | 298 | MAP NO. 6/C-1 |
| Sushi Kanesaka | ✿✿ | ✕ | 300 | MAP NO. 6/C-2 |
| Sushiko Honten | ✿ | ✕ | 302 | MAP NO. 6/C-1 |
| Sushi Mizutani | ✿✿✿ | ✕ | 304 | MAP NO. 6/C-2 |
| Sushi Musashi | ✿ | ✕ | 306 | MAP NO. 9/A-2 |
| Sushi Nakamura | ✿ | ✕ | 308 | MAP NO. 10/A-4 |
| Sushi Ohno | ✿ | ✕ | 310 | MAP NO. 6/C-1 |
| Sushi Saito | ✿✿ | ✕ | 312 | MAP NO. 9/B-2 |
| Sushisho Saito | ✿ | ✕ | 314 | MAP NO. 9/B-1 |
| Taku | ✿✿ | ✕✕ | 322 | MAP NO. 9/A-2 |
| Umi | ✿✿ | ✕ | 356 | MAP NO. 9/A-2 |
| Yuta | ✿ | ✕ | 396 | MAP NO. 9/A-2 |


## JAPANESE TEMPURA


| | | | | |
|---|---|---|---|---|
| Asagi | ✿ | ✕ | 64 | MAP NO. 6/C-1 |
| Fukamachi | ✿ | ✕ | 108 | MAP NO. 6/D-1 |
| Kondo | ✿✿ | ✕✕ | 166 | MAP NO. 6/C-1 |
| Mitsuta | ✿ | ✕✕ | 214 | MAP NO. 6/D-2 |
| Raku-tei | ✿ | ✕ | 250 | MAP NO. 9/B-2 |
| 7 chome Kyoboshi | ✿✿ | ✕ | 278 | MAP NO. 6/C-1 |
| Tensei | ✿ | ✕ | 334 | MAP NO. 9/A-2 |
| Yokota | ✿ | ✕ | 378 | MAP NO. 10/A-4 |
| Yokoyama | ✿ | ✕ | 380 | MAP NO. 24/B-4 |
| Yotaro | ✿ | ✕ | 388 | MAP NO. 9/B-2 |


## JAPANESE TEPPANYAKI


| | | | | |
|---|---|---|---|---|
| Keyakizaka | ✿ | ✕✕ | 150 | MAP NO. 10/A-4 |

| | | | | |
|---|---|---|---|---|
| Morimoto XEX | ✿ | XXX | 222 | MAP NO. 10/A-4 |
| Ukai-tei Ginza | ✿ | XXX | 352 | MAP NO. 6/D-2 |
| Ukai-tei Omotesando | ✿ | XXXX | 354 | MAP NO. 16/C-2 |
| Yebisu | ✿ | XXX | 376 | MAP NO. 7/C-2 |


## JAPANESE UNAGI


| | | | | |
|---|---|---|---|---|
| Chikuyo-tei Honten | ✿ | XX | 82 | MAP NO. 6/C-2 |
| Yamanochaya | ✿ | XX | 372 | MAP NO. 3/A-3 |


## CHINESE


| | | | | |
|---|---|---|---|---|
| China Blue | ✿ | XXX | 84 | MAP NO. 9/C-1 |
| Chugoku Hanten Fureika | ✿ | XX | 86 | MAP NO. 10/A-4 |
| Hei Fung Terrace | ✿ | XXX | 122 | MAP NO. 4/C-3 |
| Maison d'Umemoto Shang-hai | ✿ | XXX | 204 | MAP NO. 9/A-2 |
| Momonoki | ✿ | X | 216 | MAP NO. 10/B-3 |
| Reikasai | ✿✿ | XX | 252 | MAP NO. 10/A-4 |
| Sense | ✿ | XXX | 276 | MAP NO. 5/A-1 |


## FRENCH


| | | | | |
|---|---|---|---|---|
| Aimée Vibert | ✿✿ | XXXX | 54 | MAP NO. 3/A-2 |
| Chez Matsuo | ✿ | XXX | 78 | MAP NO. 16/C-2 |
| Chez Tomo | ✿ | XX | 80 | MAP NO. 10/A-3 |
| Cogito | ✿ | X | 88 | MAP NO. 10/A-4 |
| Crescent | ✿✿ | XXXX | 92 | MAP NO. 9/B-2 |
| Gordon Ramsay | ✿ | XXX | 114 | MAP NO. 9/C-1 |
| Hiramatsu | ✿ | XXXX | 128 | MAP NO. 9/A-2 |
| L'Anneau d'Or | ✿ | XX | 174 | MAP NO. 20/C-3 |
| La Tour | ✿ | XXX | 180 | MAP NO. 6/C-2 |
| La Tour d'Argent | ✿ | XXXXX | 182 | MAP NO. 3/A-2 |
| L'Auberge de l'Ill | ✿ | XXXX | 184 | MAP NO. 10/A-4 |
| Le Bourguignon | ✿ | XX | 186 | MAP NO. 10/A-4 |

## FRENCH CONTEMPORARY

| | | | | |
|---|---|---|---|---|
| Tateru Yoshino Shiodome | ✿ | XXX | 330 | MAP NO. 9/C-1 |

## FUSION

| | | | | |
|---|---|---|---|---|
| Tapas Molecular Bar | ✿ | XX | 326 | MAP NO. 5/A-1 |
| Yonemura | ✿ | XX | 382 | MAP NO. 6/C-2 |

## ITALIAN

| | | | | |
|---|---|---|---|---|
| Bice | ✿ | XXX | 74 | MAP NO. 9/C-1 |
| Faro | ✿ | XXX | 104 | MAP NO. 6/C-2 |
| Piatto Suzuki | ✿ | XX | 244 | MAP NO. 10/A-4 |

## ITALIAN CONTEMPORARY

| | | | | |
|---|---|---|---|---|
| Argento Aso | ✿✿ | XXXX | 60 | MAP NO. 6/D-1 |
| Aroma-Frèsca | ✿ | XXX | 62 | MAP NO. 10/B-3 |
| Ristorante Aso | ✿✿ | XXXX | 254 | MAP NO. 16/C-3 |
| Ristorante Honda | ✿ | XX | 256 | MAP NO. 9/A-2 |
| Ristorante La Primula | ✿ | XX | 258 | MAP NO. 10/A-4 |

## SPANISH CONTEMPORARY

| | | | | |
|---|---|---|---|---|
| Ogasawara Hakushaku-tei | ✿ | XXXX | 234 | MAP NO. 20/C-2 |
| Sant Pau | ✿✿ | XXXX | 268 | MAP NO. 5/B-1 |

## STEAKHOUSE

| | | | | |
|---|---|---|---|---|
| Aragawa | ✿ | XXX | 58 | MAP NO. 9/C-1 |
| Dons de la Nature | ✿ | XXX | 98 | MAP NO. 6/D-1 |

# RESTAURANTS PARTICULARLY PLEASANT

| | | | | |
|---|---|---|---|---|
| Aimée Vibert | ✿✿ | XXXX | 54 | MAP NO. 3/A-2 |
| Argento Aso | ✿✿ | XXXX | 60 | MAP NO. 6/D-1 |
| Aroma-Frèsca | ✿ | XXX | 62 | MAP NO. 10/B-3 |
| Beige Alain Ducasse | ✿ | XXX | 72 | MAP NO. 6/D-1 |
| Chez Matsuo | ✿ | XXX | 78 | MAP NO. 16/C-2 |
| China Blue | ✿ | XXX | 84 | MAP NO. 9/C-1 |
| Chugoku Hanten Fureika | ✿ | XX | 86 | MAP NO. 10/A-4 |
| Coucagno | ✿ | XXX | 90 | MAP NO. 16/C-3 |
| Cuisine[s] Michel Troisgros | ✿✿ | XXXX | 94 | MAP NO. 19/A,B-3 |
| Daigo | ✿✿ | XXXX | 96 | MAP NO. 9/B-2 |
| Fukudaya | ✿✿ | XXXXX | 110 | MAP NO. 3/A-2 |
| Hamadaya | ✿✿✿ | XXXX | 116 | MAP NO. 5/B-1 |
| Hei Fung Terrace | ✿ | XXX | 122 | MAP NO. 4/C-3 |
| Hinokizaka | ✿ | XXX | 126 | MAP NO. 9/A,B-2 |
| Hiramatsu | ✿ | XXXX | 128 | MAP NO. 9/A-2 |
| Ichimonji | ✿✿ | XX | 138 | MAP NO. 20/D-1 |
| Ishikawa | ✿✿✿ | XX | 140 | MAP NO. 20/D-1 |
| Joël Robuchon | ✿✿✿ | XXXXX | 142 | MAP NO. 7/C-2 |
| Kanda | ✿✿✿ | XX | 148 | MAP NO. 10/A-4 |
| Keyakizaka | ✿ | XX | 150 | MAP NO. 10/A-4 |
| Kikunoi | ✿✿ | XXXX | 156 | MAP NO. 9/B-2 |
| Koju | ✿✿✿ | X | 162 | MAP NO. 6/C-2 |
| La Bombance | ✿ | X | 170 | MAP NO. 9/A-2 |
| L'Atelier de Joël Robuchon | ✿✿ | XX | 178 | MAP NO. 10/A-4 |
| La Tour d'Argent | ✿ | XXXXX | 182 | MAP NO. 3/A-2 |
| L'Auberge de l'Ill | ✿ | XXXX | 184 | MAP NO. 10/A-4 |

# RESTAURANTS OPEN ON SUNDAY

| | | | | |
|---|---|---|---|---|
| Au Goût du Jour Nouvelle Ère | ✿ | XX | 66 | MAP NO. 4/C-2 |
| Beige Alain Ducasse | ✿ | XXX | 72 | MAP NO. 6/D-1 |
| Bice | ✿ | XXX | 74 | MAP NO. 9/C-1 |
| Chemins | ✿ | XXX | 76 | MAP NO. 9/B-1 |
| Chez Matsuo | ✿ | XXX | 78 | MAP NO. 16/C-2 |
| Chez Tomo | ✿ | XX | 80 | MAP NO. 10/A-3 |
| China Blue | ✿ | XXX | 84 | MAP NO. 9/C-1 |
| Chugoku Hanten Fureika | ✿ | XX | 86 | MAP NO. 10/A-4 |
| Coucagno | ✿ | XXX | 90 | MAP NO. 16/C-3 |
| Cuisine[s] Michel Troisgros | ✿✿ | XXXX | 94 | MAP NO. 19/A,B-3 |
| Daigo | ✿✿ | XXXX | 96 | MAP NO. 9/B-2 |
| Hei Fung Terrace | ✿ | XXX | 122 | MAP NO. 4/C-3 |
| Hinokizaka | ✿ | XXX | 126 | MAP NO. 9/A,B-2 |
| Hosokawa | ✿ | X | 136 | MAP NO. 24/A-4 |
| Joël Robuchon | ✿✿✿ | XXXXX | 142 | MAP NO. 7/C-2 |
| Keyakizaka | ✿ | XX | 150 | MAP NO. 10/A-4 |
| L'Anneau d'Or | ✿ | XX | 174 | MAP NO. 20/C-3 |
| L'Atelier de Joël Robuchon | ✿✿ | XX | 178 | MAP NO. 10/A-4 |
| La Tour | ✿ | XXX | 180 | MAP NO. 6/C-2 |
| La Tour d'Argent | ✿ | XXXXX | 182 | MAP NO. 3/A-2 |
| Le Bourguignon | ✿ | XX | 186 | MAP NO. 10/A-4 |
| Le Jeu de l'Assiette | ✿ | XX | 188 | MAP NO. 16/C-3 |
| Les Enfants Gâtés | ✿ | XXX | 196 | MAP NO. 16/C-3 |
| Les Saisons | ✿ | XXXXX | 200 | MAP NO. 4/C-3 |
| Miravile | ✿ | XX | 212 | MAP NO. 7/B-1 |
| Momonoki | ✿ | X | 216 | MAP NO. 10/B-3 |

# RESTAURANTS TO HAVE A LATE DINNER

| | | | | |
|---|---|---|---|---|
| Abe | ✻ | X | 52 | MAP NO. 9/B-2 |
| Ajiman | ✻ | X | 56 | MAP NO. 10/A-4 |
| Aragawa | ✻ | XXX | 58 | MAP NO. 9/C-1 |
| Aroma-Frèsca | ✻ | XXX | 62 | MAP NO. 10/B-3 |
| Bice | ✻ | XXX | 74 | MAP NO. 9/C-1 |
| Chez Tomo | ✻ | XX | 80 | MAP NO. 10/A-3 |
| Chugoku Hanten Fureika | ✻ | XX | 86 | MAP NO. 10/A-4 |
| Cogito | ✻ | X | 88 | MAP NO. 10/A-4 |
| Coucagno | ✻ | XXX | 90 | MAP NO. 16/C-3 |
| Harutaka | ✻ | X | 118 | MAP NO. 6/C-2 |
| Hei Fung Terrace | ✻ | XXX | 122 | MAP NO. 4/C-3 |
| Hishinuma | ✻✻ | XX | 132 | MAP NO. 10/A-4 |
| Ishikawa | ✻✻✻ | XX | 140 | MAP NO. 20/D-1 |
| Joël Robuchon | ✻✻✻ | XXXX | 142 | MAP NO. 7/C-2 |
| Kadowaki | ✻✻ | X | 144 | MAP NO. 10/A-4 |
| Kanda | ✻✻✻ | XX | 148 | MAP NO. 10/A-4 |
| Keyakizaka | ✻ | XX | 150 | MAP NO. 10/A-4 |
| Koju | ✻✻✻ | X | 162 | MAP NO. 6/C-2 |
| La Bombance | ✻ | X | 170 | MAP NO. 9/A-2 |
| La Table de Joël Robuchon | ✻✻ | XXX | 176 | MAP NO. 7/C-2 |
| L'Atelier de Joël Robuchon | ✻✻ | XX | 178 | MAP NO. 10/A-4 |
| Les Saisons | ✻ | XXXX | 200 | MAP NO. 4/C-3 |
| Maison d'Umemoto Shang-hai | ✻ | XXX | 204 | MAP NO. 9/A-2 |
| Morimoto XEX | ✻ | XXX | 222 | MAP NO. 10/A-4 |
| Muroi | ✻ | X | 224 | MAP NO. 6/C-2 |
| Ohno | ✻ | X | 238 | MAP NO. 6/C-1 |

| Restaurant | Stars | Comfort | Page | Map |
|---|---|---|---|---|
| Okina | ✿ | ✕✕ | 240 | MAP NO. 16/C-3 |
| Ozaki | ✿ | ✕ | 242 | MAP NO. 10/A-4 |
| Piatto Suzuki | ✿ | ✕✕ | 244 | MAP NO. 10/A-4 |
| Ristorante Honda | ✿ | ✕✕ | 256 | MAP NO. 9/A-2 |
| Ryugin | ✿✿ | ✕✕✕ | 260 | MAP NO. 10/A-4 |
| Sawada | ✿✿ | ✕ | 272 | MAP NO. 6/D-2 |
| Sense | ✿ | ✕✕✕ | 276 | MAP NO. 5/A-1 |
| Shin | ✿ | ✕ | 282 | MAP NO. 9/A-2 |
| Signature | ✿ | ✕✕✕✕ | 284 | MAP NO. 5/A-1 |
| Sushi Aoki Nishiazabu | ✿ | ✕ | 292 | MAP NO. 9/A-2 |
| Sushi Fukumoto | ✿ | ✕ | 294 | MAP NO. 14/C-1 |
| Sushi Isshin Asakusa | ✿ | ✕ | 296 | MAP NO. 26/C-2 |
| Sushi Iwa | ✿ | ✕ | 298 | MAP NO. 6/C-1 |
| Sushi Nakamura | ✿ | ✕ | 308 | MAP NO. 10/A-4 |
| Sushi Ohno | ✿ | ✕ | 310 | MAP NO. 6/C-1 |
| Sushi Saito | ✿✿ | ✕ | 312 | MAP NO. 9/B-2 |
| Sushisho Saito | ✿ | ✕ | 314 | MAP NO. 9/B-1 |
| Taku | ✿✿ | ✕✕ | 322 | MAP NO. 9/A-2 |
| Tamao | ✿ | ✕ | 324 | MAP NO. 10/A-4 |
| Umi | ✿✿ | ✕ | 356 | MAP NO. 9/A-2 |
| Usukifugu Yamadaya | ✿✿ | ✕✕✕ | 360 | MAP NO. 9/A-2 |
| Yebisu | ✿ | ✕✕✕ | 376 | MAP NO. 7/C-2 |
| Yotaro | ✿ | ✕ | 388 | MAP NO. 9/B-2 |
| Yuta | ✿ | ✕ | 396 | MAP NO. 9/A-2 |

# RESTAURANTS WITH PRIVATE ROOMS

| | | | | |
|---|---|---|---|---|
| Abe | ✿ | X | 52 | MAP NO. 9/B-2 |
| Aimée Vibert | ✿✿ | XXXX | 54 | MAP NO. 3/A-2 |
| Ajiman | ✿ | X | 56 | MAP NO. 10/A-4 |
| Argento Aso | ✿✿ | XXXX | 60 | MAP NO. 6/D-1 |
| Ayumasa | ✿ | X | 68 | MAP NO. 9/C-1 |
| Banrekiryukodo | ✿ | XXX | 70 | MAP NO. 9/B-2 |
| Bice | ✿ | XXX | 74 | MAP NO. 9/C-1 |
| Chemins | ✿ | XXX | 76 | MAP NO. 9/B-1 |
| Chez Matsuo | ✿ | XXX | 78 | MAP NO. 16/C-2 |
| Chikuyo-tei Honten | ✿ | XX | 82 | MAP NO. 6/C-2 |
| China Blue | ✿ | XXX | 84 | MAP NO. 9/C-1 |
| Chugoku Hanten Fureika | ✿ | XX | 86 | MAP NO. 10/A-4 |
| Cogito | ✿ | X | 88 | MAP NO. 10/A-4 |
| Coucagno | ✿ | XXX | 90 | MAP NO. 16/C-3 |
| Crescent | ✿✿ | XXXX | 92 | MAP NO. 9/B-2 |
| Cuisine[s] Michel Troisgros | ✿✿ | XXXX | 94 | MAP NO. 19/A,B-3 |
| Daigo | ✿✿ | XXXX | 96 | MAP NO. 9/B-2 |
| Édition Koji Shimomura | ✿✿ | XXX | 100 | MAP NO. 9/B-2 |
| Esaki | ✿✿ | XX | 102 | MAP NO. 16/D-2 |
| Fugu Fukuji | ✿ | X | 106 | MAP NO. 6/D-2 |
| Fukudaya | ✿✿ | XXXXX | 110 | MAP NO. 3/A-2 |
| Fukuju | ✿ | X | 112 | MAP NO. 6/C-2 |
| Hamadaya | ✿✿✿ | XXXX | 116 | MAP NO. 5/B-1 |
| Harutaka | ✿ | X | 118 | MAP NO. 6/C-2 |
| Hei Fung Terrace | ✿ | XXX | 122 | MAP NO. 4/C-3 |
| Hinokizaka | ✿ | XXX | 126 | MAP NO. 9/A,B-2 |

| | | | | |
|---|---|---|---|---|
| Morimoto XEX | ✿ | XXX | 222 | MAP NO. 10/A-4 |
| Muroi | ✿ | X | 224 | MAP NO. 6/C-2 |
| Nadaman Honten Sazanka-so | ✿ | XXXX | 226 | MAP NO. 3/A-2 |
| Nakajima | ✿ | X | 228 | MAP NO. 19/B-3 |
| Ogasawara Hakushaku-tei | ✿ | XXXX | 234 | MAP NO. 20/C-2 |
| Ohno | ✿ | X | 238 | MAP NO. 6/C-1 |
| Okina | ✿ | XX | 240 | MAP NO. 16/C-3 |
| Ozaki | ✿ | X | 242 | MAP NO. 10/A-4 |
| Pierre Gagnaire | ✿✿ | XXXX | 246 | MAP NO. 9/A-2 |
| Quintessence | ✿✿✿ | XXX | 248 | MAP NO. 10/A-3 |
| Reikasai | ✿✿ | XX | 252 | MAP NO. 10/A-4 |
| Ristorante Aso | ✿✿ | XXXX | 254 | MAP NO. 16/C-3 |
| Ristorante La Primula | ✿ | XX | 258 | MAP NO. 10/A-4 |
| Ryugin | ✿✿ | XXX | 260 | MAP NO. 10/A-4 |
| Sakuragaoka | ✿ | XX | 262 | MAP NO. 10/A-4 |
| Sakuragawa | ✿ | XX | 264 | MAP NO. 5/A-1 |
| Sankame | ✿ | X | 266 | MAP NO. 6/C-1 |
| Sant Pau | ✿✿ | XXXX | 268 | MAP NO. 5/B-1 |
| Sekiho-tei | ✿ | XX | 274 | MAP NO. 16/D-2 |
| Sense | ✿ | XXX | 276 | MAP NO. 5/A-1 |
| Shigeyoshi | ✿ | X | 280 | MAP NO. 16/C-2 |
| Signature | ✿ | XXXX | 284 | MAP NO. 5/A-1 |
| Sushi Aoki Ginza | ✿ | X | 290 | MAP NO. 6/C-1 |
| Sushi Aoki Nishiazabu | ✿ | X | 292 | MAP NO. 9/A-2 |
| Sushi Fukumoto | ✿ | X | 294 | MAP NO. 14/C-1 |
| Sushiko Honten | ✿ | X | 302 | MAP NO. 6/C-1 |
| Tahara | ✿ | XX | 318 | MAP NO. 10/A-4 |
| Takeyabu | ✿ | XX | 320 | MAP NO. 10/A-4 |
| Taku | ✿✿ | XX | 322 | MAP NO. 9/A-2 |

| | | | | |
|---|---|---|---|---|
| Tamao | ✿ | X | 324 | MAP NO. 10/A-4 |
| Tateru Yoshino Shiba | ✿ | XXX | 328 | MAP NO. 9/B-2 |
| Tateru Yoshino Shiodome | ✿ | XXX | 330 | MAP NO. 9/C-1 |
| Tatsumura | ✿ | X | 332 | MAP NO. 9/B-1 |
| Tensei | ✿ | X | 334 | MAP NO. 9/A-2 |
| Tofuya Ukai Shiba | ✿ | XXXX | 338 | MAP NO. 9/B-2 |
| Tomura | ✿✿ | XX | 340 | MAP NO. 9/B-2 |
| Totoya Uoshin | ✿ | XX | 342 | MAP NO. 9/B-1 |
| Tsujitome | ✿ | XXX | 346 | MAP NO. 9/B-1 |
| Uchiyama | ✿ | XX | 348 | MAP NO. 6/D-1 |
| Uemura Honten | ✿ | XXX | 350 | MAP NO. 6/D-2 |
| Ukai-tei Ginza | ✿ | XXX | 352 | MAP NO. 6/D-2 |
| Ukai-tei Omotesando | ✿ | XXXX | 354 | MAP NO. 16/C-2 |
| Uotoku | ✿ | XXX | 358 | MAP NO. 20/D-1 |
| Usukifugu Yamadaya | ✿✿ | XXX | 360 | MAP NO. 9/A-2 |
| Waketokuyama | ✿ | XX | 362 | MAP NO. 9/A-2 |
| Wako | ✿✿ | XX | 364 | MAP NO. 27/B-2 |
| Yamaji | ✿ | X | 366 | MAP NO. 6/C-2 |
| Yamamoto | ✿✿ | XXX | 368 | MAP NO. 6/D-2 |
| Yamane | ✿ | XXX | 370 | MAP NO. 6/C-2 |
| Yamanochaya | ✿ | XX | 372 | MAP NO. 3/A-3 |
| Yebisu | ✿ | XXX | 376 | MAP NO. 7/C-2 |
| Yoshihashi | ✿ | XX | 386 | MAP NO. 9/B-1 |
| Yukicho | ✿ | XX | 392 | MAP NO. 6/C-2 |
| Yuta | ✿ | X | 396 | MAP NO. 9/A-2 |

# Abe
## 阿部

¥ LUNCH 6

Obscurely located across from Akasaka Arc Hills - look for a small sign on a white building - with a table that seats 12 at its centre, it also has four private dining rooms of varying size. Here you can enjoy fresh vegetables, fish and Shonai beef shipped directly from Yamagata and dishes such as *kandarajiru* hotpot with cod in winter which are unconventional in their execution. Reservations are not accepted for lunch, when one reasonably priced set menu is offered. Not only does the restaurant get crowded but the number of lunch servings is limited so it's best to get there as soon as the doors open. For dinner, two set menus which change monthly are offered in addition to à la carte dishes. Reservations are needed for the *omakase* (chef's choice) set menu. Steaming hot rice -*Haenuki* produced in Yamagata- is served at the end of dinner. With a wide selection of *sake* brewed in Yamagata, the set of smaller tasting cups is the best option. The owner also runs two Japanese hot spring inns in Yamagata, both of which provide inspiration for Abe: Kameya in Yunohama Onsen and Yudono-An in Yutagawa Onsen in Tsuruoka.

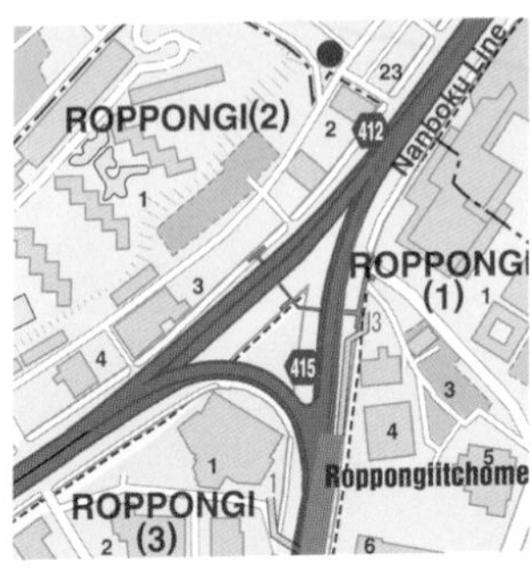

■ Opening hours, last orders
Lunch=11:30-14:30 L.O.14:00
Dinner=18:00-23:00 L.O.22:00

■ Annual and weekly closing
Closed mid-August, late December-early January, Saturday, Sunday and Bank Holidays

■ Price
Lunch= menu ¥ 1,365
Dinner= menu ¥ 5,775-15,750
carte ¥ 3,000-8,000
Service charge= 10% (dinner)

**TEL. 03-3568-2350**
FAX. 03-3568-2355
2-22-11 Akasaka, Minato-ku
www.kameya-net.com/akasaka-abe

# Aimée Vibert

This French restaurant near Kojimachi Station is housed in an Ile de France-style mansion. It is named after the rose, also known as *Bouquet de la Mariée* for its wedding bouquet appearance and is often used for wedding receptions. The second-floor salon and bar feature elegant furniture as well as some antique pieces. During the day, the skylight fills the spacious dining room with natural light while at night subtle lighting and candles provide a romantic atmosphere. Traditional French cuisine is the order of the day. The hors-d'œuvre of crustacean gelée dressed with sea urchin and cauliflower cream is one example. Many ingredients are imported from France: the lobster and sea bass from Brittany, foie gras from Landes, chicken and guinea fowl from Bresse. Dishes for which the meat is grilled in a cocotte provide wonderful balance as the accompanying vegetables become saturated with the flavour of the meat. Desserts include Crêpe Suzette and Grand Marnier soufflé.

■ Opening hours, last orders
Lunch=11:30-14:00 (L.O.)
Dinner=18:00-21:00 (L.O.)

■ Annual and weekly closing
Closed mid-August, late December-early January and Tuesday

■ Price
Lunch= menu ¥ 5,250-8,400
carte ¥ 10,000-19,000
Dinner= menu ¥ 10,500-21,000
carte ¥ 10,000-19,000
Private room fee= ¥ 21,000
Service charge= 10%

**TEL. 03-5216-8585**
FAX. 03-5216-7588
14-1 Nibancho II, Chiyoda-ku
www.aimeevibert.com

# Ajiman
## 味満ん

12

A fugu restaurant in Roppongi whose ageing yet simple interior adds to its authentic downtown Tokyo atmosphere. Run by owner-chef Sadao Matsubara and four of his family members, this cozy restaurant is packed night after night, thanks to the appealing service which is friendly and unaffected and the large numbers of regular customers. The chef only uses firm and flavoursome wild *shiro tora-fugu* (white-finned puffer fish) from Shimonoseki. Most diners opt for *omakase*, the chef's choice. Thick slices of white transparent *fugu* arranged on the plate in a peony shape are served with a *ponzu* dipping sauce made of soy sauce and *kabosu* citrus juice. Other *fugu* dishes include grilled *shirako* (milt) bursting with aroma, *shioyaki* (broiled with salt), *karaage* (deep-fried), *shabu-shabu* and richly flavored *zosui* (risotto) with *shirako* as the final dish. While *fugu* is considered a winter dish, here the delicacy can be enjoyed up to May and in the peak season, the restaurant opens daily. The name "Aji-man," which is literally translated as "filled with taste," symbolizes the chef's commitment to fully satisfying his customers.

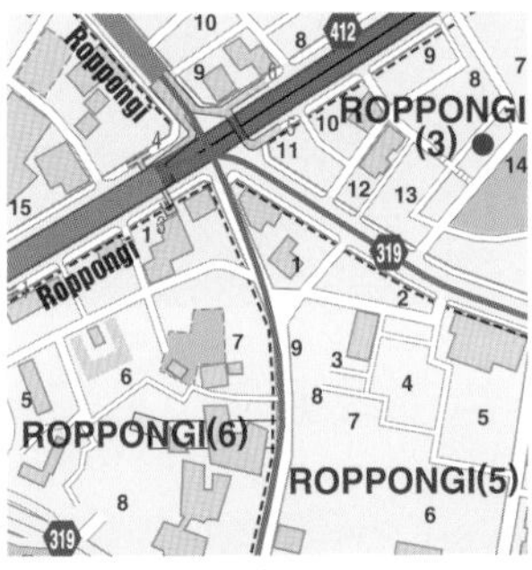

■ Opening hours, last orders
Dinner=18:00-24:00 L.O.22:00

■ Annual and weekly closing
Closed July, August, 31 December-4 January and Sunday from April-June

■ Price
Dinner= menu ¥ 35,000-45,000
carte ¥ 30,000-40,000

TEL. 03-3408-2910
3-8-8 Roppongi, Minato-ku

# Aragawa
## 麤皮

This char-grilled steakhouse has been operating in Shinbashi since 1967 and offers the same appeal now than it did back then; regular customers span three generations. The original obscurely-placed sign as well as the interior décor and even the quality of ingredients remain unchanged. The golden-hued silk walls and Swedish chandelier have also been there since the beginning. There are no menus; instead the head waiter explains the day's offerings at the table. A 400-gram steak, which can feed two people, is the minimum size available, so an appetiser should be enough. Only purebred Tajima Sanda cattle from Hyogo are used and only salt and pepper are used to season the beef thus focusing on the tenderness of the meat and the softness of the fat. A brick oven with *Bincho* charcoal from Wakayama is used for grilling. The meat is skewered and grilled from four sides at more than 800°C. Although brown on the surface, it is burgundy on the inside and keeps in the full flavour. Sirloin is usually served; if you prefer fillet it might be better to check when reserving. Also check the address, as Aragawa may move.

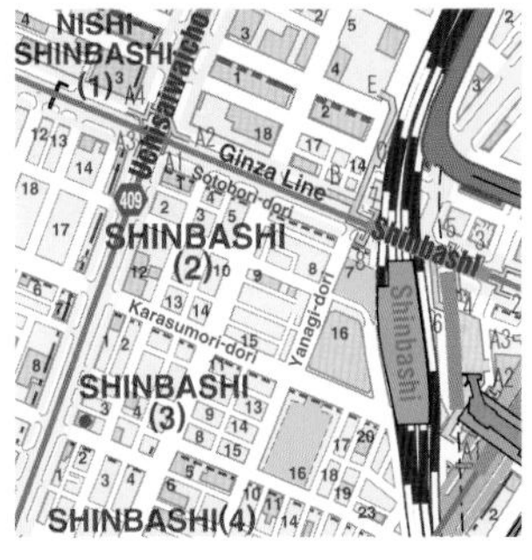

■ Opening hours, last orders
12:00-22:00 (L.O.)

■ Annual and weekly closing
Closed late December-early January, Sunday and Bank Holidays

■ Price
Lunch= menu ¥ 52,500
carte ¥ 40,000-80,000
Dinner= menu ¥ 52,500
carte ¥ 40,000-80,000
Service charge= 12%

**TEL. 03-3591-8765**
FAX. 03-3591-8768
Hankyukotsusha Building B1F,
3-3-9 Shinbashi, Minato-ku

# Argento Aso

10

The entrance and the bar lounge of this Italian restaurant -sister to Daikanyama's Ristorante Aso- are on the eighth floor. The private rooms behind the lounge are decorated with mirrors to reflect the chandeliers. The ninth-floor dining room, featuring stunning Venetian chandeliers and an array of glassware, is bright and sunny by day, romantic and softly lit by night. Dishes come in glasses adding a touch of fun to the dining experience. Marinated lobster with white balsamic vinegar jelly, served as an hors-d'œuvre, and spaghetti *alla pescatora* with a separate glass containing the seafood are house specialities, while smoked Iberico pork with garlic-infused cream is a meat speciality. The chef's original smoky butter is tasty. At lunch, dessert comes courtesy of the trolley and the small bouquets of sweets follow after the meal. The extensive wine list is heavy on Italian and French regions but also offers a wide selection of Armagnac.

■ Opening hours, last orders
Lunch=11:30-15:30 L.O.13:30
Dinner=18:00-23:00 L.O.20:30

■ Annual and weekly closing
Closed 1 week in January

■ Price
Lunch= menu ¥ 4,000-8,400
carte ¥ 13,000-20,000
Dinner= menu ¥ 10,500-21,000
carte ¥ 13,000-20,000
Service charge= 13%

**TEL. 03-5524-1270**
FAX. 03-5524-1273
ZOE Ginza 8F,
3-3-1 Ginza, Chuo-ku
http://www.hiramatsu.co.jp/restaurants/argento-aso

# Aroma-Frèsca

Aroma-Frèsca is located on the second floor of a modern building with a wine shop on the first floor. There are two set menus, both with the same number of dishes. The standard menu dates back to the chef's former premises in Hiroo and remains unchanged throughout the year; the other is a seasonal menu. The chef uses the principle of ensuring maximum freshness by minimal cooking and he only starts to cook when an order has been received. Dishes generally feature light and subtle flavours and tastes that do not overwhelm the palate. Grapefruit used in the grilled king crab salad gives a pleasantly sour touch; the conger eel steamed in herbs is delicate and the freshness of the tomato stands out while fresh fish, giant clams and seasonal vegetables are oven-baked en cocotte. After refreshing the palate with citrus sorbet, he serves Japanese beef charcoal-roasted. The extensive wine list is well selected. Due to the popularity of this restaurant, it is essential to make reservations well in advance.

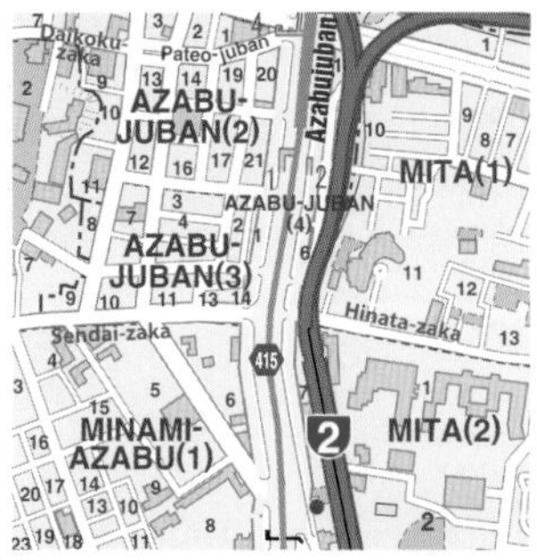

■ Opening hours, last orders
Dinner=18:00-22:30 (L.O.)

■ Annual and weekly closing
Closed mid-August, late December-early January, Sunday and Monday

■ Price
Dinner= menu ¥ 13,125-16,275
Service charge= 10%

**TEL. 03–5439–4010**
FAX. 03–5439–4170
M Tower 2F,
1-7-31 Minami-Azabu, Minato-ku

# Asagi
## あさぎ

A *tempura* restaurant in Ginza. The modern dining room features high ceilings and a counter crafted from a single Japanese cypress tree which creates a natural line. Seating just eight, the restaurant is run by owner-chef Hiroshi Asagi and his wife; their daughter helps out at dinner. Using a large frying pot positioned at the centre of the cooking counter, the chef delicately fries each ingredient using sesame oil. Biting into the shrimp *tempura*, it feels as if you are eating pure shrimp as the chef's unique technique allows the taste of the seafood to permeate the batter. The passion he displays when talking about this traditional Japanese fare shows the consideration he has for his customers. Asagi first opened in Tokyo's Sendagi district and operated for 13 years before moving to Nishi-Azabu. Since relocating to Ginza in 1999, the chef visits nearby Tsukiji market daily to select fresh ingredients. Reservations are strongly recommended during the busy dinnertime hours.

■ Opening hours, last orders
Lunch=12:00-13:00 (L.O.) except Sat. and Bank Holidays
Dinner=17:30-20:30 (L.O.)

■ Annual and weekly closing
Closed Golden week, mid-August, late December-early January, Sunday and Bank Holiday Mondays

■ Price
Lunch= menu ¥ 5,775-7,875
Dinner= menu ¥ 12,000-15,000

**TEL. 03-3289-8188**
6-4-13 Ginza, Chuo-ku

FRENCH CONTEMPORARY MAP NO. 4/C-2

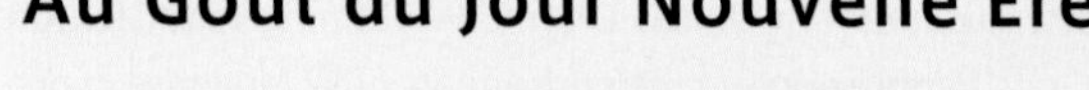

# Au Goût du Jour Nouvelle Ère

This French restaurant looks out onto the red brick façade of Tokyo Station. Fresh and simple, food here is complemented with light, fragrant sauces. It considers its cuisine to be of a "new era," as the restaurant name suggests. Seafood is purchased at Tsukiji market while wild sea bream, sea bass and tilefish are sent from Yamaguchi; Lacan pigeon and Challans duck are chosen by the chef during visits to France and sides of pork hail from the Basque region. The flavour-laden pork back ribs and shoulder loin, cooked for two days and served with a port sauce, are worth trying. The foie gras, a speciality, is simply broiled, coated with *pain d'epices* crumbs to elevate the natural flavour and served with a seasonal fruit purée. Lobster, with its firm texture, is flown in from Brittany, while the Hokkaido veal is tender but has a robust flavour. The chef was a former pâtissier so dinner sees a variety of desserts. The savarin is served with a dash of cointreau; in winter, try the apple *chiboust* with salted caramel ice cream. Well-priced wines and no service charge add to the pleasure.

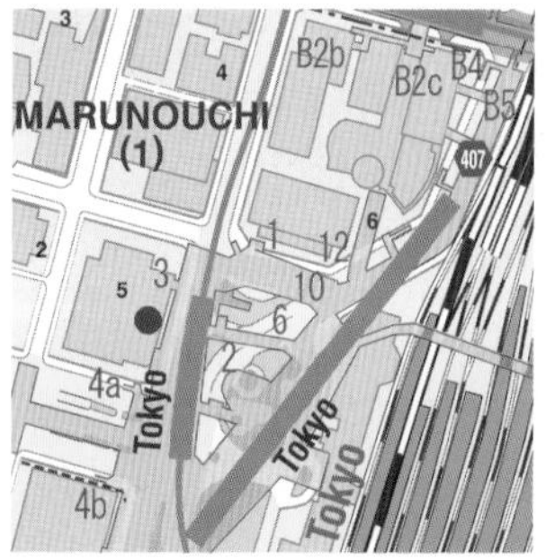

■ Opening hours, last orders
Lunch=11:00-13:30 (L.O.)
Dinner=18:00-21:30 (L.O.)

■ Annual and weekly closing
Closed 1 January

■ Price

| | | |
|---|---|---|
| Lunch= | menu | ¥ 3,800-10,000 |
| Dinner= | menu | ¥ 7,500-15,000 |
| | carte | ¥ 9,200-10,300 |

**TEL. 03–5224–8070**
FAX. 03–5224–8060
Shin-Marunouchi Building 5F,
1-5-1 Marunouchi, Chiyoda-ku
www.augoutdujour-group.com/no

# Ayumasa
## 鮎正

16

A *kappo* (counter style restaurant) known for *ayu* (sweetfish) located in the shopping and dining street near the West Exit of Shimbashi Station. Here, Tsunetaka Yamane, the second-generation owner-chef, serves mainly local cuisine of Shimane, from where wild ayu are sent, during the *ayu* season of June to October. Large and plump *ayu* smoked for the *ayu-no nama-aburi-yaki*, is a house speciality; smoking, with straw, starts an hour before the scheduled reservation, so don't be late. The smoked *ayu* with roe in mid-October is recommended. *Ayu-jiru* (*ayu miso* soup) is flavoured with *koji miso* (soybean paste) and exudes a slight sweetness. The dish made of eggplant and *uruka* (salted *ayu* innards) and *Ayu-gohan*, a rice dish cooked with *ayu* flesh and its stock allow customers to savour a wide variety of *ayu* dishes. In the *ayu* off-season, *matsubagani* crabs, *fugu* (puffer fish), duck and other seasonal ingredients are available. Large wild *fugu,* chosen according to designated weights, is popular. Between November and May, the restaurant is closed on the second and fourth Saturdays of the month.

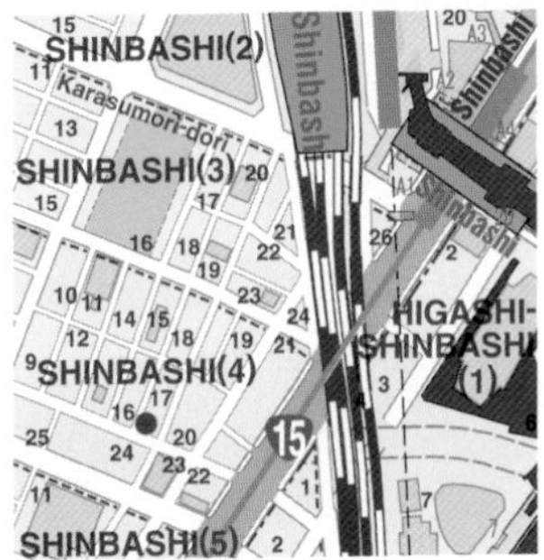

■ Opening hours, last orders
Dinner=17:00-22:00 L.O.21:30

■ Annual and weekly closing
Closed late December-early January, Sunday and Bank Holidays

■ Price
Dinner= menu ¥ 11,550-15,750
carte ¥ 9,000-20,000
Private room fee= 10%

TEL. 03-3431-7449
4-17-5 Shinbashi, Minato-ku

# Banrekiryukodo
## 万歴龍呼堂

10

The striking wooden door of this Japanese restaurant in Higashi-Azabu is framed by a wall of glass and the interior is simple and modern. A large counter is positioned in the centre of the first floor and at the back you will find a private room with a high ceiling that seats up to 10 guests. The cavern-like basement has a low ceiling and secluded semi-private table seating. The head chef worked in Kyoto and offers appealing cuisine. *Suppon-jiru* (soft-shelled turtle soup) is sealed with a buckwheat pastry to lock in the aroma. Here, even *sashimi* is unique: sea bream from Naruto is served with a dipping sauce made of *karami-daikon* (piquant Japanese radish) and white *ponzu*. The smooth-textured *chawanmushi* (savoury egg custard) is made with *konoko* (salted sea cucumber ovaries), shark fin and lily roots. Four set menus are available, which change every month. The restaurant's unique flair is displayed in its food as well as in its use of tableware. Banrekiryukodo offers a new style of Japanese cuisine while respecting tradition. It is popular with couples and foreign nationals and also used for business occasions.

■ Opening hours, last orders
Lunch=11:30-14:00 (L.O.)
Dinner=18:00-21:00 (L.O.) Bank Holidays 17:00-20:30 (L.O.)

■ Annual and weekly closing
Closed mid-August, late December-early January and Sunday

■ Price
Lunch= menu ¥ 8,400-15,750
Dinner= menu ¥ 10,500-26,250
Service charge= 10%

**TEL. 03-3505-5686**
FAX. 03-3505-5693
2-33-5 Higashi-Azabu, Minato-ku
www.banreki.com

# Beige Alain Ducasse

This restaurant is a collaboration between fashion brand Chanel and restaurateur Alain Ducasse. Rather than classic French cuisine, Ducasse proffers cutting-edge French fare that incorporates unique Japanese ingredients. The lunchtime menu offers an all-vegetable "végétal", a "mer/terre" of only seafood and meat, and also a full set menu combining the two. In the evening two set menus are offered, both including cheese. Specialities are braised green asparagus and morel, and terrine of local breed chicken and foie gras served with sweet-and-sour seasonal vegetables. For dessert, Carré Chanel, a concoction of chocolate, praline and hazelnut ice cream is designed to reflect the Chanel image. The main dining room is decorated in tones of beige with Chanel tweed as its theme. From April through November, guests can enjoy afternoon tea, aperitifs or after-dinner cognac and cigars on the rooftop terrace, Le Jardin de Tweed, which overlooks Ginza and thus is worth a visit.

■ Opening hours, last orders
Lunch=11:30-16:30 L.O.14:30
Dinner=18:00-23:30 L.O.21:30

■ Annual and weekly closing
Closed mid-August, late December-early January

■ Price

| | | |
|---|---|---|
| Lunch= | menu | ¥ 6,000-15,000 |
| | carte | ¥ 15,000-20,000 |
| Dinner= | menu | ¥ 17,000-30,000 |
| | carte | ¥ 15,000-20,000 |

Service charge= 10%

**TEL. 03-5159-5500**
FAX. 03-5159-5501
Chanel Building 10F,
3-5-3 Ginza, Chuo-ku
www.beige-tokyo.com

# Bice

The first Bice was established in 1926 in Milan, called by the nickname of its founder, Beatrice Ruggeri. To reach it, take the lift from the basement to the 46th floor, and then take either another lift or the stairs to the 47th floor. From a height of 200m, the view -which takes in the area from around Tokyo Bay to the Boso Peninsula- is breathtaking. Inside, the space has a simple, contemporary look. The cuisine is based on a similar theme of "simple yet sophisticated"; traditional regional Italian recipes are transformed for today's palates and offered on an à la carte menu. From northern Veneto, lightly steamed, sliced cod served with paprika sauce is available as an appetiser, while tagliolini pasta from northwestern Liguria comes with artichoke and scampi. Meat in the style of Sardinia is sautéed with aromatic herbs and served with sweet-and-sour shallots. The wine list features an assortment of regional Italian wines.

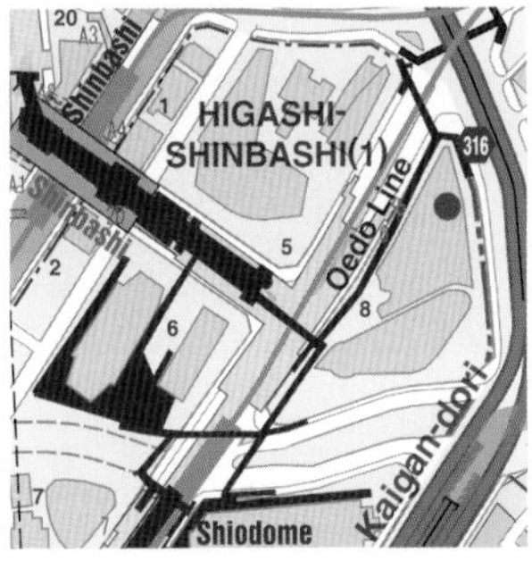

■ Opening hours, last orders
Lunch=11:30-15:30 L.O.14:00
Dinner=17:30-23:30 L.O.22:00
Sat., Sun. and Bank Holidays
17:00-23:30 L.O.22:00

■ Annual and weekly closing
Closed 1 January

■ Price
Lunch= menu ¥ 3,675-9,450
carte ¥ 10,000-13,000
Dinner= menu ¥ 9,450-18,900
carte ¥ 10,000-13,000
Private room fee= ¥ 10,500
Service charge= 10% (dinner)

**TEL. 03-5537-1926**
FAX. 03-5537-1929
Caretta Shiodome 47F,
1-8-1 Higashi-Shinbashi, Minato-ku
www.bicetokyo.com

# Chemins

10

Simple and modern, the dining room has a pleasant atmosphere and, in the warmer months, open-air dining is possible. The owner, a sommelier, went out on his own after gaining experience at a Tokyo restaurant and training in France. In the autumn of 2008 he welcomed a new chef who is seeking to introduce new dishes while remaining faithful to the Chemins' style. He provides vegetables from his parents' farm in Okayama, along with organic vegetables from Shizuoka. The fish arrives fresh from Fukushima and, for the meat, he makes good use of domestic products such as shorthorn, duck, Shamo gamecock and lamb. One of the more popular dishes here is carrot mousse with consommé jelly served with sea urchin; you can also find boudin noir and, in winter, roasted wild pigeon. The wine menu offers more than 500 bins at attractive prices; be sure to make use of the sommelier's advice in choosing one to accompany your meal.

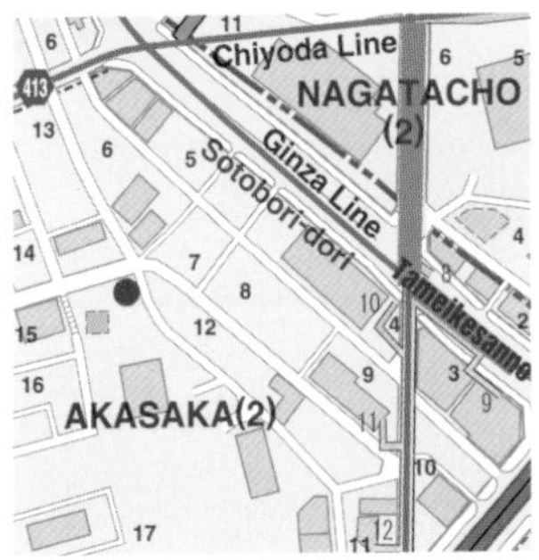

■ Opening hours, last orders
Lunch=11:30-16:00 L.O.13:30
Dinner=18:00-24:00 L.O.21:30

■ Annual and weekly closing
Closed late December-early January and Monday

■ Price
Lunch= menu ¥ 2,800-5,300
carte ¥ 7,000-10,000
Dinner= menu ¥ 5,900-11,500
carte ¥ 7,000-10,000
Service charge= 10%

**TEL. 03-3568-3344**
FAX. 03-3568-3344
Akasaka Tameike Tower Annex,
2-17-7 Akasaka, Minato-ku
www.chemins.jp

# Chez Matsuo

16

This French restaurant near the Toguri Museum of Art in Shoto, Shibuya, opened in 1980 as Tokyo's first restaurant in a detached house. As a preferred destination of the imperial family, it gained prominence on the Tokyo dining scene. Just off the entrance is a salon bar fitted with a fireplace and furniture from the early 1900s. Private rooms past the bar have wooden flooring and panelling as well as elegant lighting fixtures and mirrors, all of which create a traditional atmosphere. The main dining room looks onto a garden overflowing with greenery. The lobster *mi-cuit* flavoured with argan oil and paired with small turnips marinated in raspberry vinegar is outstanding. Recommended in season are the stewed baby boar served with white bean purée, and venison caught in Nara. Only fixed price options are available for both lunch and dinner, with the latter being rather expensive. The menu cover features a vividly coloured illustration drawn by the owner, Kozo Matsuo. At Chez Matsuo diners can take time to enjoy meals in a relaxed environment.

■ Opening hours, last orders
Lunch=12:00-15:00 L.O.13:00
Dinner=18:00-23:00 L.O.20:30

■ Annual and weekly closing
Closed 31 December-4 January

■ Price
Lunch= menu ¥ 8,400
Dinner= menu ¥ 21,000-52,500
Private room fee= ¥ 31,500
Service charge= 10%

**TEL. 03-3485-0566**
FAX. 03-3485-0766
1-23-15 Shoto, Shibuya-ku
www.chez-matsuo.co.jp

# Chez Tomo

It may be small, but this restaurant of Tomoji Ichikawa offers good fare at reasonable prices. The menu features both traditional cuisine and contemporary recipes developed by the chef; in addition to standard seasonal dishes, the menu is changed monthly. While there is an à la carte menu, the fixed price option is particularly popular and offers plenty of choice. House specialities include a warm hors-d'œuvre of sea urchin and soft scrambled egg served in a sea urchin shell and gateau-style *boudin noir*. In winter, the foie gras, *poireau* leek and consommé jelly, served Mille-feuille style, is recommended. The assortment of organic vegetables is a colourful and beautiful dish with more than 25 types of vegetable, each prepared and seasoned differently. The shrimp and fish quenelle, Paul Bocuse style, is also popular. For dessert, there is *brioche perdu*—a traditional dish of steamed homemade brioche with custard cream.

■ Opening hours, last orders
Lunch=11:30-16:00 L.O.15:00
Dinner=18:00-24:00 L.O.23:00

■ Annual and weekly closing
Closed late December-early January and Monday except Bank Holidays

■ Price

| | | |
|---|---|---|
| Lunch= | menu | ¥ 2,890 |
| | carte | ¥ 6,000-7,000 |
| Dinner= | menu | ¥ 5,780 |
| | carte | ¥ 6,000-7,000 |

Service charge= 10%

**TEL. 03–5789–7731**
FAX. 03–5789–7732
5-15-5 Shirokane, Minato-ku
www.chez-tomo.com

# Chikuyo-tei Honten
## 竹葉亭 本店

This *unagi* (eel) restaurant has been in business since the late Edo Period (1603-1867). Now in the hands of the seventh-generation owner, it started out as an eatery for *samurai* in town to safeguard their lord's Edo mansion. The current building has been in use since 1924 when the eatery relocated from Shintomicho and it also has historical value as one of the few buildings unscathed in World War II. Surrounded by office blocks, it has four *tatami* rooms and a banquet room on the second floor; there is also a house for tea ceremonies on the premises that stores antique tea ceremony instruments. *Unagi* served here is generally sent from Shizuoka and Aichi; *Shirayaki* (broiled unseasoned *unagi* fillet) is enjoyed with a little *wasabi* and soy sauce; for *kabayaki*, *unagi* fillets are rendered plump and filled with aroma through a process that involves broiling and basting them with the house's special sauce simply made by combining soy sauce and *mirin* (sweet cooking *sake*). At Chikuyo-tei Honten, diners can enjoy a traditional Japanese atmosphere free of formality. Waiting staff in *kimono* offer attentive and pleasant service.

■ Opening hours, last orders
Lunch=11:30-15:00 L.O.14:30
Dinner=16:30-21:00 L.O.20:00

■ Annual and weekly closing
Closed late December-early January, Sunday and Bank Holidays

■ Price
Lunch= menu ¥ 7,350-10,500
Dinner= menu ¥ 12,600-14,700
Service charge= 10%

**TEL. 03-3542-0789**
FAX. 03-3542-0788
8-14-7 Ginza, Chuo-ku

# China Blue

10

A Chinese restaurant opened on the 28th floor of the Conrad hotel in the Tokyo Shiodome Building. Lights covered in blue cloth hang from the 8m high ceiling and the windows offer views of Hamarikyu Onshi Teien Garden and the Tokyo Bay area. The restaurant, bright with sunshine during the day, becomes a cosy, softly illuminated space in the evening. There are three private rooms; the one situated in a corner and surrounded on two sides by glass is particularly popular. The glass-encased wine cellar fulfils an aesthetic function as well as housing a variety of French and assorted wines. Dishes are served Western style on individual plates and guests can enjoy not only traditional Cantonese cuisine but also contemporary creations accented with flavours of other Asian countries. Typical dishes include braised shark fin and paper-baked crab meat served with soup, prawns dressed with a mayonnaise made with *wasabi*, and stir-fried beef fillet with black pepper.

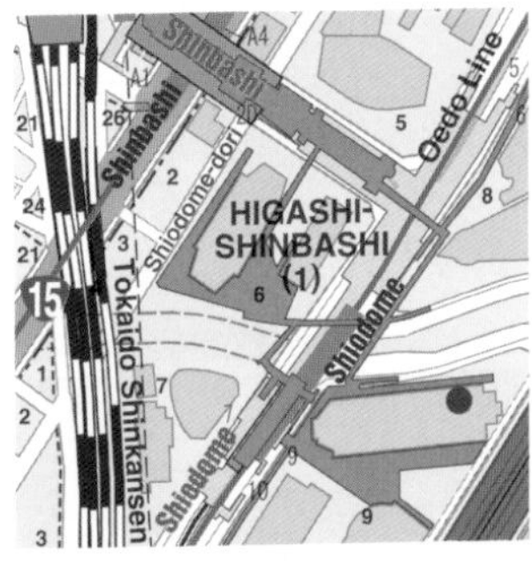

■ Opening hours, last orders
Lunch=11:30-14:00 (L.O.)
Dinner=17:30-21:00 (L.O.)

■ Price
Lunch= menu ¥ 3,800-7,800
carte ¥ 6,000-13,500
Dinner= menu ¥ 13,800-26,800
carte ¥ 6,000-13,500
Private room fee= ¥ 15,000-25,000

**TEL. 03-6388-8000**
FAX. 03-6388-8001
Conrad Hotel 28F,
1-9-1 Higashi-Shinbashi, Minato-ku
www.conradtokyo.co.jp

# Chugoku Hanten Fureika
## 中国飯店 富麗華

P 100

This restaurant is affiliated with a Chinese restaurant in Roppongi which has a history spanning more than three decades. The menu offers a large variety of dishes focusing on Cantonese and Shanghainese culinary culture, which come not only on large plates but are also served in individual portions. The team of chefs, hired in Hong Kong and Shanghai and led by a master from Hong Kong, work in different kitchens, depending on the cuisine, which makes it quite unique. Recommended is the roasted pork dish prepared by the specialist Grill and Roast food chef. *Shao lon bao* (Shanghai soup dumplings) bursting with juicy meat are prepared from scratch only after an order. The fried rice is seasoned with Chinese soy sauce and has an intense flavour. Live performances featuring classical Chinese instruments showcase the subtlety and depth of Chinese culture. The inexpensive lunch menu served during the week is not available on holidays or weekends.

■ Opening hours, last orders
Lunch=11:30-14:00 (L.O.)
Dinner=17:30-22:00 (L.O.)

■ Annual and weekly closing
Closed 31 December-1 January

■ Price

| | | |
|---|---|---|
| Lunch= | menu | ¥ 2,000-6,000 |
| | carte | ¥ 6,000-12,000 |
| Dinner= | menu | ¥ 8,400-33,600 |
| | carte | ¥ 6,000-12,000 |

Service charge= 10% (dinner)

**TEL. 03-5561-7788**
FAX. 03-5561-7878
3-7-5 Higashi-Azabu, Minato-ku
www.chuugokuhanten.com

# Cogito

Housed in a detached building across from Roppongi Hills, this restaurant has a bistro-style look. Jitsuhiro Yamada, the owner-chef, started his first solo venture in 1994 after returning from Europe where he honed his culinary skills. The décor featuring *muku* wood evokes images of Vienna in the early C20. Not only do they do a fixed menu but also an à la carte; with lunch having a more casual menu, the chef's potential is more evident at dinner, especially with his wintry game dishes. He hunts the game himself between early November and the end of February and the meat is dressed immediately and shipped to the kitchen within a few hours. Roasted Yezo Sika deer served with wild mushrooms and black truffles comes with a sauce made by gravy and wild grape. Cogito has a wide-ranging wine list with a large choice of Burgundy. The liqueur selection encompasses 60 types of Chartreuse, including some early-1900s vintages. For a digestive and cigar, head to the basement salon.

■ Opening hours, last orders
Lunch=12:00-14:00 (L.O.)
Dinner=18:00-22:30 (L.O.)

■ Annual and weekly closing
Closed late December-early January and Sunday

■ Price

| | | |
|---|---|---|
| Lunch= | menu | ¥ 3,800-8,000 |
| | carte | ¥ 6,000-8,000 |
| Dinner= | menu | ¥ 5,800-15,000 |
| | carte | ¥ 6,000-8,000 |

Service charge= 10%

**TEL. 03-3796-3838**
FAX. 03-3796-2277
3-2-15 Nishi-Azabu, Minato-ku

# Coucagno

12

With its name meaning "earthly paradise", this restaurant is in the Cerulean Tower Tokyu Hotel near Shibuya Station. The modern interior, in shades of brown and ivory, has large windows providing sweeping vistas of Odaiba, Ebisu and even as far as Yokohama. Simply designed silverware, and crystal and ceramic vases decorate the dining room where good-sized tables are evenly spaced. Charges for the two private rooms for both lunch and dinner vary depending on the number of guests -check when making a reservation as one of the private rooms does not have the view. The menu changes each season, but generally offers Provençal Mediterranean-style cuisine focusing on tapenades, olive oil, tomato confit and so on. Dishes feature mainly domestic ingredients and are executed with a contemporary twist in line with the chef's desire to provide colourful, tempting fare. The wine list offers about 200 bins from France and other parts of the world.

■ Opening hours, last orders
Lunch=11:30-14:00 (L.O.)
Dinner=17:30-22:00 (L.O.)

■ Price

| | | |
|---|---|---|
| Lunch= | menu | ¥ 4,100-10,000 |
| | carte | ¥ 7,000-11,000 |
| Dinner= | menu | ¥ 10,000-18,000 |
| | carte | ¥ 9,000-14,000 |

Private room fee= less than 6 persons ¥ 10,000-20,000

**TEL. 03-3476-3404**
FAX. 03-3476-3493
Cerulean Tower Tokyu Hotel 40F,
26-1 Sakuragaokacho, Shibuya-ku
www.ceruleantower-hotel.com

# Crescent

24

A restaurant that occupies a five-storey late Victorian-style building near the lush Shiba Park, and one of the few in Tokyo that can be described as being "aristocratic". Guests will not fail to notice the chandelier, silverware and assorted decorative touches. The chef took charge of the kitchen in 1997 after honing his culinary skills in famous restaurants in France and Switzerland. The house speciality, *compression de tomate*, combines two types of tomato with complementary layers of mousse, tartar and jelly. Lamb comes from Shiranuka in Hokkaido and various cuts are roasted on the bone and served on one plate with a sauce typical of the season—salted lemon sauce in summer, for example, or truffle sauce in winter. A dessert of lightly warmed raspberries from Nagano served with meringue, pistachio nuts and caramel ice cream is available just in summer and autumn. The wine cellar holds a variety of bottles, including some rare vintages. This restaurant is particularly suitable for those formal or special occasions that you'll want to remember.

■ Opening hours, last orders
Dinner=17:30-22:30 L.O.20:30

■ Annual and weekly closing
Closed mid-August, late December-early January, Sunday and Bank Holidays

■ Price
Dinner= menu ¥ 26,250
Service charge= 10%

**TEL. 03-3436-3211**
1-8-20 Shiba-Koen, Minato-ku
www.restaurantcrescent.com

# Cuisine[s] Michel Troisgros

12

A French restaurant opened in 2006 in the Hyatt Regency, next to the Tokyo Metropolitan Government buildings. Michel Troisgros is the third-generation owner-chef of Troisgros, a famed restaurant in Roanne, northwest of Lyons, and looks to Japanese cuisine as a source of inspiration. The French and Japanese chefs entrusted by Troisgros, offer contemporary French cuisine with accents of citrus fruit, herbs and spices incorporating Japanese ingredients and tastes. There are two dining rooms: modern and elegant with a natural stone floor, from which customers can see the glass-enclosed kitchen; and a more warming space reminiscent of a French countryside inn with a carpeted floor and exposed wooden pillars and beams. The menu changes every two months. Aside from poultry imported from France, all ingredients are sent directly from throughout Japan. The wine list, featuring mainly French wines, is noted for both its breadth and depth.

■ Opening hours, last orders
Lunch=11:30-14:00 (L.O.)
Dinner=18:00-21:30 (L.O.)

■ Annual and weekly closing
Closed Wednesday from May-October

■ Price
Lunch= menu ¥ 5,300-10,500
carte ¥ 12,500-17,500
Dinner= menu ¥ 14,700-18,900
carte ¥ 12,500-17,500
Service charge= 10%

**TEL. 03-5321-3915**
FAX. 03-3340-3722
Hyatt Regency Hotel 1F,
2-7-2 Nishi-Shinjuku, Shinjuku-ku
www.cuisinesmicheltroisgros.com

# Daigo
醍醐

48

Located at the foot of Atago Hill near Atagoyama Shrine, this *shojin ryori* restaurant started out in the grounds of the nearby Soto Zen temple Seishoji in 1950, before relocating to the second floor of the Forest Tower in 2002. *Shojin ryori* is rooted in Zen Buddhism, is meat-free and based on the simple concept of appreciating simple food. Various root vegetables and legumes are used as a starting point. Close attention is also paid to seasonal ingredients and, in the formal *kaiseki* style, dishes are served one at a time. For taste differentiation, various flavoured broths are used: dried bonito, kelp and *shiitake* mushroom. Stepping inside the Japanese-style entrance after passing the moss-covered yard, you are met with a dignified silence. The dining room exerts the refined *wabi-sabi* essence of Zen Buddhism, complemented by *ikebana* floral arrangements. In the evening, the illuminated garden can be seen from all the *tatami* rooms. The *kaiseki* lunch menu (¥10,000) served with a drink is well priced and includes the service charge.

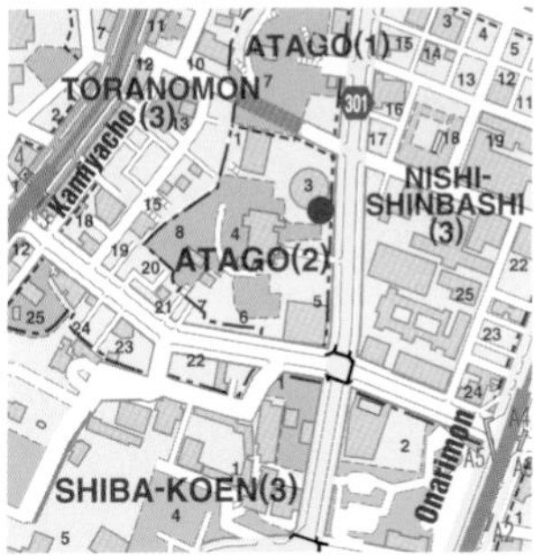

■ Opening hours, last orders
Lunch=12:00-15:00 L.O.14:00
Dinner=17:00-22:30 L.O.20:00

■ Annual and weekly closing
Closed early January

■ Price
Lunch= menu ¥ 10,000-19,000
Dinner= menu ¥ 15,000-19,000
Service charge= 15%

**TEL. 03-3431-0811**
FAX. 03-3431-1382
Forest Tower 2F,
2-3-1 Atago, Minato-ku
www.shiba-daigo.com

# Dons de la Nature

The French name of this steakhouse means "gifts of nature." There is a striking counter and tables facing the open kitchen; oil landscapes of Amsterdam and La Rochelle adorn the walls and classical music plays in the background. Yoshiji Otsuka, the owner-chef, is experienced in French cuisine and opened this restaurant having honed his skills at another Tokyo steakhouse. The appeal of his restaurant comes down to the beef. His use of a unique cooking method that forgoes the usual hot-plate style and the selection of meat—only Japanese black-haired cattle is used—as well as its preparation demonstrate his attention to detail. Only cuts from heifers aged around 33 months old are considered; the meat is aged in a special locker and later smaller cuts are carved and swathed in cloth to absorb excess moisture. Aged for another seven to 10 days in a vacuum, an original salt blend and black pepper are rubbed into the meat before it is grilled. Orders start at 400 grams as this, the restaurant claims, is the minimum weight at which the best results can be expected. It may therefore be wise to bring a dining companion.

■ Opening hours, last orders
Dinner=17:00-22:00 L.O.21:00

■ Annual and weekly closing
Closed mid-August, late December-early January, Sunday and Bank Holidays

■ Price
Dinner= menu ¥ 21,000
carte ¥ 21,000-34,000
Service charge= 10%

**TEL. 03-3563-4129**
FAX. 03-3563-4130
Kawai Building B1F,
1-7-6 Ginza, Chuo-ku
www.dons-nature.jp

# Édition Koji Shimomura

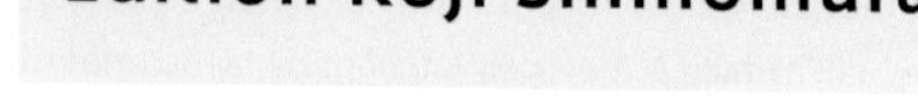

6

Backed by his experience at some famous restaurants in France and Tokyo, Koji Shimomura opened this Roppongi eatery in 2007. The modern French cuisine he serves is not too heavy, with the use of oil and fat kept to a minimum. His specialities combine techniques he learnt as a young chef and include an hors-d'œuvre of rich and creamy chilled oysters from Miyagi lightly boiled in sea water and served with dried *iwanori* (rock laver) and a jelly of sea water and citrus fruit. Fried John Dory wrapped in finely shredded *kadayif* pastry is served with broccoli purée and lemon jam. The grilled Challans duck is a house speciality that pays homage to Bernard Loiseau and his well-known duck dishes, but clearly has the Shimomura touch. The reconstituted strawberry tart offered for dessert adopts a novel concept: while using regular strawberry tart ingredients, this version comes uniquely constructed. Private room charges vary depending on the number of guests and therefore should be checked in advance. Since there are no fixed closing days, be sure to call ahead.

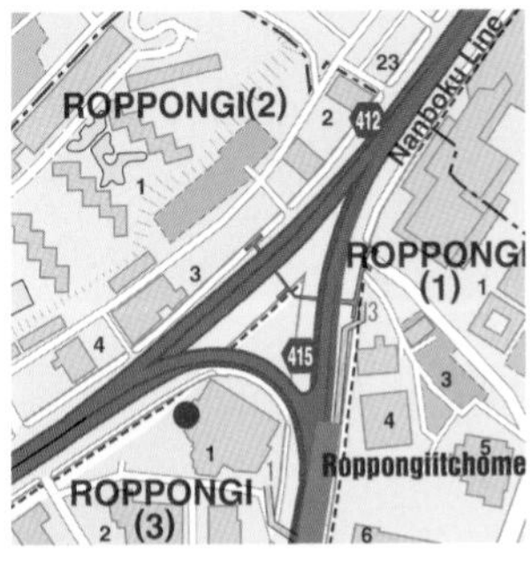

■ Opening hours, last orders
Lunch=12:00-16:00 L.O.13:30
Dinner=18:00-0:30 L.O.21:30

■ Annual and weekly closing
Closed late December-early January

■ Price
Lunch= menu ¥ 4,200-13,650
Dinner= menu ¥ 9,450-21,000
Private room fee= less than 5 persons ¥ 5,250-31,500
Service charge= 10%

**TEL. 03-5549-4562**
FAX. 03-5549-4563
Roppongi T-Cube 1F,
3-1-1 Roppongi, Minato-ku
www.koji-shimomura.jp

# Esaki
## えさき

10

It's located in a quiet residential area - look out for the sign and menu board. Inside, there is both counter and table seating, as well as private rooms with sunken seating. Wheat and bamboo reliefs on the walls were brought from Bali. Shintaro Esaki, the owner-chef, uses only fresh ingredients and his organic vegetable dishes form an important part of the menu. Only two set menus are available for both lunch and dinner. *Yurine manju senbei zutsumi* is a signature dish of deep-fried balls of steamed lily root and Yamato yam coated with pieces of unseasoned rice crackers served in a kudzu broth. In summer when lily root is not available, *ayu* (sweetfish) soup is offered instead. Each portion of soup, only available in-season (late June to August), generously uses three *ayu* sourced from the Shimanto-gawa river. The same dishes are incorporated into both the lunch and dinner set menus, the prices of which differ according to the number of courses. The dinner set menu that includes a whole *kinki* fish is particularly recommended. Only open for lunch on Thursdays, Fridays and Saturdays.

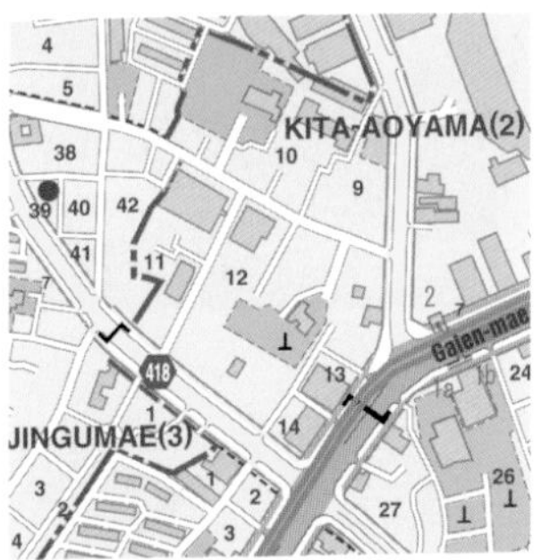

■ Opening hours, last orders
Lunch= Thu.-Sat.12:00-14:00
L.O.13:30
Dinner=18:00-23:00 L.O.21:30

■ Annual and weekly closing
Closed Golden week, mid-August, late December-early January, Sunday and Bank Holidays

■ Price
Lunch= menu ¥ 3,675-5,250
Dinner= menu ¥ 8,400-10,500
Service charge= 10% (dinner)

**TEL. 03-3408-5056**
FAX. 03-3408-5056
Hills Aoyama B1F,
3-39-9 Jingumae, Shibuya-ku
www.aoyamaesaki.net

# Faro

With its name meaning "lighthouse", this restaurant is located in the eye-catching red Tokyo Ginza Shiseido Building. The peppermint-coloured dining room, reminiscent of a crystal-clear sky, provides an airy but elegant backdrop. Porthault linens and Christofle flatware add to the sophistication. Here, traditional Italian recipes are executed with the *esprit* of French cuisine. House specialities include carpaccio of marbled Wagyu beef served with tomato and avocado in summer or truffles in winter. Homemade spaghetti with snow crab, cooked with a fresh tomato reduction that goes well with the flavour of the roasted crab, is another highlight. One of the best winter choices is a risotto with black truffles made with Carnaroli rice imported from Lombardy in Italy. As well as typical Italian desserts such as tiramisu and panna cotta, it offers *Paris-Brest, ile flottante* and other French favourites. The wine list is extensive and the service pleasant.

■ Opening hours, last orders
Lunch=11:30-15:30 L.O.14:30
Dinner=17:30-23:00 L.O.21:30

■ Annual and weekly closing
Closed late December-early January, Sunday and Bank Holidays

■ Price

| | | |
|---|---|---|
| Lunch= | menu | ¥ 2,800-8,000 |
| | carte | ¥ 7,000-21,000 |
| Dinner= | menu | ¥ 6,800-15,000 |
| | carte | ¥ 7,000-21,000 |

Service charge= 10%

**TEL. 03-3572-3911**
FAX. 03-5537-6230
Shiseido Building 10F,
8-8-3 Ginza, Chuo-ku
www.shiseido.co.jp/faro

# Fugu Fukuji
## ふぐ 福治

15

Takeshi Yasuge, the owner-chef, uses only wild tiger *fugu* (puffer fish) from the Bungo Strait, which he purchases daily from a local supplier. Two set menus are available: "Take" consists of standard *fugu* courses—namely, an hors-d'œuvre, *sashimi*, *fuguchiri* (hotpot) and *zosui* (risotto); "Matsu" offers an extra fried dish in addition to the regular courses. For *sashimi*, *fugu* is aged for several days to develop the taste and sliced thicker than usual; a 1-kilogram fish is divided into four portions of *sashimi* for generous servings. *Fugu* feed on crustaceans, which gives their flesh a pinkish hue. The *ponzu* sauce is made with hand-squeezed *daidai* (sour oranges) juice harvested in November. The red chili pepper used for the *momiji-oroshi* (red pepper-spiced grated *daikon*) condiment is ground with a stone mill to enhance aroma. Shiitake mushroom is not used in the *fuguchiri* to highlight the taste of the *fugu*. As the end of course, the chef or manageress prepares *zosui* using eggs, *koto-negi* (scallion) and the soup from the hotpot dish, which exhibits a strong *fugu* flavour.

■ Opening hours, last orders
Dinner=17:00-23:00 L.O.21:30

■ Annual and weekly closing
Closed mid-August, late December-early January, Saturday, Sunday and Bank Holidays from April-October

■ Price
Dinner= menu ¥ 27,300-34,650
Service charge= 10%

**TEL. 03–5148–2922**
Koda Building 3F,
5-11-13 Ginza, Chuo-ku
www.fukuji.jp

# Fukamachi
深町

The owner-chef Masao Fukamachi's *tempura* is thinly battered and lightly fried so as not to spoil the original taste of the ingredients. The chef uses two deep fryers with only high-quality white sesame oil, set at a different temperature for precision-cooked *tempura*, soft on the palate. Vegetables are fried at a lower temperature to maintain their freshness and colour, and seafood at a higher temperature to ensure a crisp tastiness. *Uni-no obamaki* (sea urchin wrapped in a perilla leaf), puffer fish milt, and *hamo* (pike conger) served with salt-pickled *ume* (Japanese apricot) sauce are recommended, depending on the season. *Kuchiko tempura* made of sea cucumber ovaries is a one of the more unique choices. Kyoyaki and Imari vessels from the end of the Edo Period (1603-1867) are among the chef's collection used to serve starters. Fukamachi is a stylish restaurant where you can appreciate both *Edomae tempura* and antiques.

■ Opening hours, last orders
Lunch=11:30-14:00 L.O.13:30
Dinner=17:00-22:00 L.O.21:00

■ Annual and weekly closing
Closed mid-August, late December-early January, Monday, 1st and 3rd Sunday

■ Price

| | | |
|---|---|---|
| Lunch= | menu | ¥ 6,300-8,400 |
| | carte | ¥ 7,000-12,000 |
| Dinner= | menu | ¥ 10,500-15,750 |
| | carte | ¥ 7,000-12,000 |

**TEL. 03–5250–8777**
FAX. 03–5250–8777
2-5-2 Kyobashi, Chuo-ku

# Fukudaya
## 福田家

40

This *ryotei* in Kioicho opened in 1939 in Toranomon as a restaurant-inn and moved to Kioicho, where it was re-branded as an exclusive *ryotei*, following renovations in 1995. Fukudaya is well known for its close relationship with Rosanjin Kitaoji, a distinguished calligrapher, ceramicist and master chef. Now run by the third-generation owner, the spacious restaurant is located in an office building in a prime area of the capital. It has seven bi-level dining rooms that are fine examples of traditional Japanese architecture. The valuable antiques and Japanese garden views behind the *shoji* screens make you forget that you are in the middle of the city. The feature of the upper level is a country house of a *shoya* (town official) built about 750 years ago and restored after careful dismantling. After appetisers in the *tatami* room, diners can move fireside and enjoy precision-cooked *tempura* and *teppan-yaki*, prepared right in front of them. Fukudaya is ideal for business occasions and is also popular with foreign nationals. If requested in advance, elaborate set menus served on valuable Rosanjin tableware can be arranged.

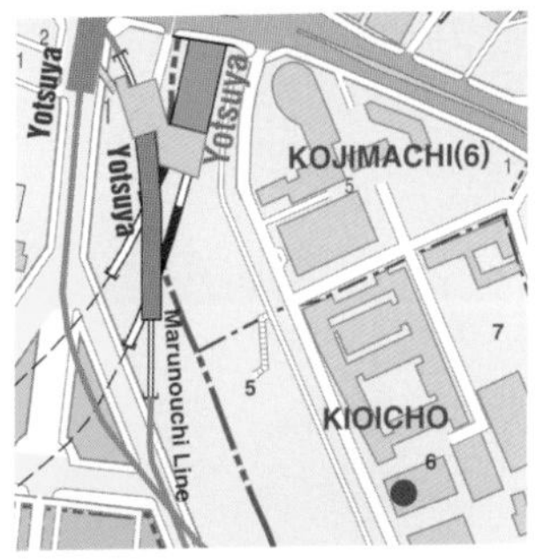

■ Opening hours, last orders
Lunch=11:00-15:00 L.O.13:30
Dinner=17:30-22:30 L.O.20:00

■ Annual and weekly closing
Closed late December-early January, Sunday and Bank Holidays

■ Price
Lunch= menu ¥ 21,000-26,250
Dinner= menu ¥ 26,250-36,750
Private room fee= ¥ 5,250/person
Service charge= 20%

**TEL. 03-3261-8577**
FAX. 03-3261-1518
6-12 Kioicho, Chiyoda-ku

# Fukuju
## 福樹

¥ LUNCH 8

A small Japanese restaurant run by the owner-chef, Katsuhiro Onodera, and his manageress. Inside you will find a counter made from a single thick plank of *hinoki* (Japanese cypress) and a private dining space in the style of a tea ceremony room, where, if reserved, guests can enjoy a tea ceremony and meal put together by the chef who is also a certified tea ceremony instructor. Composed of well-selected ingredients, dishes are prepared carefully to retain their flavour and aroma and are served in moderately sized portions. The Japanese-style shark fin braised in bonito stock, invented by the chef with inspiration from Chinese cuisine, is the house speciality. The disk abalone from Iwate's Sanriku coast served in a soup with a freshwater clam base that combines Shinshu *miso* (soybean paste) and Saikyo *miso* is also delicious. Beautiful serving vessels, including some from the Edo Period, make each dish even more appealing. Rare varieties of *sake* are available, most of which have a clear, sharp taste that complements the food. Only one party is accepted at lunchtime.

■ Opening hours, last orders
Lunch=12:00-15:00 L.O.13:00
Dinner=18:00-22:30 L.O.20:30

■ Annual and weekly closing
Closed mid-August, late December-early January, Sunday and Bank Holidays

■ Price
Lunch= menu ¥ 15,750-21,000
Dinner= menu ¥ 18,900-52,500
Service charge= 10%

**TEL. 03-3571-8596**
FAX. 03-3571-8596
Iseyoshi Building 5F,
8-8-19 Ginza, Chuo-ku

# Gordon Ramsay

A French restaurant produced by British chef Gordon Ramsay, located on the 28th floor of the Conrad hotel in Shiodome. The open kitchen that can be seen upon emerging from the chic entrance is striking. The chef's table with stool seating in front of the kitchen can take a group of up to eight; behind which there are three booths. The spacious, open main dining area has floor to ceiling windows. Just two set menus are offered at lunch, with a main of either meat or fish. For dinner, à la carte dishes are also available. For example, an appetiser of foie gras served cold with Sauternes gelée and fig sauce might be followed by a main of either steamed red sea bream with celeriac purée and dried tomato or roasted lamb accompanied by ratatouille and potato, finishing with tart tatin with vanilla ice cream for dessert. The chef's policy is to not weigh down dishes with too many ingredients: simple dishes are accented by the accompaniments and sauces. The wine list features selections from all over the world. Sunday lunch sees a special fixed price menu.

■ Opening hours, last orders
Lunch=11:30-14:00 (L.O.)
Sun. and Bank Holidays 12:00-14:00 (L.O.)
Dinner=17:30-21:00 (L.O.) except Sunday

■ Price
Lunch= menu ¥ 4,000-6,500
Dinner= menu ¥ 15,500-22,000
carte ¥ 11,000-18,000

**TEL. 03-6388-8000**
FAX. 03-6388-8001
Conrad Hotel 28F,
1-9-1 Higashi-Shinbashi, Minato-ku
www.conradtokyo.co.jp

# Hamadaya
## 濱田家

60

This prestigious restaurant is one of the few *sukiya*-style buildings remaining today. Each of its eight private Japanese-style rooms has a charming garden while each set menu consists of about eight courses. The dishes are given a subtle variation of flavours depending on the ingredients used and their serving order. Using *Katsuo-bushi* (dried bonito) from Makurazaki in Kagoshima, the stock for the clear soup of *shinjo* (steamed fish balls) and *karasumi* (dried and salted grey mullet roe) is flavoured lightly, while the richer stock is used for clear *hamo* (pike conger) soup and other more delicate ingredients. The *shinogi* (intermezzo) course is a rice dish: *saba-zushi* (chub mackerel *sushi)* or *anago-no ii-mushi* (conger eel steamed with glutinous rice). For the grilled course, there is fish, duck or quail depending on the season, while the *takiawase* course offers herring simmered in a sweet salty sauce and served with lightly seasoned bamboo shoots. The last course before dessert is *takikomi-gohan (*a rice dish seasoned with soy sauce and boiled with various ingredients) or buckwheat noodles from Tokamachi in Niigata.

■ Opening hours, last orders
Lunch=11:00-15:00 L.O.14:00
Dinner=17:30-23:00 L.O.20:00

■ Annual and weekly closing
Closed mid-August, late December-early January, Sunday and Bank Holidays

■ Price
Lunch= menu ¥ 15,750-24,150
Dinner= menu ¥ 26,250-52,500
Private room fee= ¥ 3,150/person (dinner)
Service charge= 20% (lunch 15%)

**TEL. 03-3661-5940**
FAX. 03-3808-0801
3-13-5 Nihonbashi-Ningyocho, Chuo-ku
www.hamadaya.info

# Harutaka
## 青空

4

After 12 years training at Sukiyabashi Jiro, Hokkaido-born Harutaka Takahashi opened this *Edomae*-style sushi restaurant in Ginza in 2006. His day begins with a trip to Tsukiji market, where he deals with suppliers depending on the fish or shellfish. The taste and aroma of *hatsu gatsuo* (bonito in May) seared over a straw fire gives diners a sense of summer to come. Wild *madaka* abalone is also delicious between May and June. *Shako* (mantis shrimp) is purchased alive and quickly steamed ensuring freshness. *Hon-maguro* (bluefin tuna), from different parts of Japan depending on the season, is aged for varying periods according to its fattiness. *Karasumi* (salted and dried grey mullet roe) pickled in *miso* (soybean paste) and goes well with *sake*. The temperature ensures each topping for *sushi* is kept at its very best. The rice, which is a special blend combining sweet-tasting rice with a variety that is less sticky, is cooked to ensure a slightly harder texture than usual. It is then generously seasoned with rice vinegar and kept at body temperature.

■ Opening hours, last orders
Dinner=17:00-24:00 (L.O.)
Saturday 17:00-22:30 (L.O.)

■ Annual and weekly closing
Closed Golden week, mid-August, late December-early January, Sunday and Bank Holidays

■ Price
Dinner= menu ¥ 15,000-25,000

**TEL. 03-3573-1144**
FAX. 03-3573-1144
Kawabata Building 3F,
8-5-8 Ginza, Chuo-ku

# Hatsunezushi

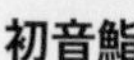

初音鮨

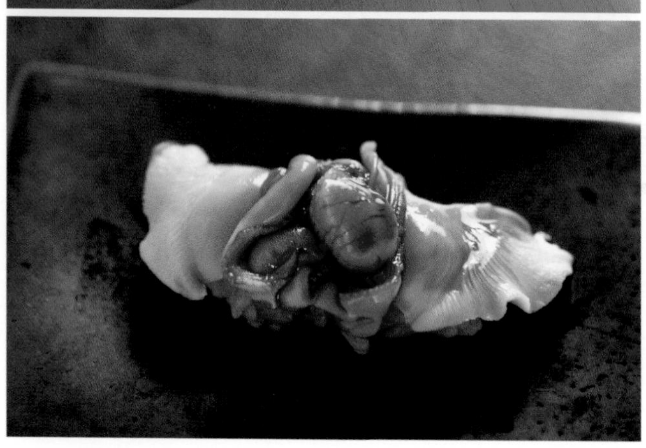

This *sushi* restaurant is on the left as you walk toward Nihon Kogakuin from the West Exit of Kamata Station. From the raised counter, owner-chef Katsu Nakaji carefully prepares *sushi* while talking with customers. He believes that the most important factor in making good *sushi* is the way it is seasoned and he follows the traditional *Edomae* technique. He prefers to use slightly firmer rice and flavours it with *akazu* (red vinegar made from *sake* lees), with which Nakaji never blends sugar so as to bring out the taste of the seafood without overwhelming it. Special care is taken to ensure the rice and the topping are the right temperature. In winter, large yellowtail is cut into pieces for a *shabu-shabu*-style dish; the pieces are only briefly dipped in boiling water to heat the surface and are then served with *ponzu* dipping sauce containing grated radish and *yuzu* pepper. Being away from central Tokyo means that the prices are very reasonable, considering the quality of cooking. As Nakaji prepares all the dishes himself, reservations are limited and diners can take their time. Lunch is only served on Saturday.

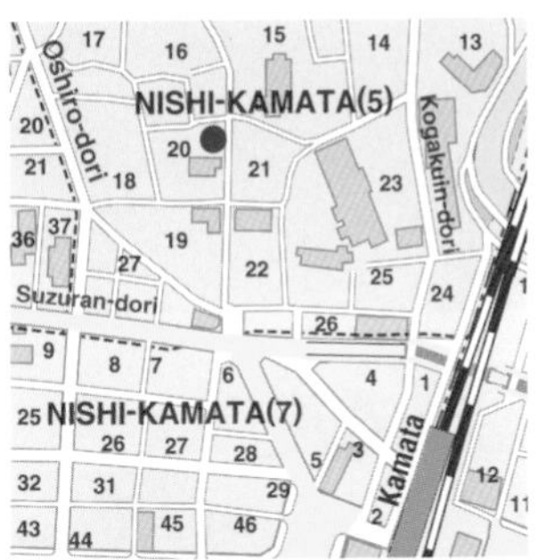

■ Opening hours, last orders
Dinner=17:30-21:30 (L.O.)

■ Annual and weekly closing
Closed Golden week, mid-August, late December-early January, Sunday and Bank Holidays

■ Price
Dinner= menu ¥ 10,500-15,750

**TEL. 03-3731-2403**
5-20-2 Nishi-Kamata, Ota-ku

# Hei Fung Terrace

♿ 13

This softly lit dining room is beautifully decorated with gently curving walls, a stone-paved floor and birdcages hanging from above. The three private rooms come with antique wooden accessories and furnishings imported from China; especially recommended is the room for 12, which provides a relaxed setting with a large window overlooking the Imperial Palace Outer Garden. There is no extra fee to use the rooms, but each has a different minimum charge, so be sure to check in advance. The menu features a number of dishes prepared in typical Cantonese style, such as chicken, abalone or other seafood cooked with shark fin. Recommendations include braised duck web with black mushrooms stewed in oyster sauce; sliced garoupa rolled with shark's fin; deep-fried bean curd with spicy salt and braised minced beef with vermicelli and XO sauce. Two reasonably priced set menus are offered at lunchtime. This Chinese restaurant is located on the second floor of The Peninsula hotel and is a good place to enjoy fine Cantonese cuisine in an exotic and relaxed setting.

■ Opening hours, last orders
Lunch=11:30-14:30 (L.O.)
Dnner=18:00-22:00 (L.O.)

■ Price

| | | |
|---|---|---|
| Lunch= | menu | ¥ 4,280-8,880 |
| | carte | ¥ 6,000-15,000 |
| Dinner= | menu | ¥ 8,880-19,880 |
| | carte | ¥ 6,000-15,000 |

**TEL. 03-6270-2738**
FAX. 03-6270-2693
The Peninsula Hotel 2F,
1-8-1 Yurakucho, Chiyoda-ku
www.tokyo.jp.peninsula.com

JAPANESE

MAP NO. 16/C-2

# Higuchi

**樋口**

With only a counter and two tables, the interior of this *kappo* (counter style restaurant) in Jingumae has a pure Japanese aesthetic. The owner-chef Kazuhito Higuchi trained in several *ryotei* and *kappo* before opening Higuchi. Although dishes are rooted in Kyoto-style cuisine, efforts are made to accommodate Kanto preferences. Soup stock made of sea bream enhances the taste of the *bafun-uni-no nikogori* (Japanese green sea urchin jelly), available throughout the year. For the *hamo* (pike conger) *shabu-shabu*, you briefly dip pieces of raw *hamo* into a soup stock made with *hamo* bones—a pleasant choice in summer. In early autumn, *matsutake* mushrooms are added; in winter, *konowata-no chawan-mushi* (savoury egg custard made with sea cucumber gut) and *saba zushi* (chub mackerel *sushi*) are recommended. The last course before a dessert is either handmade buckwheat noodles or *tai meshi* (sea bream with rice). For dessert, try the *wafu-jitate-no annin-dofu* (Japanese-style almond tofu). The chef works alone, so sit back and enjoy the leisurely pace. This restaurant is a good one to visit with friends.

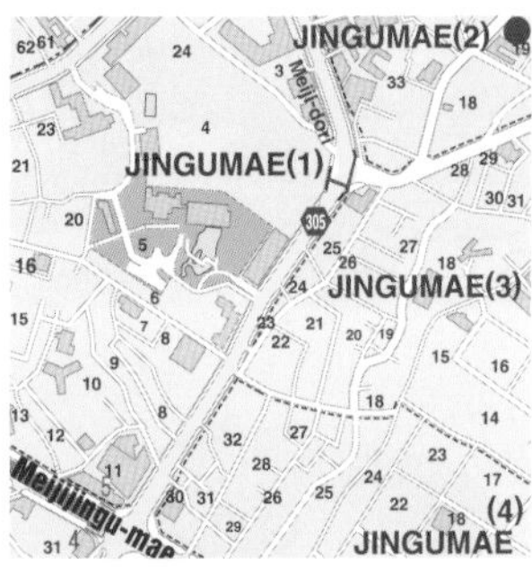

■ Opening hours, last orders
Dinner=18:00-21:00 (L.O.)

■ Annual and weekly closing
Closed Golden week, mid-August, late December-early January, Sunday and Bank Holidays

■ Price
Dinner= menu ¥ 12,600-18,900
Service charge= 10%

**TEL. 03–3402–7038**
FAX. 03–3402–7038
2-19-12 Jingumae, Shibuya-ku

JAPANESE MAP NO. 9/A,B-2

# Hinokizaka

**ひのきざか**

10

Located in The Ritz-Carlton, it offers four types of Japanese cuisine—*kaiseki*, *sushi*, *teppanyaki* and *tempura*—in designated sections. The *kaiseki* section selected for inclusion in this guide is a table-seating area located to the right of the entrance. The large windows offer views of Meiji Shrine, Shinjuku Gyoen National Garden and the Shinjuku skyscraper; even Mt. Fuji can be seen, weather permitting. Each of the set menus include dishes where seasonal ingredients are prepared so as to bring out their natural flavours. Presentation is colourful and eye-catching and care is taken to complement the food with the beautiful tableware. There are two private rooms at the back: Kokushoan, with a seating capacity of six, is a 200-year-old tea house that was rebuilt here; and Karin, a larger room that seats 10. The traditional Japanese architecture blends well with the modern refinements in these rooms. The *horigotatsu*-style sunken seating is also comfortable.

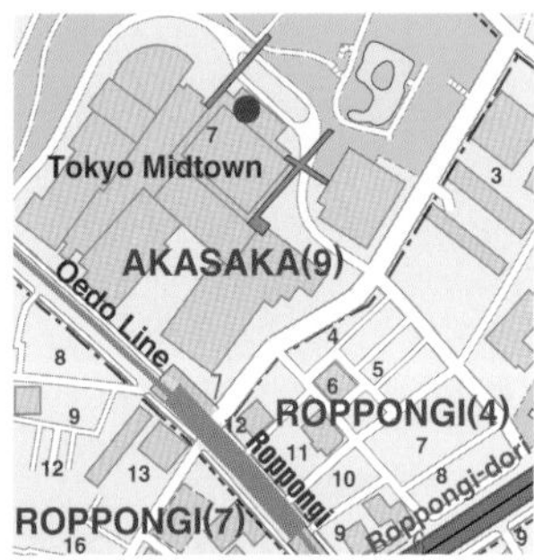

■ Opening hours, last orders
Lunch=11:30-14:00 (L.O.)
Dinner=17:30-21:30 (L.O.)

■ Price
Lunch= menu ¥ 7,900-23,000
Dinner= menu ¥ 15,000-25,000
Private room fee= ¥ 5,000-30,000
Service charge= 10%

**TEL. 03-3423-8000**
FAX. 03-3423-8001
The Ritz-Carlton Hotel 45F,
Tokyo Midtown, 9-7-1 Akasaka,
Minato-ku
www.ritzcarlton.com/ja/tokyo

# Hiramatsu

14

Owner-chef Hiroyuki Hiramatsu's culinary career was decided after reading a book by 20th century French chef Fernand Point. The stylish first-floor reception features antique French furnishings, while the gallery on the first basement level exhibits paintings by his brother. A bar and a private dining room are located on the second floor and the main dining room is on the third. The food is a contemporary take on traditional French cuisine and the specialities are duck foie gras rolled in cabbage with truffle sauce and roast lamb slices and onion compote with truffle sauce, with *gâteau au chocolat "Hiramatsu"* for dessert. The menu changes with every season and lunchtime set menus change weekly; the inexpensive lunch menu is not available on weekends or holidays. The wine list of 800 French wines is impressive. This restaurant, located near Hiroo Station, is suitable for both special celebrations and business entertaining.

■ Opening hours, last orders
Lunch=12:00-14:00 (L.O.)
Dinner=18:00-21:30 (L.O.)

■ Annual and weekly closing
Closed mid-August, late December-early January and Monday except Bank Holidays

■ Price
Lunch= menu ¥ 4,200-8,400
carte ¥ 14,000-18,000
Dinner= menu ¥ 12,600-21,000
carte ¥ 14,000-18,000
Private room fee= less than 5 persons ¥ 31,500
Service charge= 15%

**TEL. 03-3444-3967**
FAX. 03-3444-3991
5-15-13 Minami-Azabu, Minato-ku
www.hiramatsu.co.jp/restaurants/hiramatsu-hiroo

# Hirosaku
## ひろ作

A *kappo* (counter style restaurant) run by a friendly couple in an old detached house in Shinbashi. Owner-chef Satoshi Watanabe trained at a *ryotei* in Akasaka in his 20s and worked at several other establishments before opening Hirosaku in 1983. The simple dining room brings to mind the Showa Era (1926-1989). Tuna, with a deep Cardinal colour, is full of flavour. The side dish of soft octopus from Akashi in Hyogo and *shuto* (salted and fermented bonito gut) is also delicious. Loin of Japanese black cattle from Otawara in Tochigi is simply charcoal-grilled with salt. As the last dish of the menu, enjoy *soba* noodles made with a blend of buckwheat flour from Hokkaido and Nagano; lightly coloured, translucent and lustrous, the noodles slide down the throat smoothly, and are in perfect harmony with the rich but light bonito broth. The side dishes to complement *sake* are another feature of this restaurant. Come for dinner to really experience the chef at his best.

■ Opening hours, last orders
Lunch=11:45-13:00 (L.O.)
Dinner=18:00-20:00 (L.O.)

■ Annual and weekly closing
Closed mid-August, late December-early January, Saturday, Sunday and Bank Holidays

■ Price
Lunch= menu ¥ 8,400-12,600
Dinner= menu ¥ 26,250-31,500

**TEL. 03-3591-0901**
FAX. 03-3593-3886
3-6-13 Shinbashi, Minato-ku

# Hishinuma
## 菱沼

12

The owner-chef, Takayuki Hishinuma, who has made it his goal to "serve society through food," has done his best to break down barriers at this restaurant—both literally and figuratively. Hishinuma is wheel-chair accessible and the menu transcends the conventional boundaries of Japanese cuisine. A vegetarian set menu is offered as is a *Hiyoko-san* menu for children. The latter is designed not only to pique kids' interest in good food but also to provide nutritional education. While *kaiseki* is kept as the base, he combines it with meat dishes as well as creative Western-inspired dishes. Tableware enhancing the beautifully arranged food lends added seasonal emphasis. The tranquil dining room, with its wooden floor and soft lighting, is modern in style with ornate cabinets and woodblock prints of various Japanese festivals. There is a wide counter and table seating as well as two private rooms that have tables rather than *tatami*. From his love of wine, chef suggests pairings of Japanese cuisine and wines. For those who enjoy informal Japanese cuisine, Hishinuma is a worthy destination.

■ Opening hours, last orders
Lunch=11:30-13:30 (L.O.)
Dinner=17:30-22:00 (L.O.)

■ Annual and weekly closing
Closed mid-August, late December-early January, Sunday and Bank Holidays

■ Price
Lunch= menu ¥ 3,570-7,350
Dinner= menu ¥ 12,600-18,900
Service charge= 10%

**TEL. 03-3568-6588**
FAX. 03-3568-6335
Axis Building B1F,
5-17-1 Roppongi, Minato-ku

# Horikane
## 堀兼

16

A *kappo* (counter style restaurant), located in Shirokanedai's residential area, where owner-chef Hidehiro Horiuchi's kitchen is a place of focused concentration. The restaurant has a counter with eight seats, two private rooms with table seating and a small private room with sunken seating. The counter seats are booked first, so make a reservation for them as early as possible. Combining Chinese and Japanese styles, a spiced stew of Jinhua ham and vegetables is served on steamed papaya with Peking duck and has a tempting, charred aroma. Crab meat and white asparagus wrapped in *namayuba* (fresh bean curd skin) is served with a unique foie gras sauce. In November, when milt of *fugu* (puffer fish) is available, the restaurant offers *shirako* (milt) risotto with white truffles from Alba, while in winter, *shabu-shabu* of *kanburi* (winter yellowtail) and wild *nameko* mushrooms is delicious. The set menu -which changes three times a month- always includes a *nabe ryori* (hotpot), no matter what the season. The *reishu* (cold *sake*) on offer only comes in 720-ml bottles.

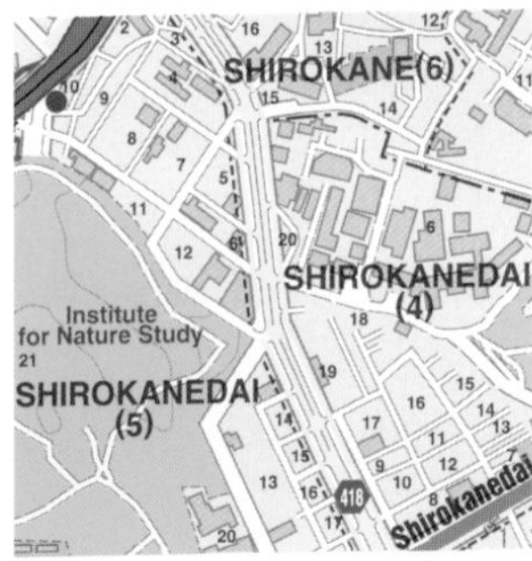

■ Opening hours, last orders
Dinner=18:30-23:00 L.O.21:00

■ Annual and weekly closing
Closed Golden week, mid-August, late December-early January, Sunday and Bank Holidays

■ Price
Dinner= menu ¥ 21,000-26,250

**TEL. 03-3280-4629**
FAX. 03-3280-4669
5-10-13 Shirokanedai, Minato-ku

# Hosokawa
## ほそ川

Go along Hokusai-dori Avenue from the Edo-Tokyo Museum near the Ryogoku Station, turn right into the first alley to find this *soba* restaurant. Believing that "the quality of *soba* is determined by its ingredients", owner-chef Takashi Hosokawa grows his own buckwheat on his farm in Ibaraki. The thin noodles are made from 100% buckwheat flour freshly ground every day and they slide easily down the throat, especially when matched with the thick broth. Appetisers include *sobagaki* (buckwheat dumpling) with a pleasant texture, *soba-dofu* (tofu made from buckwheat flour) containing buckwheat grains and *Edomae anago-no tempura* (conger eel *tempura*). These straightforward dishes allow the flavour of each fastidiously selected ingredient to assert itself. The interior is simple, with only four shared tables and one private room; red earthen walls and warm lighting create a comfortable mood. Reservations can be made for weekday dining, but not on weekends or public holidays. As the restaurant is intended to be a retreat for adults wishing to enjoy *soba* in a quiet environment, guests are requested not to bring small children.

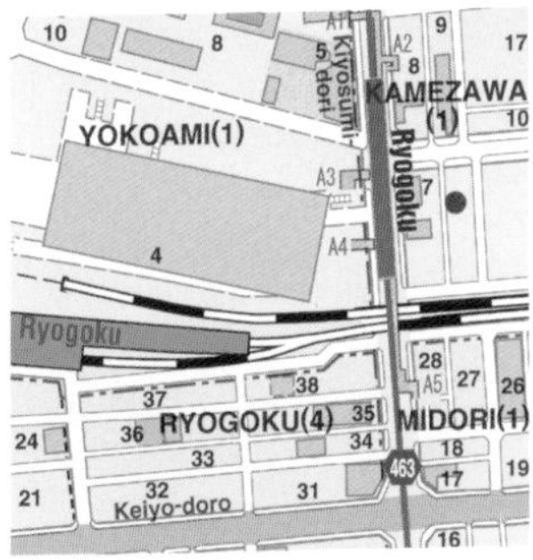

■ Opening hours, last orders
Lunch=11:45-15:00
Dinner=17:30-21:30 L.O.21:00

■ Annual and weekly closing
Closed mid-August, early January, Monday and 3rd Tuesday

■ Price

| | |
|---|---|
| Lunch= carte | ¥ 3,000-6,000 |
| Dinner= carte | ¥ 3,000-6,000 |

**TEL. 03–3626–1125**
FAX. 03–3626–1125
1-6-5 Kamezawa, Sumida-ku
www.edosoba-hosokawa.jp

# Ichimonji
## 一文字

Kazuhiko Hirose, the owner-chef, provided the catering for tea ceremonies for 13 years (and continues to do so) before opening this *kaiseki* restaurant in 2005. An *ichimonji* is a narrow strip of cloth placed horizontally at the top and bottom of the artwork on a scroll. Since it is used in all schools, the chef chose it to indicate his intention of transcending ceremonial boundaries. The interior has sunken seating for seven at the counter on the first floor and a *tatami* room on the second floor. Both dining spaces reflect the beauty of traditional tea houses while also providing a relaxing atmosphere. Each dish is in harmony with the colour and feel of the tableware on which it is served, elegantly conveying a sense of the season. The soft and plump *hotate-shinjo* (steamed scallop balls) served with Kintoki carrot and *yuzu* is a colourful dish with the white, red and yellow standing out in the clear soup stock. The *sawara-no yuan-yaki* (grilled Japanese Spanish mackerel marinated in *yuzu*) is served with *ikura* (salmon roe) in *yuzu* skin and *Tanba-kuromame* (black soybeans).

■ Opening hours, last orders
Lunch=12:00-14:00 (L.O.)
Dinner=18:00-21:00 (L.O.)

■ Annual and weekly closing
Closed Golden week, mid-August and late December-early January

■ Price
Lunch= menu ¥ 8,400-16,800
Dinner= menu ¥ 12,600-21,000
Private room fee= ¥ 5,250
Service charge= 10%

**TEL. 03–5206–8223**
FAX. 03–5206–8227
3-6 Kagurazaka, Shinjuku-ku

# Ishikawa
## 石かわ

Originally established by Hideki Ishikawa in 2003, this restaurant moved to its current location behind Zenkokuji Temple –known as Bishamonten- in January 2008. The interior, with a seven-seater counter made of 400-year-old Bishu *hinoki* (Japanese cypress) and four small private rooms, has a warm, comfortable feel. The cuisine is described as "Ishikawa-style", bounded only by the chef's imagination. Various innovations are incorporated into each dish to highlight the unique characteristics of each ingredient. Stewed beef tendon and wax gourd in soup stock is refined and creamy. The spiny lobster and abalone that are added to enhance the flavour of the wax gourd—the dish's main ingredient—also add a luxurious element. *Takikomi-gohan* (a rice seasoned with broth and boiled with various ingredients) with firefly squid and onion pan-fried in advance to intensify its taste and texture, is a full-bodied, flavoursome dish permeated with the strong taste of squid gut. Also on offer is a variety of *sake*, mainly from Niigata, the chef's birthplace, and the Hokuriku region.

■ Opening hours, last orders
Dinner=17:30-24:00 L.O.22:00

■ Annual and weekly closing
Closed mid-August, late December-early January, Sunday and Bank Holidays

■ Price
Dinner= menu ¥ 15,750-19,950
Service charge= 10%

**TEL. 03-5225-0173**
FAX. 03-5225-0173
5-37 Kagurazaka, Shinjuku-ku

# Joël Robuchon

30

A restaurant located on the second floor of the 18C French-style château at Yebisu Garden Place, named after the eponymous chef, Joël Robuchon. The dining room is furnished with a black arabesque-pattern carpet, black tablecloths and chairs, Swarovski crystal adorning the golden walls and a Baccarat chandelier hanging dazzlingly from the ceiling. This is a charming setting in which to enjoy the food, which is itself impressive in both taste and presentation. The menu changes frequently, but the house specialities, ossetra caviar and crustacean gelée served with smooth cauliflower cream, mille-feuille of tomato and horse crab, and ravioli stuffed with langoustine and truffles, are highly recommended. Wine lovers can consult with the sommelier in choosing an appropriate bottle from the extensive wine list. The restaurant also has three private salons on the third floor. This is an elegant restaurant, suitable for celebrating special occasions.

■ Opening hours, last orders
Lunch=11:30-14:30 (L.O.)
Dinner=18:00-22:00 (L.O.)

■ Price

| | | |
|---|---|---|
| Lunch= | menu | ¥ 8,200-12,300 |
| | carte | ¥ 15,000-30,000 |
| Dinner= | menu | ¥ 22,500-36,000 |
| | carte | ¥ 15,000-30,000 |

Service charge= 12% (private room 15%)

**TEL. 03-5424-1347**
Yebisu Garden Place,
1-13-1 Mita, Meguro-ku
www.robuchon.jp/ebisu

# Kadowaki
## かどわき

High-quality ingredients carefully selected by owner-chef Toshiya Kadowaki and his creative techniques are the star attractions here. As well as traditional Japanese ingredients, he looks to Western produce like truffles and foie gras as part of his desire to make "dishes to impress". In April, the peak season for *hanasansho* (Japanese pepper flowers), *hanasansho-nabe* (hotpot with fish or beef and *hanasansho*) is available. In autumn, *matsutake* mushroom and beef *shabu-shabu* is recommended. *Fukahire-no-karaage* (deep-fried shark fin) and *soba* (buckwheat noodles) with foie gras dipping sauce are served year-round and are also good. Truffle rice, a house speciality, fuses Japanese and Western ingredients. Kadowaki seats six at the counter and has three private rooms with table seating. To get there, head towards TV Asahi along a shopping street as you leave Exit 4 of Azabu-Juban Station. Kadowaki is behind the red-tiled building with a supermarket on the first floor that you will see on the left. Look for the black wooden walls and a lantern at the entrance.

■ Opening hours, last orders
Dinner=18:00-1:00 L.O.24:00
Saturday L.O.22:00

■ Annual and weekly closing
Closed Golden week, mid-August, late December-early January, Sunday and Bank Holidays

■ Price
Dinner= menu ¥ 21,000-26,250
Service charge= 5%

**TEL. 03–5772–2553**
FAX. 03–5772–2533
2-7-2 Azabu-Juban, Minato-ku
www.azabu-kadowaki.com

# Kamiya Nogizaka
## 神谷 乃木坂

12

This restaurant is on your left, about 100m down the slope as you leave Exit 1 of Nogizaka Station. While respecting the basics of Japanese culinary culture, Masataka Kamiya, the owner-chef, expands its possibilities by also using French, Italian and Chinese ingredients. Meisyanton pork loin from Ibaraki is used for the *shabu-shabu,* while the belly is cooked with black vinegar in the same way as *kakuni* (Nagasaki-style braised pork) and topped with *Shimonita-negi* (scallion) sauce. French duck is slowly cooked in its own fat and flavoured with a red wine sauce that includes soy sauce. Spring choices include large short-necked clams from Mikawa in Aichi steamed in *sake*, while in summer, the wax gourd is thoroughly seasoned with the soup stock. In autumn, try the grilled sea bream coated with grated *karasumi* (salted and dried grey mullet roe). The winter menu features *fugu nabe* (puffer fish hotpot) seasoned with homemade *miso* (soybean paste), and a hotpot of Toyama's *matsubagani* crabs. The handmade *soba* served as the last course before dessert is another memorable feature of this restaurant.

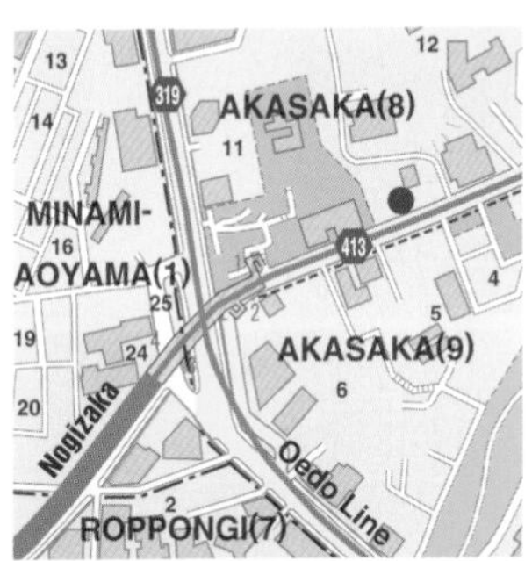

■ Opening hours, last orders
Lunch=11:30-15:00 L.O.14:30
Dinner=17:30-22:00 L.O.21:30

■ Annual and weekly closing
Closed Golden week, mid-August, late December-early January, Sunday and Bank Holidays

■ Price
Lunch= menu ¥ 5,250-10,500
Dinner= menu ¥ 10,500-21,000
Private room fee= ¥ 1,050/person
Service charge= 10%

**TEL. 03-3497-0489**
FAX. 03-3497-0489
8-11-19 Akasaka, Minato-ku
www.kamiya-m.com/nogizaka

# Kanda
## かんだ

Hiroyuki Kanda, the owner-chef of this Japanese restaurant in residential Moto-Azabu, makes the most of the natural flavour of premium ingredients to create dishes that burst with originality. For the sea bream *sashimi*, he uses a little salt, briefly sears the skin and serves it with soy sauce accented with the slightly sour taste of *bainiku* (Japanese apricot pulp). For the soup dish he uses mainly vegetables. Grilled *anago* (conger eel) has a tempting aroma and is a popular topping for *sushi*. The grilled *sakura-masu* (cherry salmon) marinated in *tsubu-miso* (coarse soybean paste) is soft and plump, and paired with slightly bitter and crisply fried *fukinoto* (butterbur sprout) reminds diners of the season. Fastidious attention is even paid to garnishes for grilled dishes, with ingredients like ginger and avocado, thinly battered and fried, further enhancing the overall taste. The chef understands his customers' preferences and adjusts the taste and quantity to suit. Here, you can really feel the enthusiasm of the chef and his staff.

■ Opening hours, last orders
Dinner=18:00-22:30 (L.O.)

■ Annual and weekly closing
Closed mid-August, late December-early January, Sunday and Bank Holidays

■ Price
Dinner= menu ¥ 13,650-24,150
Service charge= 10%

**TEL. 03-5786-0150**
FAX. 03-5786-0150
3-6-34 Moto-Azabu, Minato-ku

# Keyakizaka
## けやき坂

This *teppanyaki* restaurant is in the Grand Hyatt hotel in the Roppongi Hills complex. Since the hotel lifts are not directly linked to the restaurant, you need to take the lift to the sixth floor and then go down the stairs to the fourth floor. Alternatively, you can use the direct passage from Roppongi Hills Mori Tower West Walk. The distinguishing feature of this restaurant lies in its original approach to *teppanyaki*, which blends aspects of Western cuisine. Looking at the menu, all the standards are there -seafood, beef and other conventional ingredients- but it is the preparation that makes it unique. For example, sautéed white asparagus is topped with an orange-flavoured sabayon sauce, while warm foie gras is served with caramelised seasonal fruit. *Shirako* (milt) is coated with flour, sautéed in a brown butter sauce and served with capers; ingredients are combined effectively. Pork, lamb and duck are also available, but the beef is recommended.

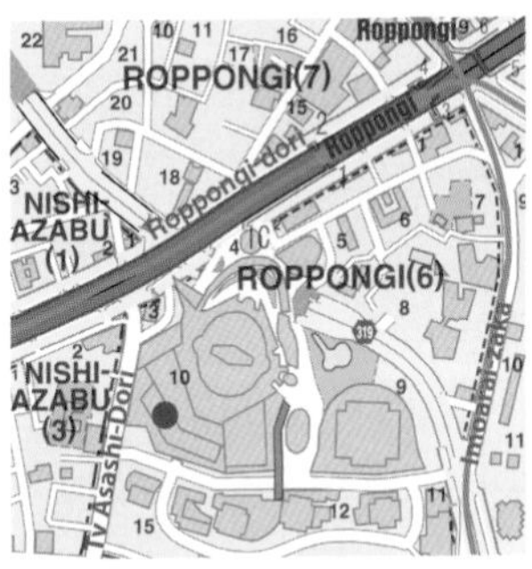

■ Opening hours, last orders
Lunch=11:30-14:30 (L.O.)
Dinner=18:00-22:00 (L.O.)

■ Price
Lunch= menu ¥ 4,000-10,500
carte ¥ 8,000-23,000
Dinner= menu ¥ 17,000-23,000
carte ¥ 8,000-23,000
Private room fee= ¥ 5,250 (lunch), ¥10,500 (dinner)
Service charge= 10%

**TEL. 03-4333-8782**
Grand Hyatt Hotel 4F,
6-10-3 Roppongi, Minato-ku
www.tokyo.grand.hyatt.jp

# Kikuchi
## き久ち

This small restaurant, with only a counter and a single table, opened in 2007 near Aoyama-bashi Bridge on Gaien-dori Avenue. Owner-chef Takashi Kikuchi trained at a wide variety of restaurants to learn various cuisines and culinary techniques and offers simply presented dishes but ones that fulfill his philosophy of leaving a lasting impression. Two *omakase* (chef's choice) set menus are available, with the number of dishes of each depending on his ingredients. For example, a menu might include a soup of *awabi* (abalone) and *awabi-dake* (abalone mushrooms) served in a silver Tame-nuri lacquered bowl. The summer speciality is a whole tomato simmered in bonito soup and topped with basil-flavoured kudzu sauce and olive oil; when placed in a *waresan-sho*-style pottery bowl pre-cooled in the refrigerator, a white vapour similar to that of dry ice is generated. The chef chooses tableware, porcelain or pottery to suit each dish. Since he runs the restaurant single-handedly and purchases only enough ingredients for the day at Tsukiji market, reservations should be made as early as possible.

■ Opening hours, last orders
Dinner=18:00-21:30 (L.O.)

■ Annual and weekly closing
Closed early January, mid-August and Sunday

■ Price
Dinner= menu ¥ 10,500-15,750

**TEL. 03-6313-5599**
Minatoya Sohonten Building 2F,
2-17-17 Nishi-Azabu, Minato-ku

# Kikumi

## きくみ

The proprietress of this Akasaka *ryotei* hails from Fukuoka and she opened this restaurant in 1962 on behalf of her parents who ran a restaurant-inn in the city's Hakata district. The large room on the first floor and four private rooms on the second floor are furnished in a Japanese style. The head chef, who has been in charge of the restaurant's menu since 2003, selects ingredients daily at Tsukiji market, buying only enough to cater to the day's bookings. *Hamo* (pike conger) from Mie are grilled and lightly seasoned with salt, while the fresh ginkgo nuts and early harvest *matsutake* mushrooms offer a pleasant texture. Pumpkin and Ishikawa taro, which are expertly carved, and *yuba* (bean curd skin) feature in a refined simmered dish. Homemade *karasumi* (salted and dried grey mullet roe) with a hint of *sake* matches favourably with the *ochazuke*-style rice and broth dish. In winter, *fugu* is used as the main ingredient for a number of dishes. The restaurant changes its menu twice a month, never digressing from authentic Japanese cuisine that highlights the natural taste of each ingredient.

■ Opening hours, last orders
Lunch=12:00-13:00 (L.O.)
Dinner=17:30-20:00 (L.O.)

■ Annual and weekly closing
Closed Golden week, mid-August, late December-early January, Sunday and Bank Holidays

■ Price
Lunch= menu ¥ 10,500-21,000
Dinner= menu ¥ 21,000-31,500
Service charge= 20%

**TEL. 03-3583-3600**
FAX. 03-3583-3635
1-9-25 Akasaka, Minato-ku

# Kikunoi
## 菊乃井

10

This is the Akasaka branch of Kikunoi, a Kyoto-based *ryotei*. Third-generation owner-chef Yoshihiro Murata reflects the four seasons with exquisite dishes, prepared according to the restaurant's long-held cooking traditions. A starter named *kakureume*, representing a scene in early spring, sees a large piece of pickled Japanese apricot with the salt removed topped with strained sea bream *shirako* (milt). The grilled dish for April is *sakuramasu-no-ibushiyaki* (smoked and grilled cherry salmon) from Himi, cooked after being dipped in *miso-yuan* paste made from soybean paste, *sake*, *mirin* (sweet cooking *sake*) and soy sauce; it is served with *Daitokuji-natto* (fermented and salted soybeans). The seasonal sense is created by grilling it with cherry tree bark for smoky flavour. Built in 2004, the restaurant has counters and also formal private rooms. On the ground floor there are two counters; upstairs, a tearoom and *tatami* rooms are based on the *sukiya* style of architecture employed for tea houses. Kikunoi's attention to detail makes one feel like one's in Kyoto.

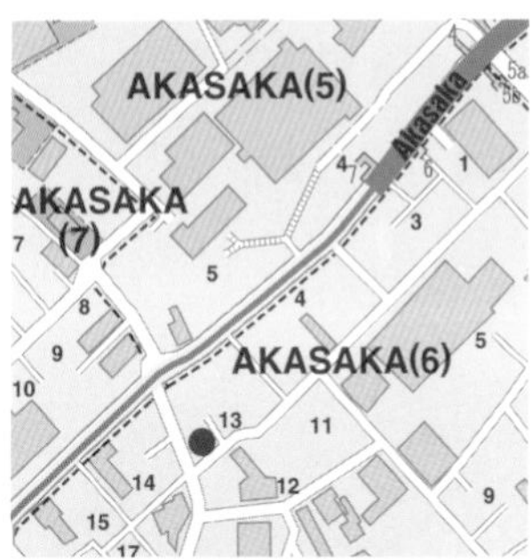

■ Opening hours, last orders
Dinner=17:00-21:00 (L.O.)

■ Annual and weekly closing
Closed mid-August, late December-early January and Sunday

■ Price
Dinner= menu ¥ 15,750-21,000
Service charge= 10% (tatami room 15%)

**TEL. 03-3568-6055**
FAX. 03-3568-6056
6-13-8 Akasaka, Minato-ku
www.kikunoi.jp/akasaka.htm

# Kodama
## こだま

You will find this Japanese restaurant on the second floor of a modern building near the Nishi-Azabu Post Office. Owner-chef Tsutomu Kodama is entirely self-taught, preferring to be guided by his instincts. He uses ingredients carefully so as not to waste even vegetable skins or usually unwanted leaves and preparation sees food transformed into inventive dishes. One of the most popular dishes here is *awabi-soba*, which is a new-take on noodles: they are made from several types of seaweed instead of flour and the sauce used is made of minced abalone flesh and innards. The fish bone soup that comes served in a small pot is made by using juice taken from fresh seasonal fish after it has been stewed in soup stock, and contains plenty of gelatine, bone marrow and other fish nutrients. Among the selection of autumn appetisers, the *matsutake* mushroom ice cream- a mixture of *matsutake* with the salty milk-based ice cream- is innovative, while the ginger ice cream with large, white kidney bean purée is also creative. The interior has a large red counter and two private rooms with sunken seating.

■ Opening hours, last orders
Dinner=18:00-22:30 L.O.20:30

■ Annual and weekly closing
Closed Golden week, mid-August, late December-early January, Sunday and Bank Holidays

■ Price
Dinner= menu ¥ 15,750
Private room fee= 10%
Service charge= 10%

**TEL. 03-3408-8865**
Nishi-Azabu 1106 2F,
1-10-6 Nishi-Azabu, Minato-ku

# Kogetsu

**湖月**

6

The name "Kogetsu" has been around since the *okami* (proprietress) and her late husband ran a restaurant in Hamburg, Germany in the 1960s. In 1967 they opened this establishment in Jingumae. Whilst not spacious, the dining room goes back a long way and has nine counter seats as well as a *tatami* room at the back. *Kyo-ryori* (Kyoto-style cuisine) that uses seasonal ingredients is the main event. *Wakatakeni* uses boiled bamboo shoots from Kyoto and *hamo* (pike conger) is served with *bainiku* (Japanese apricot pulp). House specialities include *kasujiru* (*sake* lee soup) with eight kinds of vegetables, steamed Shogoin turnip with *anago* (conger eel), *tai-no-iimushi* (sea bream steamed with rice), and thinly sliced *aigamo* (crossbred duck) loin cooked in a bonito and kelp soup stock. *Tai meshi* (sea bream with rice) is recommended. The friendly head chef formerly taught Japanese cuisine overseas. Although he serves diners at the counter, there are waitresses including the *kimono*-attired *okami*. Here, you can enjoy Japanese food deeply rooted in tradition.

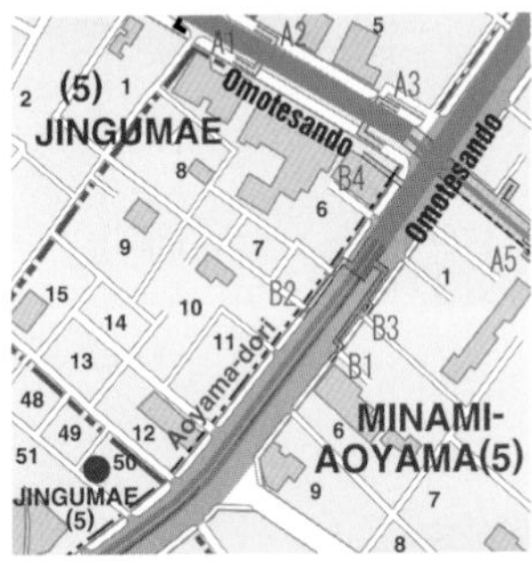

■ Opening hours, last orders
Dinner=18:00-21:30

■ Annual and weekly closing
Closed mid-August, late December-early January, Sunday and Bank Holidays

■ Price
Dinner= menu ¥ 13,650-15,750

**TEL. 03-3407-3033**
5-50-10 Jingumae, Shibuya-ku
www.aoyama-kogetsu.com

# Koju
## 小十

A Japanese restaurant run by Toru Okuda, in a back street behind the Nikko Hotel. Look for the small sign, *noren* curtain and paved entrance. In addition to seafood ordered from Omaezaki, red sea bream, *hamo* (pike conger), tilefish, prawns and others are sent daily from Naruto in Tokushima. During transit, even the position of the ice is specified as this, Okuda believes, affects freshness. Spring offerings include *tairagai shunsai zukushi* (pen shells with assorted spring vegetables), and in summer, prawns with summer vegetables grace the menu. The *unagi* (eel) is thick and both the *shirayaki* (broiled unseasoned *unagi*) and *kabayaki* (*unagi* broiled and basted with a sweet sauce) are tasty. As for dessert, the strawberry sherbet with Champagne Rosé shows the chef's creativity and ability to let go of tradition. Another attraction of Koju is the wide selection of *sake* and wine, which is carefully chosen by the owner-chef who is both a certified *sake* taster and a qualified sommelier. At Koju, you can enjoy dishes that exhibit modern flair but also make use of traditional cooking techniques.

■ Opening hours, last orders
Dinner=17:30-1:00 L.O.24:00
Saturday 17:30-24:00 L.O.21:30

■ Annual and weekly closing
Closed mid-August, late December-early January, Sunday and Bank Holidays

■ Price
Dinner= menu ¥ 13,650-24,150
carte ¥ 10,000-18,000
Service charge= 10%

**TEL. 03-6215-9544**
FAX. 03-6215-9545
8-5-25 Ginza, Chuo-ku
www.kojyu.jp

# Komuro
## 小室

Owner-chef Mitsuhiro Komuro established his own business in Kagurazaka in 2000 after training at a *chakaiseki* establishment (one specialising in simple Japanese cuisine served during tea ceremonies) in Mejiro. Diners can admire ceramic tableware created by artists such as Seika Suda or Tosai Sawamura on which Komuro, a collector, serves the food. The *hamo zukushi* set menu is a treat - although it is only available in summer - and features hamo (pike conger) from Akashi, which is well known for its quality and pleasant aftertaste. In spring, *samatsudake* mushrooms from Yamaguchi and Shimane are served with *hamo* in a flavoursome soup. In autumn, *matsutake* mushrooms from Tanba have an exceptional aroma, flavour and texture. Watching the chefs hard at work in the kitchen is also one of the pleasures. This small restaurant has one private room in addition to an eight-seat counter, but the counter is recommended. Go up Kagurazaka-dori Avenue from Iidabashi Station, turn left just before Zenkoku-ji Temple -known as Bishamonten- and follow the road until the white sign of the restaurant appears on the right.

■ Opening hours, last orders
Lunch=12:00-13:00 (L.O.) except Monday
Dinner=18:30-20:00 (L.O.)

■ Annual and weekly closing
Closed mid-August, 21 December-16 January, Sunday and Bank Holidays

■ Price
Lunch= menu ¥ 6,300-12,600
Dinner= menu ¥ 16,800-31,500
Service charge= 10%

**TEL. 03-3235-3332**
FAX. 03-3235-3338
13 Wakamiyacho, Shinjuku-ku

# Kondo
## 近藤

In order to offer fresh seasonal ingredients, owner-chef Fumio Kondo travels the country to check and purchase raw produce. The asparagus and corn from Hokkaido, log-cultivated *shiitake* mushrooms from Iwate and other vegetables used at this restaurant are highly rated by customers. One of the "musts" at this establishment is sweet potato. After being fried, the large cylindrical slices are left to sit and cook in the remaining heat. Considering the time it takes before serving, it is a good idea to order early. Carrots are julienned before going into the fryer—a method inspired by a French candy technique—to bring out their sweet flavor. Summer squash stuffed with *yuba* (bean curd skin) is a unique recipe only offered at Kondo. Here, tempura with a thin batter, fried in the restaurant's special sesame oil, holds the full flavour of the ingredients kept on ice rather than in a refrigerator to maintain freshness. The restaurant, located in Namiki do-ri avenue in Ginza, features a plain wooden counter and two bright rooms.

■ Opening hours, last orders
Lunch=12:00-15:00 L.O.13:30
Dinner=17:00-22:30 L.O.20:30

■ Annual and weekly closing
Closed Golden week, mid-August, late December-early January, Sunday and Bank Holiday Mondays

■ Price
Lunch= menu ¥ 5,250-7,350
Dinner= menu ¥ 8,400-15,750

**TEL. 03-5568-0923**
Sakaguchi Building 9F,
5-5-13 Ginza, Chuo-ku

# Kosetsu
## 古拙

A *soba* restaurant located on the second floor of an old building in a side street behind Showa-dori Avenue in Ginza 2-chome. It may be difficult to find, but the name Toni building (東二ビル) is indicated above the entrance and the restaurant's name is near the stairs. Only seasonal set menus are offered at dinner. In spring, the salad with *soba*, *zuke-maguro* (marinated tuna) and rocket is delicious. Summer choices include *awabi-to mozuku-no tsuyusoba* (*soba* served with a *tsuyu* dipping sauce featuring abalone and *mozuku* seaweed) and a small *soba* hotpot with eel and egg. Jin Ishii, the owner-chef, favours vegetables from Tochigi and Kyoto, and in spring uses plenty of mountain vegetables from Akita. His noodles are delicate and silky in the mouth, and go well with the light *tsuyu* dipping sauce. For lunch, the restaurant offers à la carte *udon* and *soba* dishes, but the *soba kaiseki* set menu available only by reservation is recommended. Substantial and innovative, it offers a range of *soba* dishes, like *soba sus*hi and even *soba* roll cake for dessert. In addition to *sake*, champagne is also available.

■ Opening hours, last orders
Lunch=11:30-14:00 L.O.13:30
Dinner=18:00-22:00 L.O.19:30

■ Annual and weekly closing
Closed mid-August, early January and Sunday

■ Price

| | | |
|---|---|---|
| Lunch= | menu | ¥ 5,250 |
| | carte | ¥ 1,125-1,890 |
| Dinner= | menu | ¥ 10,500-14,700 |
| Service charge= | | 10% (only for set menu) |

**TEL. 03-3543-6565**
FAX. 03-3543-6565
Toni Building 2F,
2-13-6 Ginza, Chuo-ku

# La Bombance

This restaurant is located in the basement of a condominium building on the right-hand side of the road, just past the Nishi-Azabu intersection as you head toward Shibuya - look for the "B" sign in the yellow light. The dimly-lit interior consisting of only a counter and a single table, with background music and soft lighting filtering through wooden lattice, boasts a gentle atmosphere. Makoto Okamoto, the owner-chef, opened this restaurant in 2004 after training at a teppanyaki restaurant and a ryotei. Underpinned by Japanese culinary traditions, he incorporates a variety of non-Japanese ingredients such as foie gras, Iberico pork and mozzarella cheese. The set menu changes monthly and foie gras appears as a constant. Speciality desserts include a decolourised white coffee blancmange and black sesame sherbet. A degustation (tasting) menu pairing a small amount of sake with each dish is also available. The restaurant's French name means "a feast" and is well suited to couples.

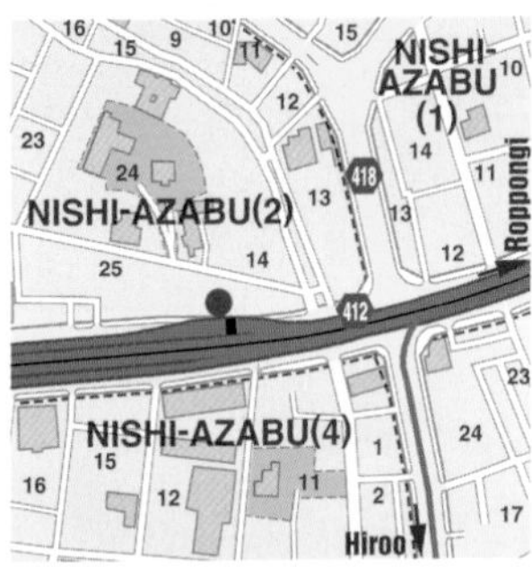

■ Opening hours, last orders
Dinner=18:00-22:00 (L.O.)

■ Annual and weekly closing
Closed mid-August, late December-early January, Sunday and Bank Holidays

■ Price
Dinner= menu ¥ 10,800
Service charge= 10%

TEL. 03-5778-6511
J-Grande Nishiazabu III B1F,
2-25-24 Nishi-Azabu, Minato-ku
www.bombance.com

# L'Alliance

20

Trained in various regions in France, the chef offers French cuisine that takes account of both seasonal ingredients and the distinct Japanese seasonal changes. One of the specialities here is the duck foie gras in a dome mold: foie gras from the Landes region is cooked over a low heat and wrapped in a jelly of duck consommé and Port, then served with 20-year aged balsamic vinegar and homemade brioche. Roasted lobster offers an original taste with a vanilla aroma. Rounds of lamb are flavoured with tapenade before being roasted - the resulting taste is enhanced by two sauces, one made of the gravy and the other with goat's cheese. For dessert, Crêpe Suzette is prepared with a showy performance at the table. The wine list is extensive and includes vintages dating back as far as 1918. This restaurant in Kagurazaka is particularly alluring at night: during dinner, there is a live piano performance and later, jazz musicians entertain in the bar.

■ Opening hours, last orders
Lunch=11:30-14:00 (L.O.)
Dinner=18:00-21:30 (L.O.)

■ Annual and weekly closing
Closed late December-early January, Saturday, Sunday and Bank Holidays

■ Price
Lunch= menu ¥ 3,900-7,500
Dinner= menu ¥ 8,500-15,000
carte ¥ 8,500-19,000
Private room fee= less than 7 persons ¥10,000
Service charge= 10% (dinner)

**TEL. 03-3269-0007**
FAX. 03-3269-0242
2-11 Kagurazaka, Shinjuku-ku
www.lalliance.jp

# L'Anneau d'Or

White leather booth seats and generous sized tables stand out in the soft lighting and the walls are decorated with a poem about the four seasons by Dogen Zenji, a teacher of Zen Buddhism, alongside illustrations by the late Raymond Peynet. L'Anneau d'Or opened in 2005 after owner-chef Yasunobu Tanikawa, who trained in several noted restaurants in Japan and Europe, wound up his Shimo-Kitazawa-based Chez Tani after 14 years in business. This latest venture is in partnership with his wife, who provides the friendly service. "The most important thing with cooking is aroma. If the aroma is good, the taste will also be", says the chef, who buys fresh seasonal ingredients from all over the country to create rich, but not heavy cuisine. Specialities here include a fastidiously selected soft-steamed egg served in a small cocotte with a sauce of truffles and foie gras; Lacan pigeon with light salmis sauce and roasted Challans duck served with a Rouennaise sauce. The quality wines on offer are reasonably priced. Reservations must be made a day in advance. This is a particularly good place for those more intimate occasions.

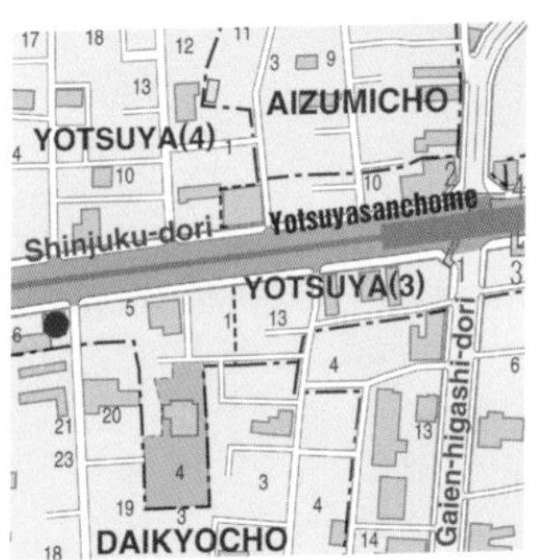

■ Opening hours, last orders
Lunch=Fri.-Sun.12:30-15:00
L.O.13:30
Dinner=18:30-22:30 L.O.20:30

■ Annual and weekly closing
Closed mid-August, late December-early January and Wednesday

■ Price
Lunch= menu ¥ 7,000-20,000
Dinner= menu ¥ 7,000-20,000
Service charge= 10% (lunch 5%)

**TEL. 03-5919-0141**
FAX. 03-5919-0152
Yotsuya Sun Heights B1F,
4-6-1 Yotsuya, Shinjuku-ku

# La Table de Joël Robuchon

Located on the first floor of what looks like an 18th-century château in the centre of Yebisu Garden Place. It has a striking décor of violet walls hung with contemporary art and a Baccarat glass chandelier that goes well with the modern furnishings. French *convivialité*, in the underlying character of the restaurant and a favourite word of Joël Robuchon, is important here. The cuisine offered is contemporary French, with original recipes combining Spanish and Italian elements; gazpacho soup, millefeuille of eggplant, tomato and mozzarella cheese, and quail with a caramelized outer layer stuffed with foie gras; the charm of each country's cuisine is delicately blended in the Robuchon style. One of the house specialities is an hors-d'œuvre of consommé jelly-covered sea urchin, served with fennel cream. Some à la carte dishes come in small portions that can be added to a set menu. The restaurant is often reserved for private parties, so it's advisable to check in advance.

■ Opening hours, last orders
Lunch=11:30-14:30 (L.O.)
Dinner=18:00-22:00 (L.O.)

■ Price
Lunch= menu ¥ 3,800-5,200
carte ¥ 7,000-14,000
Dinner= menu ¥ 6,200-12,500
carte ¥ 7,000-14,000
Service charge= 10%

**TEL. 03-5424-1338**
FAX. 03-5424-1339
Yebisu Garden Place,
1-13-1 Mita, Meguro-ku
www.robuchon.jp/ebisu

# L'Atelier de Joël Robuchon

Tokyo was the first city in the world to embrace Robuchon's concept of a new kind of restaurant. The stylish red and black interior is largely taken up by a long counter with seating for 44, in the style of a Japanese *sushi* restaurant or Spanish bar. The open kitchen is lively and the chefs and waiting staff are friendly. The restaurant has a good international atmosphere, filled with diners from all over the world. Carefully selected ingredients include fresh vegetables and fruits and seasonal seafood from Japan, foie gras, asparagus and poultry from France and, from Spain, *Jamon Iberico de Bellota*. Both the set and à la carte menus change each season. A small-portion menu (*La Carte Des Plats En Petites Portions Dégustation*) enables guests to try a variety of à la carte dishes. The wide selection of wines -about 200 choices from France and around the world- is another attraction. The restaurant also houses a boutique selling bread, pastries, cakes and delicatessen goods.

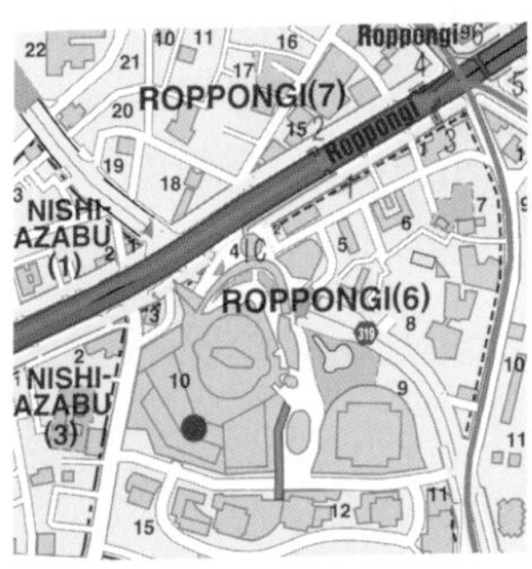

■ Opening hours, last orders
Lunch=11:30-14:00 (L.O.)
Sun. and Bank Holidays 11:30-15:00 (L.O.)
Dinner=18:00-22:00 (L.O.)

■ Price

| | | |
|---|---|---|
| Lunch= | menu | ¥ 4,100-13,800 |
| | carte | ¥ 8,000-20,000 |
| Dinner= | menu | ¥ 7,800-17,850 |
| | carte | ¥ 8,000-20,000 |

Service charge= 10%

**TEL. 03-5772-7500**
FAX. 03-5772-7789
Roppongi Hills Hillside 2F,
6-10-1 Roppongi, Minato-ku
www.robuchon.jp/roppongi

# La Tour

This French restaurant opened in 2006 in the Ginza Kojun Building. It is decorated in an elegant neo-baroque style and features a bar near the entrance where you can enjoy an aperitif while waiting for your dining companion. Tadaaki Shimizu, the owner-chef, refined his culinary skills at La Tour d'Argent in Paris and Tokyo, and opened his first restaurant in Kagurazaka in 1993 before opening in Ginza. He avoids having fixed suppliers, preferring to hand-pick ingredients from markets. The beef from Ogata Farm in Iwate can be ordered as a sautéed fillet or grilled rump and is served with its gravy. Flank is stewed in red Burgundy wine. The Royale de Foie Gras is a house speciality: foie gras is cooked for four hours at 110°C, and flavoured with Sauternes wine, accentuated by the gently aroma of Sicilian honey. Recommended are exquisite duck recipes, which go well with the green pepper, fig or citrus sauces. There is a wide selection of French cheeses to enjoy after the main course. This is a restaurant that uses reliable techniques in the classic tradition of French cuisine.

■ Opening hours, last orders
Lunch=11:30-15:00 L.O.13:30
Dinner=18:00-23:00 L.O.20:30

■ Annual and weekly closing
Closed mid-August,
31 December, 1 January
and Monday

■ Price
Lunch= menu ¥ 4,500-8,000
Dinner= menu ¥ 12,500-18,500
carte ¥ 14,000-19,000
Service charge= 10%

TEL. 03-3569-2211
FAX. 03-3569-2219
Kojun Building 5F,
6-8-7 Ginza, Chuo-ku
www.ginzalatour.com

# La Tour d'Argent

30

As the Tokyo counterpart of the venerable Parisian establishment, La Tour d'Argent -which has been serving diners since 1582-this French restaurant opened in New Otani in 1984. After passing through the blue-carpeted entrance hall towards the portrait of Henri IV on horseback, guests are greeted by a luxurious dining room reminiscent of a salon in a European castle. Large chandeliers that illuminate the spacious dining room, elegant oak-panelled walls, beautiful window furnishings, Louis XV furniture—the restaurant spells graceful luxury at every turn. Among the house specialities is roast duckling, for which the main ingredient is imported from Vendée in western France. Two sauces for this are particularly recommended: "Tour d'Argent" is a heavy sauce made from consommé and duck blood and liver, adjusted with cognac and Madeira wine; the other is "Marco Polo," which has a duck stock base and is seasoned with four types of grain pepper. The wine list features some 600 bins, mostly French. La Tour d'Argent is one of Tokyo's most luxurious restaurants in atmosphere and décor.

■ Opening hours, last orders
Dinner=17:30-22:30 L.O.21:00

■ Annual and weekly closing
Closed Monday

■ Price
Dinner= menu ¥ 21,000-35,000
carte ¥ 15,000-25,000
Private room fee= less than 12 persons
¥ 21,000
Service charge= 10%

**TEL. 03-3239-3111**
FAX. 03-3221-2874
New Otani Hotel The Main 2F,
4-1 Kioicho, Chiyoda-ku
www.newotani.co.jp/tokyo

# L'Auberge de l'Ill

Opened by the Hiramatsu Group in partnership with chef Marc Haeberlin, who runs the restaurant of the same name in Alsace in eastern France. This Tokyo restaurant is modelled on the original and offers traditional French cuisine with strong Alsatian influences. Signature dishes include *La mousseline de grenouilles 'Paul Haeberlin'* and *La côtelette de pigeon au chou et aux truffes. La pêche 'Haeberlin'* is a dessert of peach topped with champagne-flavoured sabayon sauce with pistachio ice cream. The wine list of more than 600 bins has been carefully selected by the sommelier and includes some excellent varieties from Alsace. The building formerly housed the Georgian Club and its columns and white façade give it the appearance of an 18th century British mansion. Inside, its salons on the second floor, the large horseshoe-shaped staircase, gleaming chandeliers, portraits of aristocrats, European-style fireplaces and furniture all add to the sophisticated atmosphere.

■ Opening hours, last orders
Lunch=11:30-14:00 (L.O.)
Dinner=17:30-21:00 (L.O.)

■ Price
Lunch= menu ¥ 4,200-8,400
carte ¥ 10,000-17,500
Dinner= menu ¥ 12,600-21,000
carte ¥ 10,000-17,500
Service charge= 15%

**TEL. 03-5785-8880**
FAX. 03-3470-1771
1-6-4 Nishi-Azabu, Minato-ku
www.hiramatsu.co.jp/restaurants/aubergedelill-tokyo

# Le Bourguignon

Based on traditional French regional cuisine, the dishes of owner-chef Yoshinaru Kikuchi are refined according to his own style. His speciality is the *boudin noir* terrine accompanied with apple salad and purée: normally thick in taste, here the dish is delicately flavoured and served as an hors d' oeuvre. Lamb, sent from Hokkaido by the half carcass, is served with a light sauce made of duck *bouillon* and herbs. A variety of winter *gibier* dishes are also available. The chef is also known for his interesting use of blood and organs in his extensive meat repertoire and this also keeps wastage to a minimum. Desserts are also imaginative, such as a combination of Mont Blanc with rice Bavarois maintaining the texture of rice, and the ripe red pepper pudding. Good wines, primarily from Burgundy, are offered at reasonable prices. This French restaurant was opened in Roppongi in 2000 and is a perfect place for casual dining with friends.

■ Opening hours, last orders
Lunch=11:30-15:30 L.O.13:00
Dinner=18:00-23:30 L.O.21:30

■ Annual and weekly closing
Closed 2 weeks in July, late December-early January, Wednesday and 2nd Tuesday

■ Price

| | | |
|---|---|---|
| Lunch= | menu | ¥ 2,625-4,725 |
| | carte | ¥ 7,000-11,000 |
| Dinner= | menu | ¥ 5,775-10,500 |
| | carte | ¥ 7,000-11,000 |

Service charge= 10%

**TEL. 03-5772-6244**
FAX. 03-5772-6344
3-3-1 Nishi-Azabu, Minato-ku

# Le Jeu de l'Assiette

Sophisticated cuisine that reflects the natural flavours of ingredients is what drives the young chef at this French restaurant, located midway between Daikanyama and Ebisu stations. Sea bass, grouper, sea urchin, tilefish and other seafood are sent from the chef's hometown in Yamaguchi; squab and duck are imported from France. One of the house specialities is an hors-d'œuvre of foie gras wrapped in rabbit that has been marinated in *yuzu* juice and is served with seasonal fruit. Roasted Challans duck breast also comes recommended: the accompanying two-coloured sauce with beets and onions is tasty and draws out the flavour of the duck. Each set menu offers a number of courses and portions are sized so that customers can enjoy a wide variety of dishes. The extensive wine list of 350 is well-priced; for champagne lovers, about 30 bins are available at a uniform price. Beautifully set tables and a brilliant Venetian glass chandelier round off the experience.

■ Opening hours, last orders
Lunch=11:30-13:30 (L.O.)
Dinner=18:00-21:00 (L.O.)

■ Annual and weekly closing
Closed mid-August, late December-early January, Monday and 3rd Tuesday

■ Price

| | | |
|---|---|---|
| Lunch= | menu | ¥ 3,500-12,000 |
| | carte | ¥ 8,500-12,000 |
| Dinner= | menu | ¥ 8,000-12,000 |
| | carte | ¥ 8,500-12,000 |

Service charge= 10%

**TEL. 03-6415-5100**
FAX. 03-6415-5101
Sun Village Daikanyama 2F,
2-17-5 Ebisu-Nishi, Shibuya-ku
www.lejeudelassiette.com

# Le Mange-Tout

This French restaurant, located in a detached house, initially opened in 1994 before reopening in 2006. Just 14 seats are available in a modern Italian-style dining space where the high-gloss floor and leather chairs by Italian furniture maker Cassina catch the eye. The chef Noboru Tani is an avid follower of Auguste Escoffier and he offers traditional French cuisine but with a modern twist. Tani carefully selects fresh ingredients and buys vegetables from Chiba and fish from Tsukiji market; meats are imported from Europe and in winter the restaurant offers game dishes using Japanese deer and boar from West Izu in Shizuoka. He also has a particular fondness for truffles and foie gras and cooks these dishes himself. *Omble chevalier* (Saibling), a European mountain trout, is served lightly smoked. Game Consommé is offered on the winter Game menu – this unique soup is based on a classic venison dish with sauce *poivrade*. In season, the *Pêche Melba* combines juicy, top quality peach, vanilla ice cream and raspberry sauce. Each dish showcases the chef's dedication to food and his unwavering professionalism.

■ Opening hours, last orders
Dinner=18:30-21:00 (L.O.)

■ Annual and weekly closing
Closed late December-early January and Sunday

■ Price
Dinner= menu ¥ 12,600
Service charge= 10%

**TEL. 03-3268-5911**
FAX. 03-3268-5911
22 Nandomachi, Shinjuku-ku
www.le-mange-tout.com

# L'Embellir

10

Focusing on beauty and health, this French eatery located in Minami-Aoyama with a modern and simple interior places importance on the selection of vegetables. The vegetable terrine combines between 14 and 17 different vegetables, each of which is individually seasoned. The fish hors-d'œuvre, made with whole horse crab from the Sea of Okhotsk, produces fresh and refined flavours; it is carefully prepared using crab meat and crab innards, which are delicately blended with paprika, and served with a small piece of fresh grapefruit tartlet. From spring to summer, there is milk-fed lamb roast from Hokkaido in northern Japan, a recommended dish served with a gravy that uses home-made coffee liquor. In winter, *suppon* (soft-shelled turtle) consommé is served along with small spear squid stuffed with scallop mousse and *tonsoku* (pig's feet). Food here is fragrant and displays a certain sophistication. Some à la carte dishes can be selected by the half portion upon request.

■ Opening hours, last orders
Lunch=11:30-14:00 (L.O.)
Dinner=18:00-21:30 (L.O.)

■ Annual and weekly closing
Closed mid-August, late December-early January, Sunday, 1st and 2nd Monday

■ Price
Lunch= menu ¥ 4,410-12,600
carte ¥ 10,000-13,000
Dinner= menu ¥ 12,600-21,000
carte ¥ 10,000-13,000
Private room fee= ¥ 10,500 (dinner)
Service charge= 10%

**TEL. 03-3423-0131**
B1F,
4-17-33 Minami-Aoyama, Minato-ku
www.lembellir.com

FRENCH CONTEMPORARY MAP NO. 9/A-1

# Les Créations de Narisawa

A French restaurant in Minami-Aoyama located behind the Sony Computer building. Opened in 2003, Les Créations de Narisawa adopts a distinctive honeybee logo, whose image of working hard to collect the blessings of nature corresponds with the resolve of owner-chef Yoshihiro Narisawa to provide diners with quality food. The dining room offers a chic harmony of white walls, dark flooring and modern furniture. Many of the vegetables come from the chef's garden in Mochizuki in the Shinshu region, while others come from organic farmers in Nagano. The fish is sourced nationwide and sent directly to the restaurant. The set menu, which changes monthly according to the available seasonal ingredients, offers modern cuisine based on traditional French recipes enlivened with the chef's original ideas. Specialities here are foie gras with strawberry; vanilla and tomato-flavoured roasted lobster; lamb with a hint of lavender; and the fondant chocolate and rose sorbet for dessert.

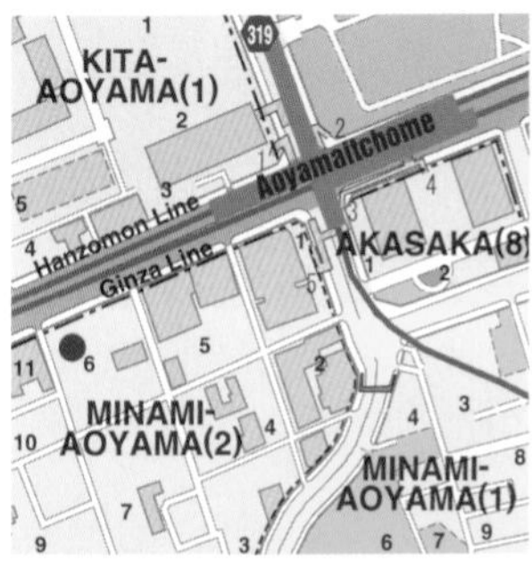

■ Opening hours, last orders
Lunch=12:00-13:00 (L.O.)
Dinner=18:30-21:00 (L.O.)

■ Annual and weekly closing
Closed late December-early January and Sunday

■ Price

| | | |
|---|---|---|
| Lunch= | menu | ¥ 7,350-12,600 |
| | carte | ¥ 13,000-16,000 |
| Dinner= | menu | ¥ 21,000 |
| | carte | ¥ 13,000-16,000 |

Service charge= 10%

TEL. 03-5785-0799
2-6-15 Minami-Aoyama, Minato-ku
www.narisawa-yoshihiro.com

# Les Enfants Gâtés

8

Just inside the entrance, you will find a refrigerator filled with terrines in colourful containers that will catch your eye. Hiroshi Haraguchi, the owner-chef, is an expert of terrines: a typical French deli food offered every day in at least eight varieties. Flavours vary from the traditional to the more inventive, such as the country-style pâté aged for more than two weeks after being cooked, and the pressed terrine of organic vegetables. The duck foie gras terrine served with fresh brioche is a house speciality. Fresh seafood, including lobster, is also made into sublime terrines. The winter *gibier* terrine that combines *colvert* duck, pigeon and venison is recommended. Aside from terrine, a range of sophisticated dishes based on traditional recipes created using contemporary techniques includes a lighter Royal hare stew, and roasted *colvert* duck. The wide selection of wines by the glass can be enjoyed with a terrine at the bar. The restaurant's name means "spoiled children."

■ Opening hours, last orders
Lunch=12:00-14:00 (L.O.)
Dinner=18:00-21:30 (L.O.)

■ Annual and weekly closing
Closed late December-early January and Monday

■ Price

| | | |
|---|---|---|
| Lunch= | menu | ¥ 3,150-5,775 |
| | carte | ¥ 6,000-11,000 |
| Dinner= | menu | ¥ 7,140-11,550 |
| | carte | ¥ 6,000-11,000 |

Service charge= 10%

**TEL. 03-3476-2929**
FAX. 03-3476-2928
2-3 Sarugakucho, Shibuya-ku
www.club-nyx.com/gates

# Le 6eme Sens

12

A French restaurant hidden behind a café on Corridor Street –look out for the "secret door" next to the reception desk that leads to the dining room. The interior is simple and modern, with an eye-catching fireplace built by an Italian craftsman. The basement private room is a must-see: it's a contemporary-styled space surrounded by glass with a curved brick ceiling and it doubles as a wine cellar storing around 10,000 bottles. It's only available to groups of six or more but no room fees are charged and it's particularly good for special occasions, small parties and business entertaining. The dishes conceived by chef Dominique Corby –who previously worked at La Tour d'Argent in Tokyo are creative; both French and Japanese seasonal ingredients are used and plates come attractively presented. Specialities include wild duck, sabayon of *homard* lobster and a dessert soufflé. Set menus change monthly and the à la carte every season. Lunchtime set menus are well priced.

■ Opening hours, last orders
Lunch=12:00-14:00 (L.O.)
Dinner=18:00-21:00 (L.O.)

■ Annual and weekly closing
Closed mid-August, late December-early January, Sunday and Bank Holidays

■ Price

| | | |
|---|---|---|
| Lunch= | menu | ¥ 4,500-10,000 |
| | carte | ¥ 12,500-21,000 |
| Dinner= | menu | ¥ 12,000-18,000 |
| | carte | ¥ 12,500-21,000 |

**TEL. 03–3575–2767**
FAX. 03–3289–5937
6-2-10 Ginza, Chuo-ku
www.6eme.com

# Les Saisons

16

This French restaurant can be found on the second-floor mezzanine of the Imperial Hotel Main Building. The interior underwent a complete transformation in 2005, led by a French designer who instilled a "classic-modern" style that fuses traditional design elements with a contemporary elegance. The glass pane at the entrance immortalises the words of well-known French gastronome Jean Anthelme Brillat-Savarin. The interior décor, tableware and even the menu cover were updated and a new chef was also brought over from France. The menu changes seasonally, but may include, for example, an appetiser of lightly smoked salmon with potato and caviar, served with cumin salad. Other offerings may include a roasted French flounder served with truffles and a white asparagus purée; and Bresse chicken breast stuffed with morels and served with a Comté cheese gnocchi. While the menu is grounded in traditional French fare, dishes incorporate a modern esprit.

■ Opening hours, last orders
Lunch=11:30-14:30 (L.O.)
Dinner=17:30-22:00 (L.O.)

■ Price
Lunch= menu ¥ 6,825-10,500
carte ¥ 13,000-28,000
Dinner= menu ¥ 16,800-29,400
carte ¥ 13,000-28,000
Private room fee= ¥ 10,500-21,000
Service charge= 10%

**TEL. 03-3539-8087**
FAX. 03-3581-9146
Imperial Hotel-Main Building M2F,
1-1-1 Uchisaiwaicho, Chiyoda-ku
www.imperialhotel.co.jp

# L'Osier

The beautiful stone façade of the Shiseido building, where this restaurant is housed, provides a nice contrast with the trees that line the street. The styling of the first floor is Art Deco, while the second-floor dining room harmoniously blends elements of Art Deco and Modernism; artworks on display include a flower vase by Jean Cocteau and pieces by Salvador Dali. The elegant ambience is further enriched with Bernardaud porcelain, Puiforcat flatware and Porthault linens. Bruno Menard has been head chef since 2005; original and contemporary, his dishes are rich in colour and variety. Recommendations include the Breton lobster salad with a hint of vanilla; duck foie gras confit; and roast suckling pig with truffle-flavoured polenta. There is a far-reaching selection of French wines - at moderate prices. Waiting staff work well as a team, further exemplifying the high levels of professionalism.

■ Opening hours, last orders
Lunch=12:00-14:30 (L.O.)
Dinner=18:00-21:00 (L.O.)

■ Annual and weekly closing
Closed Golden week, 2 weeks mid-August, late December-early January, Sunday and Bank Holiday Mondays

■ Price

| | | |
|---|---|---|
| Lunch= | menu | ¥ 6,800-11,000 |
| | carte | ¥ 17,000-25,000 |
| Dinner= | menu | ¥ 19,000-35,000 |
| | carte | ¥ 17,000-25,000 |

Service charge= 12%

**TEL. 03-3571-6050**
FAX. 03-3571-6080
7-5-5 Ginza, Chuo-ku
www.shiseido.co.jp/losier

# Maison d'Umemoto Shang-hai

Something of a retreat, this Chinese restaurant offers home-style food of the French Concession in Shanghai. Owner-chef Nobuhisa Umemoto recreates these dishes using recipes passed down from the Chinese owner of the Shinjuku restaurant where he trained. He uses only premium ingredients, which he flavours with the merest hint of seasoning. Only set menus are offered, and each guest is served with an individual plate; condiments and portion sizes can be adjusted on request. The chef travels bi-monthly to Hong Kong to purchase delicacies difficult to find in Japan. He also uses French ingredients to prepare Beggar's chicken; Bresse chicken seasoned with sansho pepper and salt, wrapped in lotus leaves and clay, and baked in an oven. Shanghai crab dishes available from mid-September are recommended. Fried rice and tantan-men (spicy noodles) with crab innards, as well as a shark fin simmered with crab innards, are especially good. The restaurant's interior mirrors the elegant milieu of a high-ranking family in the old French Concession. The large tables allow one to enjoy the flavour of Shanghai in a relaxing setting.

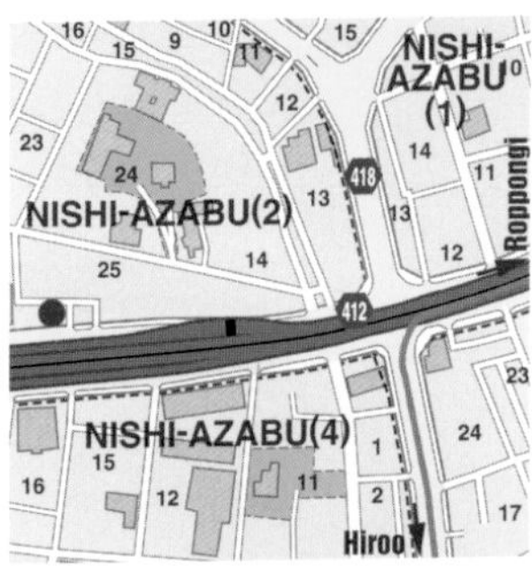

■ Opening hours, last orders
Lunch=11:30-13:00 (L.O.)
Dinner=18:00-22:00 (L.O.)

■ Annual and weekly closing
Closed mid-August, late December-early January, Bank Holidays from January-August and Sunday except December

■ Price
Lunch= menu ¥ 7,350-10,500
Dinner= menu ¥ 16,800-47,250
Service charge= 12% (lunch 10%)

**TEL. 03-5467-2837**
FAX. 03-5467-2838
New city Residence Nishi-Azabu Twin Tower II B1F,
2-26-20 Nishi-Azabu, Minato-ku

# Maison Paul Bocuse

This Daikanyama restaurant is a partnership between celebrated chef Paul Bocuse, and Hiroyuki Hiramatsu. Try specialities from the chef's Lyon restaurant: oven-baked black truffle consommé covered with pie dough, served in 1975 to then French President Valéry Giscard d'Estaing; the sea bass pie with Choron sauce uses a whole locally caught sea bass, and is therefore good to share; the Nagoya-Cochin dish is the Japanese version of *poularde de Bresse en vessie* offered at the Lyon restaurant -replacing Bresse chicken with a breed from Nagoya- served with the cream sauce combining the chicken gravy and the morels and is particularly good in spring with fresh morels. For dessert, the Grand Marnier soufflé is a good choice. Lunch is served in the mosaic-tiled dining room with the soft tones of the musette, while dinner is in the more modern-styled dining room at the back of the restaurant. As it is a popular venue for weekend wedding receptions, it is best to call in advance.

■ Opening hours, last orders
Lunch=12:00-14:00 (L.O.)
Dinner=18:00-21:00 (L.O.)

■ Annual and weekly closing
Closed late December-early January

■ Price
Lunch= menu ¥ 2,680-3,780
carte ¥ 12,000-20,000
Dinner= menu ¥ 7,000-25,000
carte ¥ 12,000-20,000
Service charge= 10%

**TEL. 03-5458-6324**
FAX. 03-5458-6328
Daikanyama Forum B1F,
17-16 Sarugakucho, Shibuya-ku
www.hiramatsu.co.jp/restaurants/maison-paulbocuse

# Makimura
## まき村

The counter seating, only available at dinner, is the more sociable choice than the tables in this Japanese restaurant. Owner-chef Akio Makimura plans the menu after ensuring the available ingredients meet his standards. So as not to detract from their original taste, he relies on a soup stock that is very light and uses *katsuo-bushi* (dried bonito), shaved fresh each morning and two different kinds: with and without *chiai* (dark-colored flesh) depending on the dish. The former is used to make soup stock with a richer taste for the fried *Kamo-nasu* (eggplant from Kyoto) dish, while the latter is for the clear soup of *hamo* (pike conger) from Hyogo and fine-textured *tamago-dofu* (egg tofu). *Tai-chazuke* (rice with sea bream topped with broth), the house speciality, has a rich flavour and aroma, and is the result of many years of being refined. Recommended is the *fugu kaiseki* (puffer fish menu) available from December to February which includes wild *tora-fugu* (tiger puffer fish) from the Bungo Strait in Oita, and is well priced considering the high quality. Reservations for lunch should be made at least a day in advance.

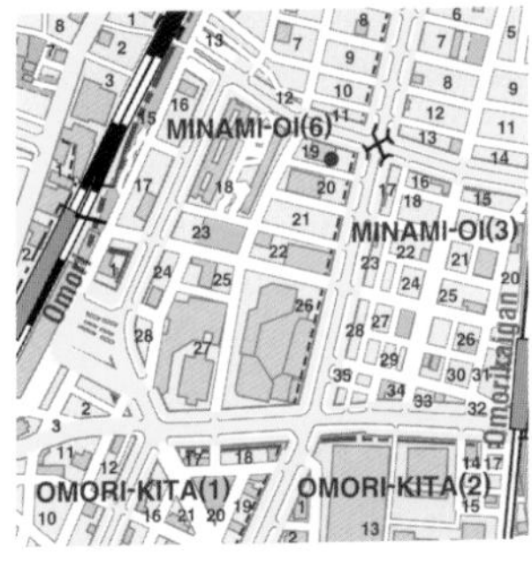

■ Opening hours, last orders
Lunch=12:00-14:00 L.O.13:00
Dinner=17:30-22:00 L.O.21:00

■ Annual and weekly closing
Closed Golden week, mid-August, late December-early January, Sunday and Bank Holiday Mondays

■ Price
Lunch= menu ¥ 6,300-8,400
Dinner= menu ¥ 10,500-13,650
Service charge= 5%

**TEL. 03-3768-6388**
FAX. 03-3768-4822
6-19-10 Minami-Oi, Shinagawa-ku

# Minoichi
## 未能一

Minoichi is located on the fifth floor of a multipurpose building in Ginza Nishi Gobangai. Owner-chef Yasuji Tatsumi and his wife run this small but charming *kappo* (counter style restaurant), paying attention to the smallest of details. There is wide array of appetisers served in small bowls matching *sake* and the *omakase* (chef's choice) set menu is recommended. The *konnyaku* and *negi* (scallion) mixed with salted and fermented bonito gut is perfectly seasoned and provides a nice chewy texture, while the sea urchin pickled in *miso* is richly flavoured. The *miso* soup served with big freshwater clams from Lake Jusanko in Aomori is also a good choice. Broad beans with *udo* and bamboo shoots are boiled and brought together in a dish that allows the taste of each ingredient to come through. The *tempura* of disk abalone and clam from Sanriku is also recommended. Every dish leaves you with a real appreciation of the skill of a traditional Japanese chef. Avoid going in a group as this is a small restaurant. Its name is derived from Chinese classical literature meaning "not yet complete."

■ Opening hours, last orders
Dinner=17:30-22:30 L.O.21:00

■ Annual and weekly closing
Closed Golden week, mid-August, late December-early January and Sunday

■ Price
Dinner= menu ¥ 12,600-21,000
Service charge= 10%

**TEL. 03-3289-3011**
FAX. 03-3289-3011
Suzuryu Building 5F,
8-7-19 Ginza, Chuo-ku

# Miravile

Seiji Tsushimi named this restaurant after a place he worked at in France that made a lasting impression on him. Inside the 18-seat restaurant, Tsushimi's own paintings hang on the walls and diners can see into the kitchen through the smoked glass. Hailing from Hiroshima, he remains loyal to his hometown and buys his fish from Setouchi while vegetables only come from known producers. The house speciality, Saint Marc-style of Japanese beef tongue, foie gras and truffles, sees each ingredient piled up like a Saint Marc cake with the crispy pie crust giving an added texture to the flavour. Vegetables grown at the foot of Mt. Fuji are used for the steamed vegetable salad. The fish of the day uses fish from Itosaki Fishing Port, sautéed and served with a vinaigrette of colza oil produced in Kumamoto. Baked Japanese ox tail, pig's feet and foie gras pie is served with a truffled red wine sauce. While traditional French cuisine remains the mainstay, there are a number of others that display originality and ingenuity, so each dish's arrival will be worth the wait.

■ Opening hours, last orders
Lunch=12:00-15:00 L.O.14:00
Dinner=18:30-23:00 L.O.21:30

■ Annual and weekly closing
Closed 1 week in September, late December-early January and Wednesday

■ Price
Lunch= menu ¥ 2,800-3,900
Dinner= menu ¥ 5,250-7,350
carte ¥ 6,000-11,000
Service charge= 10% (lunch 5%)

**TEL. 03-5738-0418**
FAX. 03-5738-0418
1-16-9 Komaba, Meguro-ku
www.miravile.net

# Mitsuta
## 三ツ田

14

Diners sit on *tatami* mats at this *tempura* restaurant near Tsukiji-gawa Ginza Park in Higashi-Ginza, which has been open since 1958. Take your shoes off at the entrance and move to one of three private rooms which are assigned depending on the number of guests; each has a counter with sunken seating. Through a specially made glass cover you can see the amber-coloured blend of four oils for the *tempura* and watch the chef at work over the counter. Meals begin with several prawns served one after the other; *Makiebi* (mid-size Japanese tiger prawns) from Kyushu are thinly battered and fried leaving the centre raw to bring out their sweetness. To cap off the meal, *ten-bara* -a bowl of rice with a *tempura* mix of small scallop eyes, *saimakiebi* and wild chervil- is recommended. The friendly proprietress is second-generation, while the head chef has more than 30 years experience. The taste of the pickled vegetables, *miso* soup and *tentsuyu* dipping sauce comes from a secret recipe from the proprietress' aunt. The warm family atmosphere has always prevailed here and this explains why this restaurant attracts so many regulars.

■ Opening hours, last orders
Lunch=12:00-14:30 (L.O.)
Dinner=17:30-20:30 (L.O.)

■ Annual and weekly closing
Closed mid-August, late December-early January, Sunday and Bank Holidays

■ Price
Lunch= menu ¥ 14,700
Dinner= menu ¥ 16,800
Service charge= 10%

**TEL. 03-3541-5577**
1-12-15 Tsukiji, Chuo-ku

# Momonoki
## 桃の木

Although culinary favourites from Canton and Shanghai make up a large part of the menu here, Beijing and Sichuan dishes are not overlooked. Preferring to serve customers "more unfamiliar home-style dishes", owner-chef Takeshi Kobayashi steers clear of pricey dried ingredients like shark's fin and abalone. The menu is wide-ranging: from spring to summer, live *watarigani* (blue crab) are plunged into hot oil and then gently simmered in soy sauce, *A-sai* (a Chinese leafy green) and *fu ru* (fermented tofu); both imported from Taiwan and sautéed with salt. Coral trout from Okinawa, containing a large amount of collagen, is cooked Cantonese-style while large prawns from Aichi provide the centrepiece for the Shanghai chili prawn dish, seasoned only with hot red peppers. *Mapo tofu*, a typical Sichuan dish, is simply made by using hot pepper rather than *dou bang jiang* (Chinese hot sauce). One unique Beijing style dish is duck tongue combined with a range of herbs and spices, including hot pepper. Set menus enable you to sample a wide variety of regional flavours.

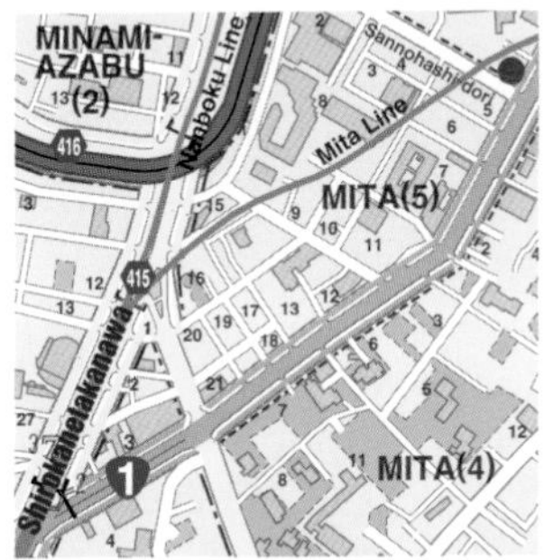

■ Opening hours, last orders
Lunch=11:30-14:30 L.O.14:00
Dinner=17:30-22:30 L.O.21:30

■ Annual and weekly closing
Closed mid-August, late December-early January, Wednesday and 3rd Tuesday

■ Price

| | | |
|---|---|---|
| Lunch= | menu | ¥ 2,500-15,000 |
| | carte | ¥ 3,000-6,500 |
| Dinner= | menu | ¥ 8,500-20,000 |

**TEL. 03-5443-1309**
FAX. 03-5443-1309
2-17-29 Mita, Minato-ku
www.mitamachi-momonoki.com

# Monnalisa Ebisu

12

Cross Komazawa-dori Avenue from the JR Ebisu Station West Exit, walk straight towards Ebisu Shrine and turn left at the second corner into a small street; owner-chef Toru Kawano's restaurant is on the right-hand side, marked by a French flag. The menu changes quarterly, with new dishes being added each year. In spring, examples include white asparagus *blancmange* and *Shamo* gamecock from Fukushima wrapped in spring cabbage and flavoured with foie gras, and in summer, crêpe of sweetfish and caviar infused with vanilla. Only a minimal amount of butter is ever used. A wide variety of desserts, often using fruit, are also on offer. All dishes beautifully match the plates they are served on—they are designed by the chef himself—making them pleasing to the eye as well as the palate. The dining room, hung with paintings, has a chic grey-toned décor that contrasts nicely with the white tablecloths. Another terrace-style space at the back of the restaurant is surrounded by greenery and is bright with sunlight during the day. The main dining room may be more suitable for those special occasions.

■ Opening hours, last orders
Lunch=11:30-15:30 L.O.14:00
Dinner=17:30-23:30 L.O.21:30

■ Annual and weekly closing
Closed late December-early January

■ Price
Lunch= menu ¥ 5,064-10,550
Dinner= menu ¥ 7,174-15,825
carte ¥ 8,000-15,000
Service charge= 10%

**TEL. 03–5458–1887**
FAX. 03–5458–9002
1-14-4 Ebisu-Nishi, Shibuya-ku
www.monnalisa.co.jp

# Monnalisa Marunouchi

♿ ⇄ < ⊡ 12 ☎ 🍴 ⚘

Monnalisa's big windows afford two magnificent views: the gardens surrounding the Imperial Palace and a panorama of the city. The white interior features oil paintings and exudes an air of elegance. Owner-chef Toru Kawano left Japan for France at the age of 25 with a desire to gain a thorough training and on his return worked at some of Tokyo's famous restaurants. He favours the concept of set menus and makes the most of them by offering a large variety of seasonal dishes, taking extra care not to overlap cooking methods and seasoning combinations. Selecting ingredients by himself, he will sometimes visit the production area to check their quality. As well as Western foodstuffs, he also looks to Japanese ingredients -wild plants in spring and ginkgo and *matsutake* mushrooms in autumn- to create a distinctly Japanese sense of the season. The house speciality is roast lamb covered with a herb and salt pie dough and this is served with a basil-flavoured cream sauce. Butter is used sparingly for a lighter texture and his food is beautifully arranged on the plates. Good to visit with friends.

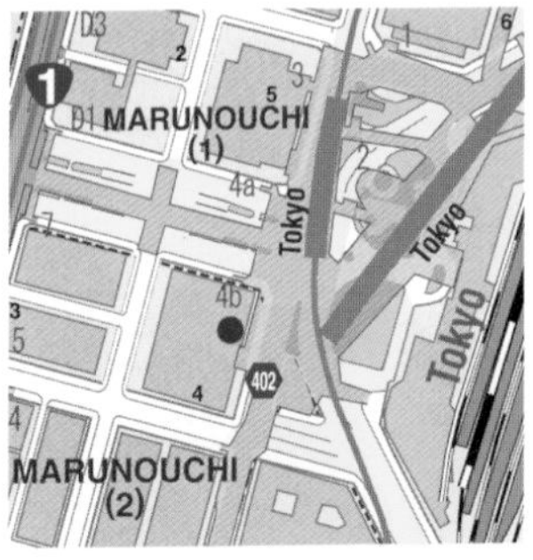

■ Opening hours, last orders
Lunch=11:30-15:30 L.O.14:00
Dinner=17:30-23:30 L.O.21:30

■ Annual and weekly closing
Closed 1 January

■ Price

| | | |
|---|---|---|
| Lunch= | menu | ¥ 3,956-10,550 |
| Dinner= | menu | ¥ 7,174-16,880 |
| | carte | ¥ 8,000-15,000 |

Service charge= 10%

**TEL. 03-3240-5775**
FAX. 03-3240-5776
Marunouchi Building 36F,
2-4-1 Marunouchi, Chiyoda-ku
www.monnalisa.co.jp

# Morimoto XEX

14

Morimoto XEX is a joint collaboration between New York-based chef Masaharu Morimoto and "Y's table corporation." Located near the Roppongi Tunnel, Morimoto XEX has lounges, bars, private rooms and *sushi* counters (not included in this guide) spread across two floors. A futuristic metallic spiral staircase leads customers to the chic main basement-level *teppanyaki* dining room. Although there are private rooms in the basement and on the second floor, the counter is recommended as you can enjoy food straight off the hot plate. The high-quality Kobe beef and marbled sirloin from Iwate and Fukushima—aged for about a month to bring out the taste— are stocked in the glass refrigerator. Spiny lobster and *kuroawabi* (black abalone) shipped direct from fishing ports are kept in the aquarium and fished out when ordered. The red manual slicer, said to be one of the few antique slicers in the world, is used to precision slice raw Kobe beef, vegetables and *prosciutto di Parma*. Desserts and digestives are served in the second-floor lounge, a comfortable space where one can truly relax.

■ Opening hours, last orders
Dinner=18:00-24:30 L.O.23:00

■ Annual and weekly closing
Closed 31 December-3 January

■ Price
Dinner= menu ¥ 10,000-15,000
carte ¥ 5,000-30,000
Service charge= 10%

**TEL. 03–3479–0065**
FAX. 03–3479–1696
7-21-19 Roppongi, Minato-ku
www.ystable.co.jp/morimoto

# Muroi
## 室井

A Japanese restaurant located in Ginza 8-chome, opened in 1980 by Masao Muroi, who started out working in *kappo* (counter style restaurant) in Ginza. The "Muroi-style" is based on the chef's culinary flexibility, which often shuns traditional cooking concepts. Original dishes include some that use wild plants from throughout Japan and are prepared during spring and summer such as carpaccio of fresh flounder served with a *bainiku* (Japanese apricot pulp) dressing, and curry made with a bonito and kelp broth. The most attracting feature of Muroi are the wild mushrooms collected by the chef and his staff in autumn in Fukushima and in Tochigi. About 40 kilograms of more than 70 varieties, including *matsutake*, *oomomitake*, *anzutake*, *tamagotake* and *akamomitake* are collected in a single day. The wild mushroom set menu offers a pasta dish, risotto and a clear Japanese soup. Recommended is the *fugu* milt served with a wild mushroom sauce. As the restaurant is sometimes closed on the weekends from late June through the end of November, it might be a good idea to call ahead.

■ Opening hours, last orders
Dinner=17:30-22:00 (L.O.)

■ Annual and weekly closing
Closed Golden week, mid-August, late December-early January, Sunday and Bank Holidays

■ Price
Dinner= menu ¥ 15,750-31,500
Service charge= 10%

**TEL. 03-3571-1421**
FAX. 03-3571-1423
Suzuryu Building 2F,
8-7-19 Ginza, Chuo-ku

# Nadaman Honten Sazanka-so
## なだ万本店 山茶花荘

16

This prestigious Japanese restaurant is located in the garden of the Hotel New Otani. All four rooms, named from The Tale of Genji, have *horigotatsu*-style sunken seating; a wide view of the carefully manicured garden can be seen from the *engawa* (external corridor). The waiting staff in *kimono* offer refined service and meals can be enjoyed at a leisurely and tranquil pace. The traditional Japanese cuisine focuses on seasonal ingredients and tastes with selected ingredients, painstaking preparation and consistent quality. The starter in winter is a dish of yellowtail covered with turnip and served with vinegar flavoured with bonito shavings, kelp, sugar and soy sauce and garnished with *kimizu* sauce. *Hassun* (appetiser plates) feature salted and steamed *ankimo* (monkfish liver), abalone steamed with *sake* and *komochi-kombu no Tosa-ae* (kelp with herring roe dressed with soy sauce, *mirin* and dried bonito). The simmered beef cheek and Sakurajima radish dish is also tasty. As the main branch of a long-established restaurant, the prices are not low but lunch menus are less expensive.

■ Opening hours, last orders
Lunch=11:30-15:00
Dinner=17:00-22:00

■ Annual and weekly closing
Closed late December-early January

■ Price
Lunch= menu ¥ 21,000-42,000
Dinner= menu ¥ 42,000
Private room fee= ¥ 8,000/person
(Mon.-Fri. for dinner)
Service charge= 20%

**TEL. 03-3264-7921**
FAX. 03-3264-7938
New Otani Hotel Japanese-Garden,
4-1 Kioicho, Chiyoda-ku
www.nadaman.co.jp/sazankaso

JAPANESE MAP NO. 19/B-3

# Nakajima

**中嶋**

LUNCH 20

The owner-chef Sadaharu Nakajima can trace his culinary roots back to his grandfather -the first chef at Hoshigaoka Saryo, a restaurant of the well-known Rosanjin Kitaoji- who later went on to open his own restaurant in Ginza in the early Showa Era. In 1962, Nakajima's father opened this restaurant, which he subsequently inherited. His efforts to create original cuisine guided by Kansai culinary traditions, while remaining loyal to his family's craft, set it apart. There are three set menus, and the quantities and seasoning can be changed accordingly. Boiled fig with *miso* (soybean paste) is served cold with sweet white *miso* in early summer; in late summer, it's served warm with boar meat. Nakajima pays attention not only to his cooking, but also to his customers; his personality has made him a popular choice for TV cooking programmes and he has published a number of cookery books. Run with the help of his wife, this cosy restaurant is always buzzing. At lunch, customers can choose from several set menus that feature sardines, as well as the more formal *kaiseki* set menu (reservation needed).

■ Opening hours, last orders
Lunch=11:30-14:00 L.O.13:45
Dinner=17:30-22:00 L.O.20:30

■ Annual and weekly closing
Closed mid-August, late December-early January, Sunday and Bank Holidays

■ Price
Lunch= menu ¥ 840-5,250
Dinner= menu ¥ 8,400-13,650
Service charge= 6% (dinner)

**TEL. 03-3356-4534**
FAX. 03-3356-7962
Hihara Building B1F,
3-32-5 Shinjuku, Shinjuku-ku
www.shinjyuku-nakajima.com

# Narukami

Masakazu Narukami, the owner-chef, first studied Italian cooking before mastering the art of French cuisine. After his training in France, he returned to Japan and opened Narukami in 2003. He places great value on his relationships with food suppliers and prefers locally sourced food. Fresh seafood such as conger eel, *hamo* (pike conger) and sea bream comes direct from Hyogo, where the chef grew up. In winter, you can enjoy game such as Yezo Sika deer from Hokkaido; to season the venison, salt pickled lemon rind is added to the reduced gravy. Another speciality is fresh oysters grown in the Seto Inland Sea served with fresh horseradish cream, seaweed and lime jelly. In summer, *Hamo* is prepared by finely cutting the bones and wrapping it around *maitake* mushrooms; it is then roasted crisp and served with a sauce combining fish liver and *ao-sansho* (young Japanese pepper). Narukami's unique dishes offer a combination of fresh ideas and quality ingredients. The red and black-themed dining space is enhanced by modern cutlery, Limoges porcelain and Japanese tableware.

■ Opening hours, last orders
Lunch=11:30-14:00 (L.O.)
Dinner=18:00-21:00 (L.O.)

■ Annual and weekly closing
Closed mid-September, late December-early January and Monday

■ Price
Lunch= menu ¥ 4,725-8,400
Dinner= menu ¥ 7,875-13,650
Service charge= 10%

**TEL. 03-6226-2225**
FAX. 03-6226-2244
Shinbo Building B1F,
6-13-7 Ginza, Chuo-ku
www.restaurant-narukami.com

# Nasubi-tei
## なすび亭

One of Nasubi-tei's largest draws is that it offers high quality cooking at reasonable prices. Three *omakase* (chef's choice) set menus are available, and the highest-grade one is particularly recommended. The house's speciality is *takikomi-gohan* (a rice dish seasoned with broth and boiled with various ingredients) served at the end of the meal. The ingredients for this dish change according to the season: *hamaguri* (clams) and bamboo shoots in spring; *ayu* (sweetfish) in summer; first-of-the-season Pacific saury, salmon and *ikura* (salmon roe) in autumn; and *matsubagani* crab in winter. Owner-chef Hidehiro Yoshioka honed his skills in upmarket *ryotei* and *kappo* restaurants before opening this establishment in 2000. In addition to the *omakase* set menus, there are also *nabe ryori* (hotpot cuisine) set menus. To get here, take the East Exit of Ebisu Station and walk towards the Ebisu 3-chome intersection; turn left just before the Shibuya Ebisu Post Office, and left again at the first corner. The dimly lit interior has a homely and relaxed atmosphere. It's particularly good for private rather than business occasions.

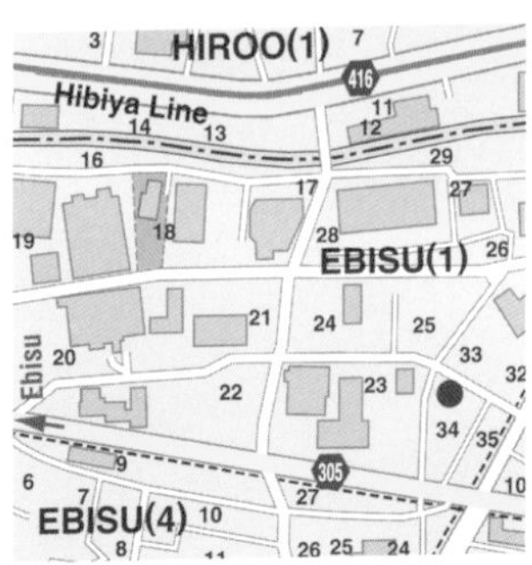

■ Opening hours, last orders
Dinner=18:00-21:00 (L.O.)

■ Annual and weekly closing
Closed Golden week, mid-August, late December-early January, Sunday and Bank Holidays

■ Price
Dinner= menu ¥ 5,000-9,000
Service charge= 5%

**TEL. 03-3440-2670**
FAX. 03-3440-2670
1-34-1 Ebisu, Shibuya-ku
www.nasubitei.com

# Ogasawara Hakushaku-tei
## 小笠原伯爵邸

20

This Spanish-style building is the former residence of Count Nagayoshi Ogasawara. Following World War II, the residence was placed under control of the General Headquarters of the Allied Forces and was later owned by the Tokyo Metropolitan Government. Empty for more than three decades, the current owner renovated the building and opened its doors to diners in 2002. Its air of elegance allows your mind to wander back in time to the life of the nobles. The main dining room is reached through the former reception room. The chef, trained in Andalusia, Catalonia and other regions in Spain, uses his skills to the full in creating modern Spanish food. Only one set menu consisting of many smaller courses is available at lunch and dinner. House specialities include cappuccino with pink shrimps and Kagoshima *mitsuimo* sweet potato in spring; a *ganache* of foie gras and *ayu* (sweetfish) in summer; Iberico pork roasted over a charcoal fire and served with acorn Mont Blanc in autumn; and a risotto of cuttlefish and *tonsoku* (pig's feet) in winter. Suitable for both business and private occasions.

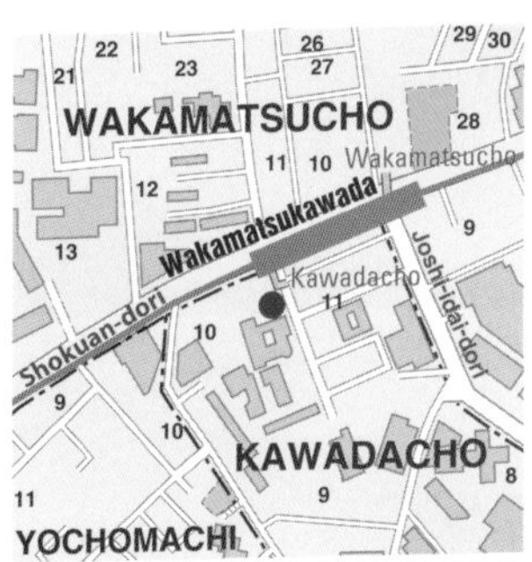

■ Opening hours, last orders
Lunch=11:30-15:00 L.O.13:30
Dinner=18:00-23:00 L.O.20:30

■ Annual and weekly closing
Closed 31 December-5 January

■ Price
Lunch= menu ¥ 7,350
Dinner= menu ¥ 10,500
Private room fee= ¥10,500
Service charge= 10%

**TEL. 03-3359-5830**
FAX. 03-3359-5831
10-10 Kawadacho, Shinjuku-ku
www.ogasawaratei.com

# Ohara's

A white awning leads guests into the basement, where the white-bright restaurant is located. Owner-chef Takashi Ohara honed his culinary skills in a number of famous restaurants in France, where he lived for a decade before returning to Japan. He offers traditional French cuisine, placing particular attention on the pairing of sauces: Choron sauce is used for fish dishes and Béarnaise is paired with grilled Hiba beef. The *boudin noir* is particularly recommended and comes served with a delicate herb salad. The restaurant also offers a varied palette of seasonal flavours such as freshly smoked Hokkaido trout served with a salad in spring; cumin-scented *gazpacho* in summer; Yezo Sika deer terrine and a pie made with truffles, foie gras and potatoes in winter. The warm service provided by the chef's German wife makes for a friendly atmosphere. The restaurant is closed on the third Tuesday of each month, and the first Tuesday, too, during summer.

■ Opening hours, last orders
Lunch=11:30-15:30 L.O.14:00
Dinner=18:00-23:00 L.O.21:30

■ Annual and weekly closing
Closed late December-early January, 15-21 January, Monday and 3rd Tuesday

■ Price

| | | |
|---|---|---|
| Lunch= | menu | ¥ 3,150-7,350 |
| | carte | ¥ 7,000-13,000 |
| Dinner= | menu | ¥ 7,350-10,500 |
| | carte | ¥ 7,000-13,000 |

Service charge= 10%

**TEL. 03-5436-3255**
FAX. 03-5436-3255
Yacmo Building B1F,
5-4-18 Osaki, Shinagawa-ku

# Ohno
## 大野

The friendly and personable head chef met the owner when he was working at a Japanese restaurant near the Paris Opera House, and has been in charge of the menu since Ohno opened in 2006. The restaurant offers three set menus, each with a different number of courses, but that which includes a seasonal hotpot and *takikomi-gohan* (a rice dish seasoned with broth and boiled with various ingredients) is recommended. The hotpot dish changes every month, and ranges widely in variety, from *madai nabe* (red sea bream hotpot) with *tororo-kombu* (dried shaved kelp) and *Shonai-fu* (Shonai-style baked wheat gluten) in spring to *jidori nabe* (local chicken hotpot) in summer, *uma-mi nabe* ("tasty" soup stock hotpot) with duck breast in autumn, and *tonyu nabe* (soybean milk hotpot) with Yezo Sika deer and mushrooms in winter. *Koshihikari* rice from Fukushima cooked in an iron pot is used for both the plain boiled rice and *takikomi-gohan*. À la carte dishes are also available from 8pm. Since the restaurant is open until 2am, customers often pop in late for assorted dishes and wine.

■ Opening hours, last orders
Dinner=17:30-2:00 (L.O.)
Saturday 17:00-23:00 (L.O.)

■ Annual and weekly closing
Closed mid-August, late December-early January, Sunday and Bank Holidays

■ Price
Dinner= menu ¥ 6,300-12,600
carte ¥ 6,000-12,000
Service charge= 10%

**TEL. 03-3571-4120**
7-2-20 Ginza,, Chuo-ku
www.auxamis.com/ginza_oono

# Okina
翁

The proprietress is an eighth-generation direct descendant of the founder of a long-established *Sarashina soba* restaurant. The buck-wheat noodles are made and boiled on the spot to offer maximum freshness and only the heart of the buckwheat kernel is ground to make the refined white *Sarashina soba*. The broth, a secret recipe inherited from the proprietress' family, is made using three types of dried bonito flakes and has a subtle flavour. While full-course set menus that end with *soba* are generally served, a range of other dishes can also be enjoyed: seaweed is sourced from Toyama; fish and shellfish from Hokkaido; and *ayu* (sweetfish) and pike con-ger from Kyoto. A variety of *soba* dishes unique to this restaurant are also available: *chasoba* (*soba* containing tea) flavoured with *yuzu*; and winter *soba* kneaded with black or white truffles. *Soba* with fresh homemade caviar—the sturgeon eggs are removed on site and cured with salt and olive oil is another speciality. All dishes succeed in reflecting the culture of this *soba* restaurant.

■ Opening hours, last orders
Dinner=18:00-22:30 (L.O.)

■ Annual and weekly closing
Closed early January, Sunday and Bank Holidays

■ Price
Dinner= menu ¥ 15,750-26,250
Service charge= 10%

**TEL. 03-3477-2648**
FAX. 03-3477-2649
Five Annex B1F,
1-3-10 Ebisu-Nishi, Shibuya-ku

# Ozaki
## おざき

A Japanese restaurant on a quiet corner in Azabu-Juban - look for a black fence on which a discreet sign is posted and *inuyarai* (bamboo screens), which protect the lower part of the building. As the son of a *sushi* chef, owner-chef Ichiro Ozaki sticks to what he knows best. He offers only an *omakase* (chef's choice) set menu, which naturally includes *sushi*. After appetisers, two pieces of tasty tuna *sushi* are served as a greeting from the chef. Grilled crab in its shell follows as a regular dish offered year-round. Seasonal dishes include cold sea-urchin *chawanmushi* (savoury egg custard), and fried *suppon* (soft-shelled turtle) seasoned with the chef's original Asian spice blend. Conger eel served with salt and grated *wasabi* offers up a delicate flavour. This small establishment has only six counter seats and a private room. In addition to the extensive *sake* list, there are more than 20 bins of champagnes and white wine. His refined taste is also evident in the tableware, including the high-quality wine glasses. If you feel like finishing your meal with *sushi*, Ozaki is highly recommended.

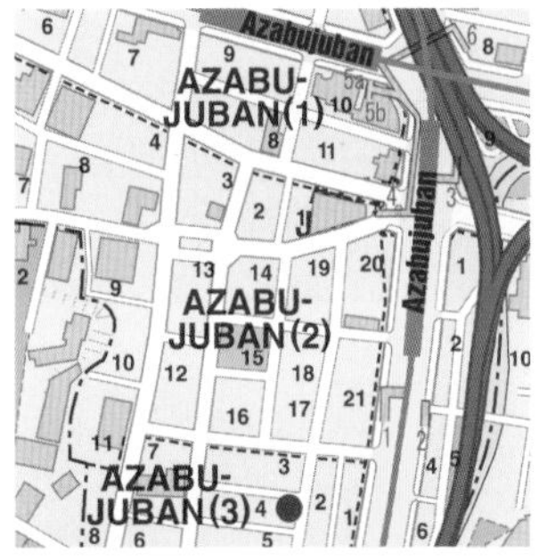

■ Opening hours, last orders
Dinner=18:00-24:00 L.O.22:00

■ Annual and weekly closing
Closed late December-early January and Sunday

■ Price
Dinner= menu ¥ 15,750
Service charge= 10%

**TEL. 03-3454-1682**
FAX. 03-3454-1682
3-4-5 Azabu-Juban, Minato-ku

ITALIAN MAP NO. 10/A-4

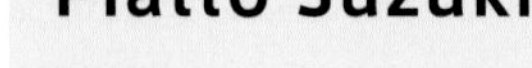

# Piatto Suzuki

With only five tables and an equal number of counter seats, this small restaurant -located four floors above the street right by Azabu-Juban Station- is a constant hive of activity. Owner-chef Yahei Suzuki serves traditional provincial Italian cuisine. Behind the counter, you can see the chefs hard at work in the small kitchen. Suzuki's day starts with the selection of high-quality ingredients. *Agu* pork, a delicacy, is ordered from Okinawa, locally produced *jidori* chicken comes from Miyazaki and beef fillet from Hitachi in Ibaraki. Most of the vegetables come directly from Kyoto and fresh fish and shellfish are purchased from Tsukiji market. The spring menu features white asparagus with fried quail eggs and smoked prosciutto as well as lamb roasted to perfection served with a complementary mustard sauce. Finish up with either an Italian or French dessert—there's a wide choice of both. Every year at the end of April during the Japanese holiday season known as Golden Week, the owner-chef heads to Italy to try out different eateries in his pursuit of even more delicious fare.

■ Opening hours, last orders
Dinner=18:00-2:00 L.O.24:00

■ Annual and weekly closing
Closed Golden week, late December-early January, Sunday and Bank Holiday Mondays

■ Price
Dinner= menu ¥ 10,500
carte ¥ 6,500-12,000

**TEL. 03–5414–2116**
FAX. 03–5414–2116
Hasebeya Building 4F,
1-7-7 Azabu-Juban, Minato-ku

# Pierre Gagnaire

10

French chef Pierre Gagnaire's Tokyo restaurant opened in 2005. There's a portrait of the chef in front of the fourth-floor lift while the kitchen on display behind plate glass adds a slight futuristic theme. The refined cuisine creatively incorporates both Japanese and French ingredients. Set menus are delivered in the conventional order, but hors-d'œuvre, fish, meat and other courses come served on several individual plates. The à la carte menu changes seasonally, the dinner set menus change every month and the lunchtime set menus even more frequently. There is a private room behind the bar counter and a doorless semi-private room in the main dining room, the latter available at no extra charge. Semi-booth seating suitable for special celebrations can be used by small parties of two or more. At La Terrasse, a bar on the building's top floor, guests can enjoy a drink before or after dinner while looking out at Tokyo Tower and the dazzling lights of Roppongi.

■ Opening hours, last orders
Lunch=11:30-14:00 (L.O.)
Dinner=18:00-21:30 (L.O.)

■ Annual and weekly closing
Closed Golden week, mid-August, late December-early January, Sunday and Bank Holidays

■ Price

| | | |
|---|---|---|
| Lunch= | menu | ¥ 6,000-10,000 |
| | carte | ¥ 17,000-29,000 |
| Dinner= | menu | ¥ 19,000-25,000 |
| | carte | ¥ 17,000-29,000 |

Private room fee= ¥ 10,000
Service charge= 12%

**TEL. 03-5466-6800**
Minami-Aoyama Square 4F,
5-3-2 Minami-Aoyama, Minato-ku
www.pierre-gagnaire.jp

# Quintessence

Chef Shuzo Kishida's interest in cooking was sparked during his youth, when he was frequently taken to restaurants by his parents. After training in Japan, he perfected his skills in France, notably at Parisian restaurant, Astrance. So inspired was he by his experience that he bases the menu *carte blanche* -under which different dishes are created for each table- on the ingredients available on the day as well as his own inclination. Dishes are prepared with the emphasis on three basic tenets: the selection of ingredients, applied heat and seasoning. Along with the stylish presentation and refined flavours, the particular attention paid to the roasting and broiling of meat and fish is remarkable and rare. Specialities include goat's milk Bavarian cream with salt and olive oil, *tarte au boudin* and foie gras, *cuisson nacrée* of matured sea bass, three-hour roast of enzyme-fed pork, and meringue ice cream. The décor of this cosy and tranquil restaurant is chic and contemporary. Reservation calls are only accepted 09:30 to 11:00, and 15:30 to 17:00.

■ Opening hours, last orders
Lunch=12:00-15:00 L.O.13:00
Dinner=18:30-23:00 L.O.20:30

■ Annual and weekly closing
Closed late December-early January and Sunday

■ Price
Lunch= menu ¥ 7,350
Dinner= menu ¥ 15,750
Service charge= 10%

**TEL. 03-5791-3715**
5-4-7 Shirokanedai, Minato-ku
www.quintessence.jp

# Raku-tei
## 楽亭

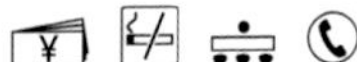

A subdued atmosphere and a plain wooden counter with seating for 12 greet you after stepping through the paper sliding doors at this *tempura* restaurant, located beside Akasaka Church. Diners can choose from two set menus. The mild, light-coloured oil is specially blended to enhance the flavour of sesame and this gives the *tempura* a light, pleasant taste. Owner-chef Shuji Ishikura prepares and fries *makiebi* (mid-size Japanese tiger prawns) only after receiving an order. Between the seafood courses, vegetables are served; *tara-no-me* (bud of the *tara* tree) and other wild plants are available in spring, eggplant and *shin-renkon* (the season's first lotus root) in summer, *matsutake* mushroom in autumn, and *kuwai* (arrowhead) in winter. Adjusting the oil temperature for each ingredient, from the shrimp starter to the final dish of *kakiage* (*tempura* fritter made with mixed ingredients), means only two groups are served at a time. Diners might need to wait while the oil is changed; so either order *sashimi* or just enjoy the sound of oil sizzling in the deep fryer. Lunchtime diners are required to arrive at noon.

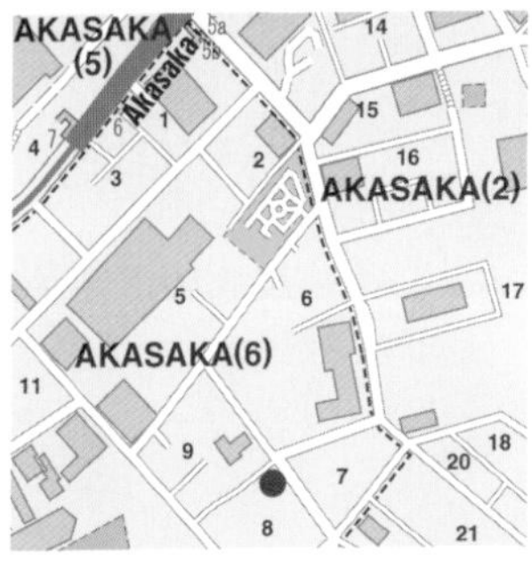

■ Opening hours, last orders
Lunch=12:00 (L.O.)
Dinner=17:00-20:30 (L.O.)

■ Annual and weekly closing
Closed Golden week, mid-August, late December-early January and Monday

■ Price
Lunch= menu ¥ 10,500-12,600
Dinner= menu ¥ 10,500-12,600

**TEL. 03-3585-3743**
6-8-1 Akasaka, Minato-ku

# Reikasai
## 厲家菜

24

The restaurant has only three private rooms, furnished with ornate Chinese furniture and ceramic ware. The owner's grandfather was a high-ranking courtier in the Qing Dynasty (1644-1911/12) and as he used to supervise the preparation of meals for Empress Dowager Cixi and other members of the imperial family, he had access to imperial recipes. The owner's parents opened the first Family Li Imperial Cuisine in Beijing, converting their home into a restaurant to offer dishes based on these secret recipes. The restaurant offers only a chef's choice set menu. Dishes such as the smoked pork flavoured with jasmine and peanuts and coloured with beetroot; shark fin simmered in chicken soup for three days and wrapped in duck; and other fastidiously cooked dishes are bound to satisfy. San Bu Nian, a dessert made of egg yolk, cornflour, sugar and lard and painstakingly prepared by hand-kneading the dough more than 600 times, is a speciality of this restaurant. Each colourful and memorable dish offers a sense of the rich history of the Li family.

■ Opening hours, last orders
Lunch=11:30-15:30 L.O.13:30
Dinner=18:00-23:30 L.O.20:30

■ Price
Lunch= menu ¥ 10,500-47,250
Dinner= menu ¥ 21,000-47,250
Service charge= 10%

**TEL. 03-5413-9561**
FAX. 03-5413-9562
Roppongi Hills, Residence B 3F,
6-12-2 Roppongi, Minato-ku
www.soho-s.co.jp/reikasai/index_fs.html

# Ristorante Aso

Built in the early Showa Era (1926-1989), this building was renovated to maintain the character of the original architecture, and evokes a Tuscan mansion with a flowered courtyard and a cloister. Ristorante Aso was opened in 1997; chef Tatsuji Aso's original and creative cooking goes far beyond the boundaries of Italian and French cuisine. Dishes overflow with innovation in terms of presentation, the way food is arranged and the colour combinations. Aso is similarly uncompromising in his selection of ingredients: *madaka* abalones between June and August, and alfonsino from Shizuoka during the winter months. Tilefish shipped directly from Yamaguchi exudes a rich taste. Miyazaki and Sendai beef are grilled on charcoal and served with black pepper-flavoured mascarpone. Sautéed foie gras topped with zabaione and black truffle sauce is also a captivating winter choice. Here, good food and warm service means customers leave immeasurably satisfied.

■ Opening hours, last orders
Lunch=12:00-15:30 L.O.13:30
Dinner=18:00-23:00 L.O.20:30

■ Annual and weekly closing
Closed 1 week in January,
Saturday and Sunday

■ Price
Lunch= menu ¥ 4,000-8,400
carte ¥ 13,000-20,000
Dinner= menu ¥ 10,500-21,000
carte ¥ 13,000-20,000
Service charge= 13%

**TEL. 03-3770-3690**
FAX. 03-3770-3554
29-3 Sarugakucho, Shibuya-ku
www.hiramatsu.co.jp/restaurants/aso

# Ristorante Honda

Owner-chef Tetsuya Honda opened this restaurant after working at various places in Japan and undergoing apprenticeships in Italy and France. His menu is characterised by sophisticated seasonal dishes that are full of originality in the way food is arranged on the plate and the colour combinations. Honda's distinct approach is reflected in his cooking methods which, although based upon Italian cooking traditions, incorporate some French elements. The tableware is also unique. Ingredients are a blend of Italian and French favourites and dishes impart a full sense of the season; the *capellini* of sweet tomato and salad with abalone and rape blossom served in spring are good examples. In summer, the jellied consommé with fish, shellfish and wax gourds, and cold pasta with caviar are very refreshing. *Tagliatelle* with porcini and *agnolotti* with Pacific saury are served in autumn, while flan with foie gras and truffles as well as roasted wild boar meat and venison from Minami Izu are satisfying winter choices. *Tagliolini* with sea urchin is a speciality that can be enjoyed throughout the year.

■ Opening hours, last orders
Lunch=12:00-15:00 L.O.14:00
Dinner=18:00-22:00 (L.O.)

■ Annual and weekly closing
Closed late December-early January and Monday except Bank Holidays

■ Price
Lunch= menu ¥ 2,940-6,825
Dinner= menu ¥ 7,875-12,600
Service charge= 10%

**TEL. 03–5414–3723**
FAX. 03–5414–3724
2-12-35 Kita-Aoyama, Minato-ku
www.ristorantehonda.jp

# Ristorante La Primula

The chef at this Italian restaurant located near the patio Azabu-Juban spent three years studying Italian cuisine in northern Italy, with stints in Emilia-Romagna, Lombardia and Piemonte. His last position in Friuli was at a restaurant called Primula, and it is from this establishment that La Primula (the primrose) takes its name. The interior décor is chic and modern with the leather chairs blending in well, while the Venetian glass lamp at the entrance draws your attention. Only set menus are served for lunch and dinner, both showcasing the flavours of regional Italian cuisine. Cjalçons, pasta stuffed with potato purée, cinnamon, mint and raisins and topped with Parmesan, is one of the Friulian speciality dishes. For its marriage of textures, the lobster risotto is a fine choice. Tasty goulash made with paprika-stewed beef cheeks is served with polenta while roasted quail thigh stuffed with foie gras and herbs is matched with an anchovy and herb sauce. The food combinations, presentation and ample portions are sure to leave customers satisfied. Reservations for lunch are required at least a day in advance.

■ Opening hours, last orders
Lunch= Wed.-Sat.12:00-15:00
L.O.13:00
Dinner=18:00-23:00 L.O.21:00

■ Annual and weekly closing
Closed late December-early
January, Sunday and 3rd Monday

■ Price
Lunch= menu ¥ 3,500-5,500
Dinner= menu ¥ 8,400-15,750
Service charge= 10%

**TEL. 03-5439-9470**
FAX. 03-5439-9469
Patio Azabu-Juban 3F,
2-8-10 Azabu-Juban, Minato-ku

# Ryugin
## 龍吟

Inside this restaurant located on a Roppongi side street, you'll find calligraphy by owner-chef Seiji Yamamoto which reads "Ryugin Unki" (Clouds rise when the dragon sings); this teaching from Chinese Zen Buddhism has served as Yamamoto's motto since his apprenticeship. Every year, the chef takes part in an international chef's meeting in Spain, which he uses as a source of new ideas. Although the menu is firmly rooted in Japanese cuisine, the chef actively seeks out new possibilities. His quest for perfection is demonstrated in the way he prepares basic stock; he shaves *katsuo-bushi* (dried bonito) only after taking an order to bring out the best possible flavour. In season, sweetfish, flown in from Tokushima every morning, is salt-grilled but its head is crisp as though deep-fried, the belly is soft, and the tail has a dry texture of *himono* (dried fish). Apple candy, a dessert, is prepared using a chemical technology that seals powder inside an apple-shaped sweet using liquid nitrogen.

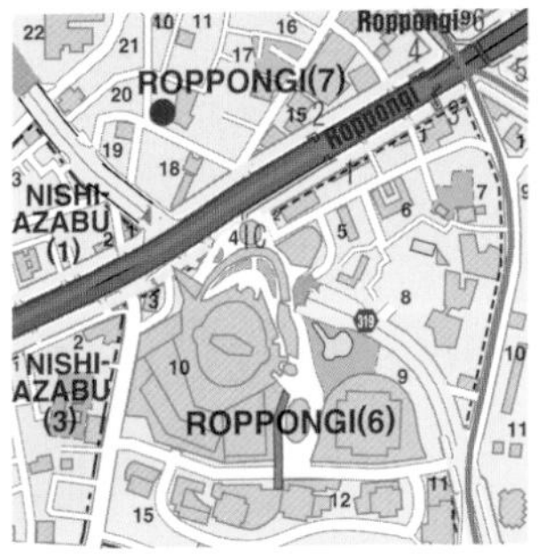

■ Opening hours, last orders
Dinner=18:00-1:00 L.O.23:00

■ Annual and weekly closing
Closed 1-6 January, mid-August, Sunday and Bank Holidays

■ Price
Dinner= menu ¥ 15,750-26,250
carte ¥ 10,000-20,000
Service charge= 10% (private room 15%)

**TEL. 03-3423-8006**
FAX. 03-3423-8003
7-17-24 Roppongi, Minato-ku
www.nihonryori-ryugin.com

# Sakuragaoka
## 桜ヶ丘

A Japanese restaurant located in Roppongi; look for a black wooden wall and paper-covered lamp stand to find the entrance. While Kyo-kaiseki (traditional Kyoto-style formal dining) is the main focus, the restaurant also offers a variety of creative dishes and the chef's repertoire goes beyond the boundaries of Japanese cuisine and encompasses recipes that combine elements of old-style yoshoku (Western dishes adapted to suit Japanese tastes) and Chinese cuisine in addition to signature dishes of Kyoto. The fukahire-no chawanmushi (savoury shark fin egg custard), a speciality, is nicely rounded with bonito stock. Other imaginative options include matsutake mushroom croquettes; a pilaf with dried fish fry; omelette stuffed with rice, bamboo shoots and yuba (bean curd skin); and Japanese-style beef stew. The omakase (chef's choice) set menus change monthly and feature many early, peak and late-season ingredients in line with the traditional leanings of formal Japanese cuisine. There is also an extensive array of original à la carte dishes.

■ Opening hours, last orders
Dinner=17:00-23:30 L.O.20:30

■ Annual and weekly closing
Closed mid-August, late December-early January, Sunday and Bank Holidays

■ Price
Dinner= menu ¥ 12,600-15,750
carte ¥ 7,000-15,000
Service charge= 15% (private room 20%)

**TEL. 03-5770-5250**
FAX. 03-5770-5250
6-8-21 Roppongi, Minato-ku
www.sakuraoka.com

JAPANESE

MAP NO. 5/A-1

# Sakuragawa

## 櫻川

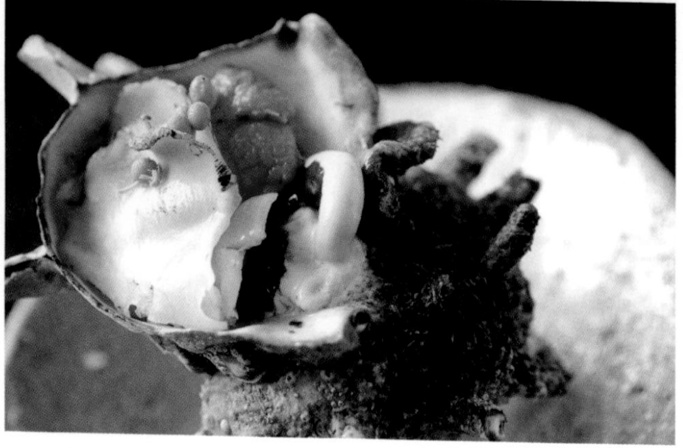

20

This Japanese restaurant was opened in Mitsui Tower, Nihonbashi in 2005; look for a sugitama (ball of Japanese cedar leaves) and the curtain at the entrance bearing the owner's family crest of cherry blossoms. "My aim is to keep traditional Japanese sensibilities alive", says owner-chef Yoshiaki Kurahashi, who attaches considerable importance to Japan's dietary culture and history. Seasonal flowers and leaves are used for hassun (little appetisers). Hassun in winter include kinkan-ikura (kumquat and salmon roe), ankimo (monkfish liver), mushi-awabi (steamed abalone), namako-zu (vinegared sea cucumber) and kani-no-daikon-zutsumi (crab wrapped in Japanese radish). Of the specialities included in the set menus, fukahire ankake gohan (rice with shark fin served with a thick dressing), which is served throughout the year, is recommended. This dish brings out the taste of the kelp and dried bonito in the broth as well as the dried shrimp and scorched rice. Only omakase (chef's choice) set menu is available and that changes every month. The lunch time set menu is good value.

■ Opening hours, last orders
Lunch=12:00-15:30 L.O.14:00
Dinner=18:00-22:00 L.O.20:00

■ Annual and weekly closing
Closed mid-August

■ Price
Lunch= menu ¥ 6,050
Dinner= menu ¥ 13,200
Private room fee= ¥ 3,150-5,250 (lunch), ¥ 5,250-10,500 (dinner)

**TEL. 03-3279-0039**
FAX. 03-3279-0040
Mitsui Tower 2F,
2-1-1 Nihonbashi-Muromachi,
Chuo-ku

# Sankame
## 三亀

¥ LUNCH 6

Situated on Sukiya-dori Avenue in Ginza 6-chome, this Japanese restaurant has been serving Kansai-style cuisine since 1946. Spring choices include *wakatakeni* (boiled bamboo shoots) and *umimasu-no kasuzuke* (sea trout marinated in sake lees) from Hokkaido. In summer, there is salt-grilled *ayu* (sweetfish) from Gujo-Hachiman in Gifu and *hamo-no yanagawa-fu nabe* (pike conger boiled in soy sauce with eggs and burdock). Autumn brings *matsutake-no dobinmushi* (clear soup of *matsutake* mushrooms served in an earthernware pot) from the Kunohe District in Iwate, and fried and salted ginkgo nuts from the Chita Peninsula in Aichi. In winter months, there is warming Shogoin radish cooked with *abura-age* (deep-fried tofu) as well as a set menu featuring *torafugu* (tiger puffer fish) from Usuki in Oita. In addition to the *omakase* (chef's choice) set menu, à la carte dishes are also available in the evening; only set menus are available at lunch. The popularity of this restaurant seems to be due not only to the food, but owner-chef Isao Nanjo's personality and sense of humour.

■ Opening hours, last orders
Lunch=12:00-14:00 L.O.13:00
Dinner=17:00-22:00 L.O.21:30

■ Annual and weekly closing
Closed mid-August, late December-early January, Saturday in July-August, Sunday and Bank Holidays

■ Price

| | | |
|---|---|---|
| Lunch= | menu | ¥ 1,950 |
| Dinner= | menu | ¥ 13,650 |
| | carte | ¥ 8,000-12,000 |

TEL. 03-3571-0573
6-4-13 Ginza, Chuo-ku

# Sant Pau

8

This Spanish restaurant is the Tokyo branch of Sant Pau in Sant Pol de Mar near Barcelona and opened in Coredo Nihonbashi Annex in 2004. It allows diners to experience traditional Spanish cuisine that makes the most of Catalonia's natural bounty, albeit with an extra twist courtesy of Carme Ruscalleda, the owner-chef of the parent restaurant in Spain, and the young chef she has entrusted to oversee the kitchen in Tokyo. Presentation is beautiful and bursts with originality. Ingredients like Iberico pork, salted cod, olive oil, Majorca salt and dried pimientos are imported from Catalonia while others are sourced domestically. The menu changes every season, and all recipes are from the kitchen of Sant Pau. A "Menu Tres Quarts", (45-minute) lunch menu is offered on weekdays, and may be ideal for businesspeople with less time to spare. There is also a large glass-encased wine cellar with about 400 bins and a smoker's lounge with a cigar cellar.

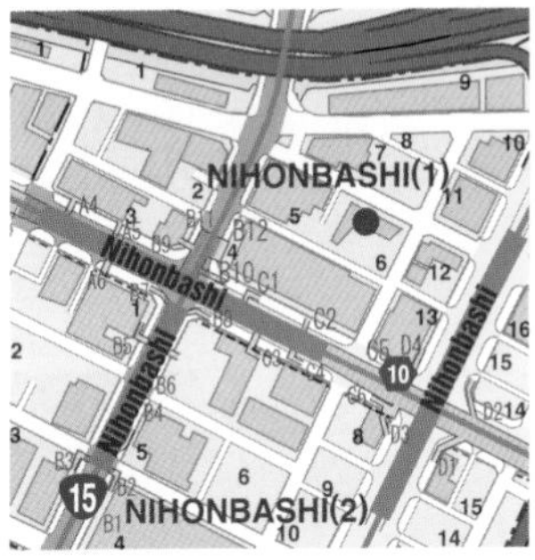

■ Opening hours, last orders
Lunch=11:30-15:30 L.O.13:30
Sat.and Sun.12:00-15:30
L.O.13:30
Dinner=18:00-23:30 L.O.21:00

■ Annual and weekly closing
Closed 1 January and Monday

■ Price
Lunch= menu ¥ 5,500-22,000
carte ¥ 16,000-17,000
Dinner= menu ¥ 18,000-22,000
carte ¥ 16,000-17,000
Private room fee= ¥ 10,000 (lunch),
¥ 18,000 (dinner)
Service charge= 10%

**TEL. 03-3517-5700**
FAX. 03-3517-5701
Coredo Nihonbashi Annex,
1-6-1 Nihonbashi, Chuo-ku
www.santpau.jp

# Sasada
## 笹田

With counter space for only eight people, this Nishi-Shinbashi restaurant has an intimacy that guarantees the individual care and attention of owner-chef Hidenobu Sasada, who runs the business with his wife. Kyoto-style seasoning features strongly here. Seasonal recommendations include *wakatakeni* (boiled bamboo shoots) in spring, *shabu-shabu-wan* (soup with pike conger and *matsutake* mushrooms picked early in the season) in summer, and *kobakogani* (female snow crab) in autumn. Try the *oden* (vegetables, fish dumplings, tofu, and other ingredients stewed in a thin soy soup, and served hot) in winter. This popular dish balances flavours such as Shamo gamecock skin and home-fried fish cakes with a Kansai-style soup stock and contains a generous amount of seasonal vegetables such as *Shogoin* turnip, *ebi-imo* (Kyoto yam) and *kyo-ninjin* carrot. The *omakase* (chef's choice) set menu ends with a serving of fragrant *Koshihikari* rice cooked in an earthenware pot. At Sasada, you will find high-quality dishes at reasonable prices.

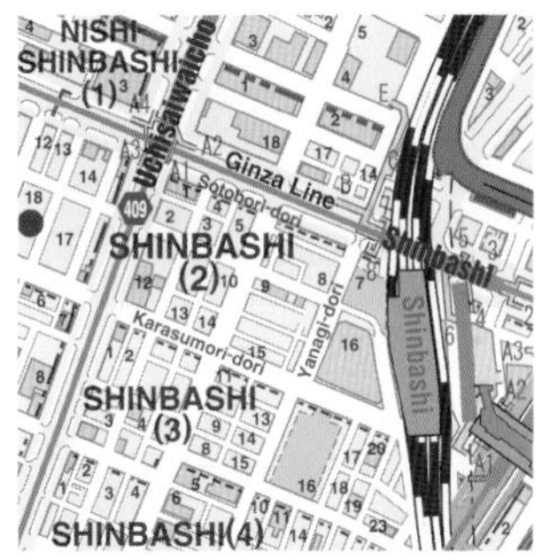

■ Opening hours, last orders
Dinner=18:00-21:30 (L.O.)

■ Annual and weekly closing
Closed mid-August, late December-early January, Sunday and Bank Holidays

■ Price
Dinner= menu ¥ 12,600-31,500

**TEL. 03–3507–5501**
FAX. 03–3507–5501
1-18-8 Nishi-Shinbashi, Minato-ku

# Sawada
## さわ田

The owner of this establishment, Koji Sawada, is a *sushi* chef with an unusual background: before setting up his own restaurant he worked not as a chef but in the transport industry. The variety of wild fish, caught by rod in the Genkai-nada sea in Kyushu, stands out as does the abalone from Sanriku and the chewy cuttlefish from Futtsu in Chiba. One of the features of this restaurant is the chef's commitment to maturing each ingredient, allowing their full flavour to come out. *Koshihikari* rice grown in Tochio is cooked so that it is not too sticky and is well seasoned with *shirozu* white vinegar. Its flavour is as distinctive as those of the ingredients that top it. *Tamagoyaki* with prawns and Japanese yams, which is served at the end of each meal, is smooth on the palate. The well-lit Japanese-style interior features a beautiful wood counter and sleek preparation area. Sawada is a reservation-only restaurant and doors are unlocked in time for the first reservation of the day. During the three-hour dining performance, you will experience a variety of tastes. Be sure to arrive with an empty stomach.

■ Opening hours, last orders
Lunch=12:00-14:00
Dinner=18:00-21:00 and 22:00-1:00

■ Annual and weekly closing
Closed mid-August, late December-early January and Monday

■ Price
Lunch= menu ¥ 21,000
Dinner= menu ¥ 32,000

**TEL. 03-3571-4711**
FAX. 03-3571-4711
MC Building 3F,
5-9-19 Ginza, Chuo-ku

# Sekiho-tei
## 赤寶亭

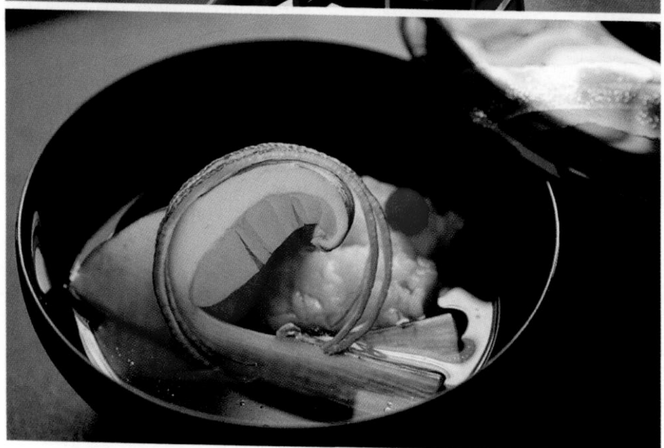

10

Owner-chef Shinichi Akatsuka opened Sekiho-tei in 2004 after working at a number of *ryotei* in Akasaka and Shiga. He cooks high-quality ingredients using traditional techniques. Tilefish comes from Wakasa, *junsai* (water shield shoots) from Hiroshima, and other edible wild plants from Yamagata, where Akatsuka grew up. Soup is created with particular care and only *honkarebushi*, a special kind of *katsuo-bushi* (dried bonito) produced in Makurazaki from the core parts of the bonito *-obushi* (back meat) and *mebushi* (belly), is used, and lavishly so. Water is purchased from Shiga to highlight the taste of the Rishiri *kombu* (kelp produced in Rishiri). The menu and decoration burst with seasonal flavour: *hagoita* (Japanese rackets) are used for *hassun* (small appetisers) at New Year; cards that read "*risshun daikichi* (with luck on the first day of spring)" are placed on plates in February; and *chimaki-zushi* (sushi rolled in the leaves of Siberian irises) are served on the May 5 Boys' Festival. Depending on set menu, you can even enjoy *matcha* (powdered green tea) and the selection of Japanese sweets after meals.

■ Opening hours, last orders
Lunch=Wed.-Sat. 12:00-14:30
L.O.13:30
Dinner=18:00-23:00 L.O.21:30

■ Annual and weekly closing
Closed Golden week, mid-August, late December-early January and Sunday

■ Price
Lunch= menu ¥ 5,250-18,900
Dinner= menu ¥ 11,500-18,900
Private room fee= ¥ 3,150-
¥ 5,250
Service charge= 10%

**TEL. 03-5474-6889**
FAX. 03-5474-6879
3-1-14 Jingumae, Shibuya-ku

# Sense

This restaurant offers modern Cantonese cuisine based on traditional recipes adapted by the head chef. Authentic Chinese ingredients and seasonings are used, such as Napoleon fish, a Hong Kong favourite, five different types of shark fin, grouper from Okinawa and Ogasawara, and rarely found Chinese vegetables grown in Japan. Vegetables offered à la carte are cooked according to each diner's preference. Recommended for dessert is mango pudding made with fresh mangoes. Lunchtime dining is appealing for its casual style, although ambient lighting and panoramic night views of the city make dinner an even more attractive option. Private rooms at the back also offer views of Tokyo Bay and Odaiba. A *yum cha* lunch service is available on weekends and public holidays, with the last orders at 16:00. The contemporary-styled interior of Sense is noteworthy for the eye-catching pink reception counter, wallpaper with a lotus motif and objets d'art placed inside the pillars.

■ Opening hours, last orders
Lunch=11:30-14:30 (L.O.) Sat. Sun. and Bank Holidays 11:30-16:00 (L.O.)
Dinner=17:30-22:00 (L.O.)

■ Price
Lunch= menu ¥ 3,800-10,000
carte ¥ 7,000-29,000
Dinner= menu ¥ 14,000-26,000
carte ¥ 7,000-35,000
Private room fee= ¥ 10,000
Service charge= 10%

**TEL. 03-3270-8188**
FAX. 03-3270-8886
Mandarin Oriental Hotel 37F,
2-1-1 Nihonbashi-Muromachi,
Chuo-ku
www.mandarinoriental.co.jp/tokyo

# 7chome Kyoboshi
## 七丁目 京星

This *tempura* restaurant of Shigeya Sakakibara moved from Ginza 7-chome to Ginza 5-chome in 2008; it is housed on the fifth floor of a modern glass building on the corner of Miyuki-dori Avenue and Nishi-5-bangai-dori Avenue. The interior has been designed in the style of a tea ceremony room, with walls constructed of both mud and dark-spotted Kitayama cedar logs. The *tempura* is made of small ingredients that can be popped into the mouth whole; small, sweet *saimakiebi* (young Japanese tiger prawns) are served with special house salt and lemon juice. Seasoned grated Japanese radish is served as a palate cleanser. Also delicious are purple asparagus, smelt-whiting and gunnel, abalone, quail eggs and figs. *Ten-cha* (*tempura* on rice in a tea broth) is recommended to finish the meal. The chef's constant trial of new ingredients accounts for his wide repertoire and gives diners the chance to savour some rare treats, albeit at a high price. The only set closure days are the New Year and summer holidays and reservations for the weekend must be made two days in advance.

■ Opening hours, last orders
Lunch=12:00-15:00 (L.O.)
Dinner=17:00-21:00 (L.O.)

■ Annual and weekly closing
Closed mid-August and late December-early January

■ Price

| | |
|---|---|
| Lunch= menu | ¥ 26,250 |
| Dinner= menu | ¥ 31,500 |

**TEL. 03-3572-3568**
Ozio Ginza Building 6F,
5-5-9 Ginza, Chuo-ku

JAPANESE

MAP NO. 16/C-2

# Shigeyoshi

重よし

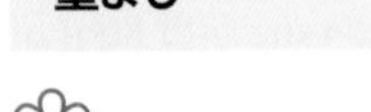

¥ 10

Head downstairs to the first floor of Co-op Olympia on Omotesando-dori Avenue near Harajuku Station. Diners can sit at the counter, where you can chat to the chefs, at tables or in a private room. Kenzo Sato opened Shigeyoshi after honing his skills and he's a devoted researcher -he developed a soup of *suppon* (soft-shelled turtle) without ginger after a year of trials. There is a good variety of ingredients: sea bream, *hamo* (pike conger) and white-fleshed fish from Naruto; *katsuo* (bonito) and *mata* abalone from Boshu; tilefish from Takeoka; and *koiwashi* (anchovies) from Kanazawa. The *satsuki-masu* (red-spotted *masu* salmon) is caught in the Nagara-gawa river and from May to September, the sea urchin from Naruto is particularly good; the *umeshiso* soup made of Japanese apricot and perilla leaf served in September is tasty. In May, the menu features a jelly made with abundant *hyuganatsu* juice (a kind of citrus) and in early summer the citrus is replaced with passion fruit.

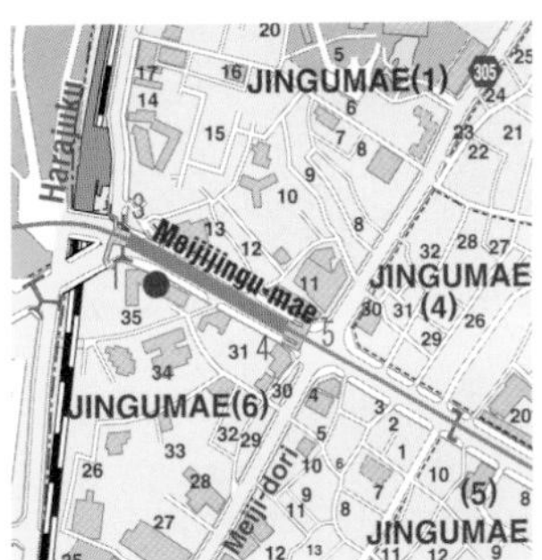

■ Opening hours, last orders
Dinner=17:30-22:00 L.O.21:00

■ Annual and weekly closing
Closed Golden week, mid-August, late December-early January, Sunday and Bank Holiday Mondays

■ Price
Dinner= menu ¥ 18,900-31,500
carte ¥ 10,000-20,000
Private room fee= 10%

**TEL. 03-3400-4044**
Co-op Olympia 1F,
6-35-3 Jingumae, Shibuya-ku

# Shin

真

A sushi restaurant in Nishi-Azabu run by owner-chef Shintaro Suzuki. Ingredients are sourced nationwide: Kasugodai (small-sized sea bream) from Kagoshima is used as a topping alongside Japanese radish and shiroitakombu (kelp); Gizzard shad from Saga is combined with shredded kelp and carefully selected oboshi (part of the flesh of trough shells) are sent from Hokkaido. Two types of sea urchin are used for the gunkan-maki (sushi wrapped in nori). The restaurant looks to traditional Edomae techniques and ingredients are either salted, vinegared or seared—sometimes with straw—to highlight the natural flavour. As for rice, two strains from Niigata and Ibaraki are blended. Nigari (brine) is added to soften the taste and it is cooked rather hard so that the texture of each grain can be distinguishable. Akazu (red vinegar made from sake lees) is the standard here. "The vinegared rice has been continuously improved since our restaurant opened in 2003, and at last, we feel we don't have to change (the recipe) anymore", says Suzuki. Different kinds of soy sauce are used depending on the topping. The good value Okimari set menu is only available during the week.

■ Opening hours, last orders
Lunch=Wed.-Sat.12:00-14:00 L.O.13:30
Dinner=18:00-23:00 L.O.22:00

■ Annual and weekly closing
Closed Monday and 3rd Sunday

■ Price

| | |
|---|---|
| Lunch= menu | ¥ 3,150-9,450 |
| Dinner= menu | ¥ 16,800 |

**TEL. 03-5485-0031**
FAX. 03-5485-0031
H·T Nishi-Azabu Building XI 3F,
4-3-10 Nishi-Azabu, Minato-ku

# Signature

With one of the best views from the entire building, Signature is divided into three sections: in one, close to the Mandarin Bar, diners can enjoy their meal while listening to live jazz in the evening. The central area features glittering partitions and has a distinctly contemporary feel, with carbon fibre lighting setting off the silver and grey tones to create a near futuristic atmosphere. Panoramic views can be had from all tables, but if you are looking for the best position to appreciate the cityscape, reserve a table near the window. The third area at the back of the restaurant has long, lavender-coloured seating with high back panels to allow guests to enjoy a semi-private, relaxed atmosphere. The menu, which changes seasonally, is composed of delicately flavoured and refined contemporary French cuisine; the lunch set menus are particularly attractive. A private room for up to 10 guests with no outside view is also available.

■ Opening hours, last orders
Lunch=11:30-14:30 (L.O.)
Dinner=17:30-22:00 (L.O.)

■ Price
Lunch= menu ¥ 5,000-12,000
carte ¥ 12,000-19,000
Dinner= menu ¥ 14,000-20,000
carte ¥ 12,000-19,000
Private room fee= ¥ 10,000
Service charge= 10%

**TEL. 03-3270-8188**
FAX. 03-3270-8886
Mandarin Oriental Hotel 37F,
2-1-1 Nihonbashi-Muromachi,
Chuo-ku
www.mandarinoriental.co.jp/tokyo

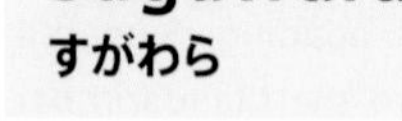

# Sugawara
## すがわら

Head to the Ebisu-Minami 1-chome intersection from Ebisu station and look for a lantern on the street just in front of the small park near Shosenji temple. Run by Shingo Sugawara, a native of Hakodate in Hokkaido, and his wife since its opening in 1992, this restaurant serves casual Japanese food in a relaxed setting. To retain the full flavour of the wild fish, it is not cut into small pieces before being grilled, giving a delicious savoury smell. A noteworthy early spring dish is the seafood salad with edible wild plants and *bainiku* (Japanese apricot pulp). In summer, dishes take on a more refreshing taste; the pike conger is lightly boiled and served with soft-boiled eggs, *junsai* (water shield shoots) and *nameko* mushrooms topped with vinegar jelly flavoured with bonito shavings, kelp, sugar and soy sauce. In autumn, mushrooms dominate the menu while in winter the *kyoage* (deep-fried tofu) cooked in an earthen pot with Japanese radish, potherb mustard and a bonito soup stock is a warming dish. As Sugawara boasts many regular customers, the menus are revised weekly.

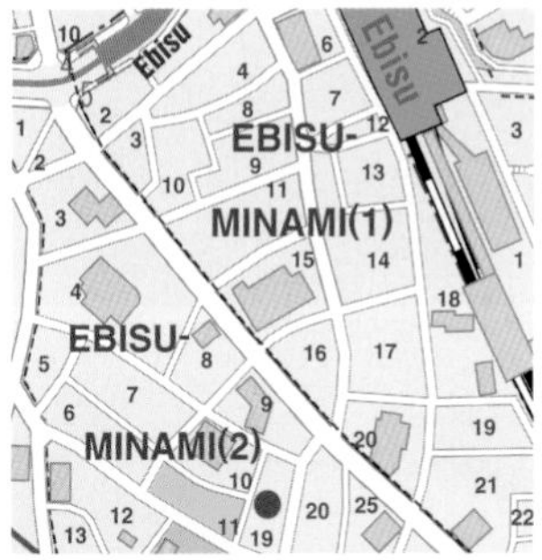

■ Opening hours, last orders
Dinner=18:30-23:00 L.O.21:00

■ Annual and weekly closing
Closed Golden week, mid-August, late December-early January, Saturday, Sunday and Bank Holidays

■ Price
Dinner= menu ¥ 6,810
Service charge= 5%

**TEL. 03–3793–0281**
FAX. 03–3793–0281
2-19-12 Ebisu-Minami, Shibuya-ku

JAPANESE SUSHI

MAP NO. 6/C-1

# Sukiyabashi Jiro
## すきやばし 次郎

This world–renowned restaurant opened in 1965. Known as the "left-handed master craftsman", owner-chef Jiro Ono is dedicated to offering customers delicious *sushi* every day. With swift and fluid movements, *sushi* is crafted using the finest ingredients, all served at different temperatures, while *shari* (vinegared rice) is kept strictly at body temperature. *Shari* seasoned with white vinegar is shaped gently to ensure the each grain of rice cling loosely together and separate easily in the mouth, harmonizing with the topping. This is a genuine *sushi* restaurant that only serves *omakase* (chef's choice) of *nigiri sushi*. Delectable dishes include tuna from local waters, *kohada* (gizzard shad), steamed *awabi* (abalone), prawn, smoked early-summer *katsuo* (bonito), *shako* (mantis shrimp), *uni* (sea urchin) from Hokkaido, simmered *anago* (conger eel) and *tamagoyaki (*omelet). The set menu consisting of about 20 pieces may be expensive but consider the exquisite tastes on offer. Everything is carefully prepared to be ready at the reserved time, so be punctual; and if you don't speak Japanese, go with someone who does.

■ Opening hours, last orders
Lunch=11:30-14:00
Dinner=17:30-20:30 except Saturday

■ Annual and weekly closing
Closed mid-August, late December-early January, Sunday and Bank Holidays

■ Price

| | |
|---|---|
| Lunch= menu | ¥ 31,500 |
| Dinner= menu | ¥ 31,500 |

**TEL. 03–3535–3600**
Tsukamoto Sozan Building B1F,
4-2-15 Ginza, Chuo-ku

# Sushi Aoki Ginza
## 鮨 青木 銀座

10

Look for the chopstick shop on the first floor of a multi-tenant building near the Kojunsha Building; go up a flight and you will find Sushi Aoki Ginza. Toshikatsu Aoki is the second-generation owner-chef, taking his lead from *Edomae sushi* techniques handed down from his father, but he also actively seeks out new possibilities. Boiled *kinjiso* (a leafy vegetable indigenous to Kanazawa) is delicately seasoned and retains a rich colour. Specialities the owner-chef inherited from his father are still favourites: *tako-no-sakurani* (simmered cherry-coloured octopus); *kisu-no-kobujime* (smelt-whiting pressed between two sheets of kelp); and *saimaki-ebi-no-karakozuke* (pickled young Japanese tiger prawns). *Koshihikari* rice from Tochio is seasoned with vinegar and kept at body temperature. Depending on the season, saw-edged perch or red rockfish from Kyushu are good either as *tsumami* eaten with salt, or lightly seared, served as *sushi*. *Shako* (mantis shrimp) and sea urchin from Aomori are also worth trying; hen clams from Hokkaido have a very nice texture. Some dishes in the *omakase* (chef's choice) set menu change each year.

■ Opening hours, last orders
Lunch=12:00-14:00
Dinner=17:00-22:00

■ Annual and weekly closing
Closed Golden week, late December-early January and Sunday

■ Price
Lunch= menu ¥ 3,150-20,000
Dinner= menu ¥ 21,000

**TEL. 03–3289–1044**
FAX. 03–3289–2350
Ginza Takahashi Building 2F,
6-7-4 Ginza, Chuo-ku
www.sushiaoki.com

# Sushi Aoki Nishiazabu
## 鮨 青木 西麻布

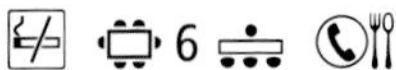


Toshikatsu Aoki, the owner-chef, believes that *sushi* can not be made alone. He also believes it is important to nurture young *sushi* chefs. While inheriting his father's technique, who was also a *sushi* chef, he integrates his own ideas and refines his dishes further. The ingredients used also make the most of his wide network of suppliers. This is an orthodox *sushi* restaurant where *nigiri sushi* holds centre stage. *Mada-ko-no sakurani* (simmered cherry-coloured common octopus), a recipe passed down from the chef's father, is served not only as an appetiser but also as *nigiri*. There is also rarely found oyster *nigiri*; the *nitsume* (soy syrup) that coats the oysters briefly steamed in *sake* is based on an *Edo-mae* technique and is prepared in a similar way to Chinese oyster sauce. The house speciality is *yaki-saba bozushi* (seared chub mackerel *sushi* pressed in a box rather than by hand) with *kombu* (kelp) that has been cooked in a pressure cooker. For Sunday lunch, only the *omakase* (chef's choice) set menu is available. Aside from the dining room counter, there is also a private room with a counter accommodating up to six guests.

■ Opening hours, last orders
Lunch=12:00-14:00
Dinner=18:00-23:00

■ Annual and weekly closing
Closed Golden week, late December-early January and Monday

■ Price
Lunch= menu ¥ 3,150-20,000
Dinner= menu ¥ 21,000

**TEL. 03-5771-3344**
FAX. 03-5771-3345
3-23-7 Nishi-Azabu, Minato-ku
www.sushiaoki.com

# Sushi Fukumoto
## 鮨 福元

Walk down the main shopping street from the South Exit of Shimokitazawa Station and turn right at the junction where you see a flower shop. Look for a modern concrete building with a dental clinic on the first floor; the clinic's green board acts as a landmark for Sushi Fukumoto, which is in the basement. Owner-chef Toshio Fukumoto visits Tsukiji market every morning, carefully selecting the best seafood—sea bream from Sajima, horse mackerel from Awaji, scallops and trough shells from Notsuke—in addition to regular items like *anago* (conger eel) from Nojima and ark shells from Yuriage. The *tsumami* (appetiser or snack) of Chinese yam and sea urchin from Toi dressed with soy sauce is served throughout the year. From spring to summer, try the raw abalone from Miyagi coated with strained innards and sea urchin. Seasonings include *mojio* (salt made by burning seaweed) from Hiroshima. *Akitakomachi* rice from Akita is boiled rather hard and is blended with a mild-tasting *akazu* (red vinegar made from *sake* lees). As the chef's aim is to "offer *sushi* that can be *tsumami*", *sushi* and *sake* can be enjoyed together.

■ Opening hours, last orders
Dinner=18:00-23:00 (L.O.)
Sun. and Bank Holidays 17:00-21:00 (L.O.)

■ Annual and weekly closing
Closed mid-August, late December-early January and Wednesday

■ Price
Dinner= menu ¥ 14,667
Service charge= 5%

**TEL. 03-5481-9537**
FAX. 03-5481-9537
Hanabu Building B1F,
5-17-6 Daizawa, Setagaya-ku
www17.ocn.ne.jp/~fuku3411

# Sushi Isshin Asakusa

## 鮨 一新 浅草

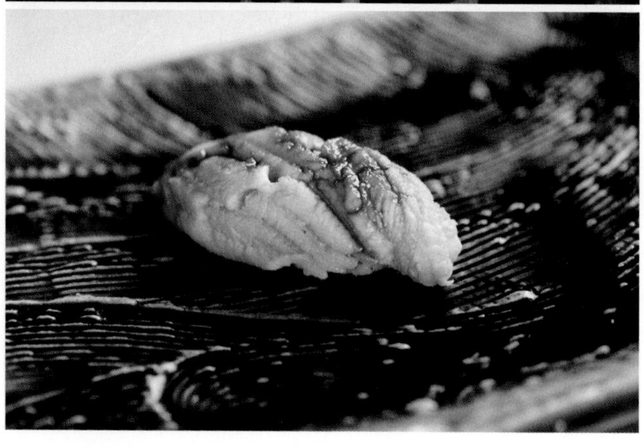

To find the restaurant, head for the Asakusa-4 Post Office or the Asakusa Police Station. Owner-chef Takashi Hashimoto runs the place single-handedly. Sit at one of the 10 counter seats and enjoy *sushi* while jazz plays in the background. Abalone from Chiba, only available from June to September, boiled in a large pan until tender is a house appetiser. *Maguro-no-zuke* sees tuna prepared in the traditional way: marinated in a blend of dried tuna soup stock and soy sauce to ensure a richer taste. *Tako* (octopus) from Sajima is also boiled until tender and can be enjoyed as a dish in itself or as *sushi*. Good winter dishes include the homemade *karasumi* (salted and dried grey mullet roe) and seared *shirako* (milt). Rice from Fukushima is steamed on a hot charcoal fire and seasoned with *akazu* (red vinegar made from *sake* lees). Popular *sushi* toppings include *kohada* (gizzard), for which the amount of vinegar and salt used depends on the condition of the fish when delivered; *anago* (conger eel) from Tokyo Bay and Nojima; *nihamaguri* (boiled clams) and *yariika* (spear squid) with egg in spring and *ikura* (salmon roe) in autumn.

■ Opening hours, last orders
Dinner=18:00-22:00(L.O.)

■ Annual and weekly closing
Closed mid-August, late December-early January, Sunday and Bank Holidays

■ Price
Dinner= menu ¥ 15,750

**TEL. 03–5603–1108**
FAX. 03–5603–1108
4-11-3 Asakusa, Taito-ku
www.sushi-issin.com

# Sushi Iwa
## 鮨 いわ

Hisayoshi Iwa's *sushi* restaurant is located near Taimei Elementary School, on a narrow lane between Ginza Corridor Street and Sukiya-dori Avenue in Ginza 6-chome; look for the tiled roof, the black wall and the bamboo screens.. The interior features seasonal flowers arranged on a hanging shelf reminiscent of a *tokonoma* alcove, and other architectural features including the woven mat ceiling. The spotless L-shaped plain wood counter has only seven white-covered chairs. To ensure the best flavour of the tuna, achieved at a specific temperature, Iwa leaves the cut slices to sit for a while before transforming them into *nigiri sushi*. Using several sections of the tuna, including *harakami* (the upper belly) -a delicacy- the chef takes particular care to entice the most flavour out of each section; three pieces of *nigiri sushi* -topped respectively with *akami* (the tuna's red flesh), *chu-toro* (the moderately fatty, sweet flesh) and *o-toro* (the more fatty, melt-in-the-mouth flesh)- are served in a well-timed succession.

■ Opening hours, last orders
Dinner=17:00-23:00

■ Annual and weekly closing
Closed mid-August, late December-early January, Saturday, Sunday and Bank Holidays

■ Price
Dinner= menu ¥ 15,750-26,250

**TEL. 03-3571-7900**
6-3-17 Ginza, Chuo-ku

# Sushi Kanesaka
## 鮨 かねさか

While the owner-chef Shinji Kanesaka attaches much importance to *Edomae sushi* techniques, new ideas are also readily adopted in pursuit of the ultimate taste: this is the style of "Sushi Kanesaka." The oft-felt barrier of respect between customers and *sushi* chefs gives way to a cosy atmosphere. The basic rules are always observed; priority is given to the freshness of ingredients and close attention is paid to the way they are matured. Recommended during the summer are the *Edomae* prawns; their flesh after being boiled and served immediately has a firm texture. Bluefin tuna from Oma or Toi, cut and trimmed on a Japanese cypress chopping board placed at a higher level so as to allow the guests to witness the show, is also highly rated. Rice is seasoned with salt and *akazu* (red vinegar made from *sake* lees) to ensure the best pairing between the rice and the toppings. The interior décor revolves around a reddish marble that runs from floor to ceiling. The service by the female waiting staff in *kimono* is also agreeable, and provides further evidence of the consideration the chef bestows on his customers.

■ Opening hours, last orders
Lunch=11:30-14:00 L.O.13:00
Dinner=17:00-22:00 L.O.21:00

■ Annual and weekly closing
Closed Golden week, mid-August, late December-early January and Bank Holiday Mondays

■ Price
Lunch= menu ¥ 5,250-15,750
Dinner= menu ¥ 15,750-21,000

**TEL. 03-5568-4411**
FAX. 03-5568-4412
Misuzu Building B1F,
8-10-3 Ginza, Chuo-ku

# Sushiko Honten
## 寿司幸本店

10

Mamoru Sugiyama, the fourth generation owner-chef uses only sun-dried rice which, when cooked, ensures that the texture is never too hard. Seasoning consists of the merest hint of salt and red vinegar and the serving temperature is key: the cooked rice is stored in a wooden container and placed in a warmed basket so as to remain at body temperature. Sweet *atsuyaki tamago* (omelette) is prepared using a technique passed down from the Edo Period (1603-1867) and is cooked under a charcoal fire to ensure a nice golden hue and a soft and fluffy texture. Sugiyama has a wine cellar at a nearby location and offers a variety of labels, premium wines included. Many regular customers enjoy wine with *sushi*, and the chef has even developed a special wine glass with a short stem to match the height of the countertops. *Barachirashi* (scattered *sushi*) using 10 different ingredients, such as vinegared gizzard shad fillet, *anago* (conger eel) fillet, *kanpyo* (dried gourd strips) and *shiitake* mushrooms, is one of the specialities and is a good choice for lunch or take-outs. The restaurant is open from lunchtime through to dinner.

■ Opening hours, last orders
11:30-23:00 L.O.21:45

■ Annual and weekly closing
Closed mid-August and late December-early January

■ Price

| | |
|---|---|
| Lunch= menu | ¥ 9,450-26,250 |
| Dinner= menu | ¥ 9,450-26,250 |

**TEL. 03-3571-1968**
FAX. 03-3571-1907
6-3-8 Ginza, Chuo-ku

# Sushi Mizutani
## 鮨 水谷

Located on the basement floor of a building opposite the Ginza Nikko Hotel, this restaurant is owned and operated by Hachiro Mizutani, one of Japan's best-known *sushi* chefs. The clean and pleasant interior has just 10 counter seats. The appeal of this restaurant lies first and foremost in the unquestionable quality of ingredients used and Mizutani's *sushi*-making techniques. *Sushi* here is slightly more slender than usual, elegant and beautifully crafted. Various innovative ideas are utilised behind the scenes to enhance the taste of the toppings, which include aromatic and tender abalone, best-quality tuna, and bonito smoked over burning straw. The chef takes pride in the rice, a blend of several varieties developed over four decades in collaboration with his rice dealer. The subtle balance between the vinegar and salt used for seasoning, the body temperature at which the rice is kept and the chef's unique *sushi*-making techniques combine to further intensify the taste of the base material. Even in the *Tamagoyaki* (omelette), available only at dinner, Mizutani's unfailing skill is demonstrated.

■ Opening hours, last orders
Lunch=11:30-13:30
Dinner=17:00-21:30

■ Annual and weekly closing
Closed Golden week, mid-August, late December-early January, Sunday and Bank Holidays

■ Price

| | |
|---|---|
| Lunch= menu | ¥ 15,000 |
| Dinner= menu | ¥ 15,000 |

**TEL. 03-3573-5258**
Seiwa Silver Building B1F,
8-2-10 Ginza, Chuo-ku

# Sushi Musashi
## 鮨 武蔵

With a cypress counter, wickerwork mat ceiling, granite floor and simply designed kitchen, this restaurant has an air of cleanliness. Owner-chef Hiroyuki Musashi places the greatest emphasis on *shari* (vinegared rice). He uses *Akita Komachi* rice from the previous year's harvest, seasoning it well with white vinegar and seaweed salt. For the same reason, his *nikiri* (condensed soy sauce) and *nitsume* (soy syrup) are subtle so as to enhance the natural taste. *Hikarimono* (silvery fish), such as *iwashi* (sardine) and *nishin* (herring) and *kohada* (gizzard shad), are thoroughly firmed up with vinegar. The chef also offers such rare ingredients as big *isaki* (chicken grunt) and *akahata* (blacktip grouper). A popular dish to complete the meal is *chu-maki* (medium-sized *sushi* rolls) containing simmered *koya-dofu* (freeze-dried tofu), *kanpyo* (dried gourd strips), rolled omelet, *shiitake* mushroom and *shibaebi-no-oboro* (seasoned mashed prawns). Sushi Musashi is located in a residential street, in the building on the left with the preserved flower shop on the first floor.

■ Opening hours, last orders
Dinner=18:00-22:00 L.O.21:00

■ Annual and weekly closing
Closed mid-August, late December-early January, Sunday and Bank Holidays

■ Price
Dinner= menu ¥ 15,750

**TEL. 03-5464-3634**
FAX. 03-5464-3634
Adessoems B1F,
5-18-10 Minami-Aoyama, Minato-ku

# Sushi Nakamura
## 鮨 なかむら

After training at a number of Japanese restaurants, Masanori Nakamura opened this establishment in Roppongi in 2000. As well as sourcing fish from Tsukiji market, white-fleshed fish and shellfish are delivered to the restaurant direct from Noto in Ishikawa. *Akanishigai* (a mollusc found exclusively in Noto) is served as *sashimi*. Meanwhile, the seared *kuchiko* (sea cucumber ovaries) is good with *sake*. *Uni* (sea urchin) from Kumamoto or Hokkaido delivered in salted water is best eaten with salt and *wasabi* to enhance the flavour. The chef is particular when it comes to tuna: in summer it comes from Sado and in winter from Oma in Aomori. Sun-dried *Koshihikari* rice from Fukushima is steamed at a high heat in a *hagama* (traditional rice cooking pot), seasoned with aged *kurozu* (black vinegar) from Kagoshima and a mild-tasting salt from Okinawa for a good match for the tuna. In summer, a soup containing slices of *ni-awabi* (boiled abalone) is recommended. Choose *sake* or *shochu* from the chef's list. Sushi Nakamura is open till late, but as it is always busy, reservations should be made well in advance.

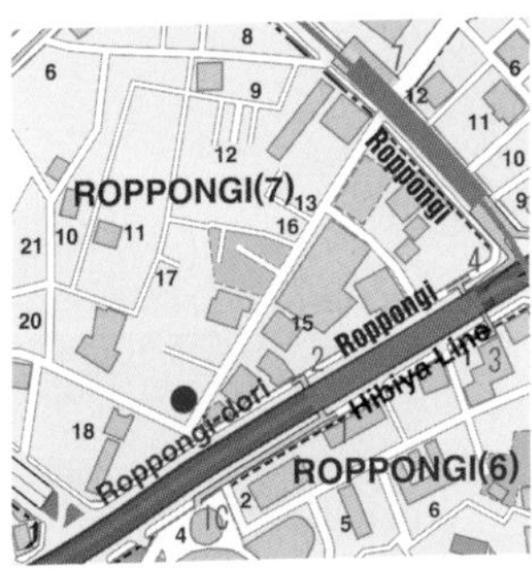

■ Opening hours, last orders
Dinner=18:00-1:00 L.O.23:30

■ Annual and weekly closing
Closed Golden week, mid-August, late December-early January, Saturday, Sunday and Bank Holidays

■ Price
Dinner= menu ¥ 15,750

TEL. 03-3746-0856
FAX. 03-3746-0856
7-17-16 Roppongi, Minato-ku

# Sushi Ohno
## すし おおの

A *sushi* restaurant with one counter that seats just eight customers. Diners generally start with a variety of appetisers before moving onto *sushi*. A key factor in the appeal of Sushi Ohno is the careful preparation and moderate seasoning. Offering variety in taste, the chef focuses on original ideas, serving not only *sashimi*, but also *kobujime* (fish pressed between two sheets of kelp) alongside dishes that may be steamed, grilled or salted. Precise attention is also paid to the temperature of each ingredient. Soft and tasty abalone is steeped in *sake* and kelp for half a day before being steamed with *sake*. The *chawanmushi* (savoury egg custard) with Japanese apricot made with a clear golden soup stock is also memorable; its cold version is recommended in summer. The fluffy flesh of local conger eel, in season throughout summer, has a distinct *umami* taste. In early autumn, hefty 1kg chub mackerel from the Miura Peninsula feature on the menu as does *karasumi* (salted and dried grey mullet roe) dried by the restaurant. *Koshihikari* rice used here is sent directly from a contract farmer in Yamagata, polished every 10 days.

■ Opening hours, last orders
Dinner=17:30-22:00 (L.O.)

■ Annual and weekly closing
Closed Golden week, mid-August, late December-early January, Sunday and Bank Holidays

■ Price
Dinner= menu ¥ 17,850-24,150

**TEL. 03-3572-0866**
FAX. 03-3572-0866
7-2-17 Ginza, Chuo-ku

# Sushi Saito
## 鮨 さいとう

As you enter the parking lot of the Nihon Jitensha Kaikan building opposite the U.S. Embassy, this *sushi* restaurant is on your right. As there is no sign, it is somewhat difficult to spot. Here, particular attention is paid by Takashi Saito, the owner-chef, in achieving the delicate balance between rice, toppings, *wasabi* and *nikiri* (condensed soy sauce). The texture of each grain of rice is constant, and while seasoning is slightly saltier than usual to enhance the taste of the toppings, the red vinegar used has a mildier flavour. This combination of seasonings is especially suited to tuna, of which the chef is particularly proud. It is aged for more than two weeks in the icebox and then sliced to the appropriate thickness. The chef keeps a sharp eye on the temperature at which it is served; when the fat begins to rise to the surface, this signals that it has reached the optimum temperature for eating. The restaurant has counter seating for just six persons, enabling the chef to give each diner his utmost attention.

■ Opening hours, last orders
Lunch=11:30-14:00 (L.O.)
Dinner=17:00-22:00 (L.O.)

■ Annual and weekly closing
Closed mid-August, late December-early January, Sunday and Bank Holidays

■ Price
Lunch= menu ¥ 5,250-15,750
Dinner= menu ¥ 15,750-26,250

**TEL. 03-3589-4412**
Nihon Jitensha Kaikan 1F,
1-9-15 Akasaka, Minato-ku

# Sushisho Saito
## すし匠 齋藤

Owner-chef Toshio Saito, who once made *sushi* in New York, opened Sushisho Saito in Akasaka in 2006. The counter has sunken seating. Only an *omakase* (chef's choice) set menu is offered and this starts with a single piece of *sushi*, followed by *sushi* and an appetiser served in a precise order. *Tsumami* (appetiser) include scallops from the Okhotsk Sea served with sesame seed oil containing salt. In addition to traditional *Edomae sushi*, which uses vinegared, boiled, seared and steamed seafood, Saito also offers his own take on this popular cuisine. *Kasugo* (small-sized sea bream) is topped with *kinome* (young Japanese pepper leaves) and seasoned with *kabosu* citrus fruit juice. Firmly steamed rice is seasoned in two different ways: red vinegar is used for *kobujime* and tuna, while white vinegar is better with lighter tasting white fish and shellfish. The body temperature of the rice is maintained by using only small tubs at a time and keeping the bulk of it warm in the kitchen. Waiting staff who serve in the *seiza* position on the Ryukyu-style *tatami* add to the overall atmosphere.

■ Opening hours, last orders
Dinner=18:00-23:30 (L.O.)

■ Annual and weekly closing
Closed Golden week, mid-August, late December-early January and Monday

■ Price
Dinner= menu ¥ 20,000

**TEL. 03-3505-6380**
FAX. 03-3505-6380
Akasaka Hogetsudo Honten Building 2F,
4-2-2 Akasaka, Minato-ku

# Suzuki
## すずき

The owner-chef Yoshitsugu Suzuki is largely self-taught in Japanese cuisine, although he did hone his skill as a *sushi* chef. He opened this restaurant near Gakugei-Daigaku Station in 1984. Much of his homely Japanese cuisine goes well with sake which, no doubt, contributes to the relaxed atmosphere. Chinese and French culinary techniques combined with unique ingredients and Suzuki's flair -which goes beyond the bounds of traditional Japanese cuisine- come together to bring out the flavour of his dishes. The chef visits Tsukiji market daily and comes up with a menu only after examining available ingredients. He favours vegetables from Kyoto and Kanazawa; *Shirako-takenoko* (bamboo shoots) brought in directly from Tanba are soft and offer a taste of spring, with the slightest hint of the bonito soup stock they are cooked in. Tilefish from Wakasa is soaked in salted water, dried for half a day, and roasted after being brushed with *sake*. As he offers a home cooking class in his kitchen every day at noon, only one lunch reservation is accepted per day and the *tatami* seating is the only option.

■ Opening hours, last orders
Lunch=12:00-14:00 L.O.12:30
Dinner=18:00-22:00 L.O.21:00

■ Annual and weekly closing
Closed Golden week, mid-August, late December-early January and Monday

■ Price
Lunch= menu ¥ 6,300
Dinner= menu ¥ 10,500-15,750

**TEL. 03-3710-3696**
FAX. 03-3710-3696
2-16-3 Takaban, Meguro-ku
www.kappou.jp

# Tahara
## 田はら

A Japanese restaurant across from the Azabu Fire Station. The detached restaurant building has a clean and simple look and diners can choose from counter-seating on the first floor, table dining on the second or third floors reached via a spiral staircase or a private room for eight with its own courtyard. Owner-chef Kazuo Tahara opened his eponymous restaurant in 1992, focusing chiefly on fish dishes. Fried horse mackerel, the restaurant's speciality, boasts a distinctive taste that is different from what one would typically expect: with thick flesh and cooked to precision, this dish is of a standard not easily found. This fish, also served as *sashimi*, comes from Okuchi Bay in Ehime. Also on offer is *jihamaguri* (clams) direct from Joban in Ibaraki which are steamed with *sake*; harvest fish pickled in sweet Kyoto-style *miso* and sablefish pickled in *sake* lees. From late November through February, oysters from Lake Hamanako in Shizuoka are an excellent choice. As the chef runs the kitchen alone, you may face a wait if the restaurant is crowded. The private room is only available for those taking the set menus.

■ Opening hours, last orders
Dinner=17:30-21:30 (L.O.)

■ Annual and weekly closing
Closed Golden week, mid-August, late December-early January, Sunday and Bank Holidays

■ Price
Dinner= menu ¥ 8,000
carte ¥ 5,000-14,500
Private room fee= ¥ 2,000/person
Service charge= 10%

**TEL. 03–5410–0200**
FAX. 03–5730–9647
3-5-4 Nishi-Azabu, Minato-ku
www.sakana-tahara.jp

# Takeyabu
竹やぶ

10

The interior of this *soba* restaurant in Roppongi Hills overflows with decorative touches that reflect owner-chef Takao Abe's personality. Un-threshed buckwheat is ground with a millstone in the restaurant and each season *soba* from various parts of Japan is featured. If you order *tempura soba*, freshly deep-fried *tempura* is added to the bowl in front of you, allowing you to enjoy the crackling sound of the crisp *tempura* hitting the soup. New ideas and methods are constantly being applied without relying on tradition, as evident in the cold buckwheat dumpling, which is not served at any other *soba* restaurant. The *galettes* made of buckwheat flour may remind you of Brittany, while the egg soufflé with balsamic vinegar topped with buckwheat seeds is another original invention. *Soba* comes served on a bamboo mat and goes well with the full-flavoured broth. Multi-course set menus that incorporate a variety of sophisticated dishes are available for groups of two or more.

■ Opening hours, last orders
Lunch=11:30-15:30
Dinner=18:00-21:30
Sunday and Bank Holidays
11:30-20:30

■ Annual and weekly closing
Closed 1-3 January

■ Price

| | | |
|---|---|---|
| Lunch= | menu | ¥ 5,250 |
| | carte | ¥ 3,000-8,000 |
| Dinner= | menu | ¥ 9,240 |
| | carte | ¥ 3,000-8,000 |

Private room fee= 10 %

**TEL. 03-5786-7500**
Roppongi Hills Residence B 3F,
6-12-2 Roppongi, Minato-ku

# Taku
## 拓

Located in Nishi-Azabu, Taku blends the modern style of exposed concrete walls with Japanese panache. Takuya Sato, the owner-chef, trained in Japanese cuisine, giving extra depth to his *sushi* craftsmanship, and his restaurant features dishes with an additional twist; high-quality fish, for example, is seasoned with *kombu* (kelp) or salt before being served, making the most of its natural taste. The *omakase* (chef's choice) set menu offers many dishes and begins with a variety of elaborate appetisers including *sashimi*, *aburi* (seared fish) and simmered dishes, and moving on to *nigiri sushi*. *Uni-no palette* (sea urchin palette), which offers several types of sea urchin from throughout Japan, is a good choice in summer. *Chu-toro* (tuna belly with medium fat) *nigiri sushi* uses two thinly cut tuna slices for each piece. The chef chooses between two types of rice, one seasoned with red vinegar and one with white vinegar, depending on the topping. As well as wine, a large array of *sake* and *shochu* is offered. Open till late.

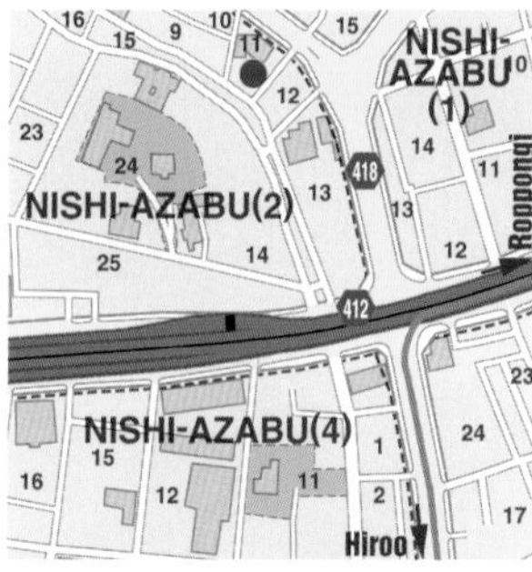

■ Opening hours, last orders
Dinner=18:00-1:00 (L.O.)

■ Annual and weekly closing
Closed mid-August, late December-early January, Sunday and Bank Holidays

■ Price
Dinner= menu ¥ 16,800-21,000

TEL. 03-5774-4372
2-11-5 Nishi-Azabu, Minato-ku

# Tamao
## 玉青

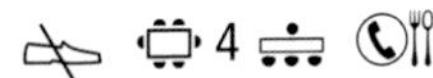

As there is no sign, look for the building entrance on the left of the *izakaya* on the first floor and call 301 on the intercom. You will then get the feeling you are invited to a private retreat; one featuring a counter and three private rooms. The restaurant is known for its *rogama* (oven) cuisine. Spring choices include roasted bamboo shoots basted with soup stock and soy sauce; in summer, the lightly baked abalone and in winter, the hotpot of salt-grilled *suppon* (soft-shelled turtle). *Namako* (sea cucumber) roasted in the oven and mixed with *konowata* (sea cucumber gut) is also a good choice in winter. In addition to seafood and vegetables, beef, Iberico pork and other meats are available. As well as oven-roasted dishes, Tamao also offers a number of other attractive options. The decoratively crafted hors-d'œuvre as well as the *hassun* (small appetisers), bursting with seasonal flavours and colours, are beautifully presented. Organic *Koshihikari* rice produced in various regions is cooked in the oven and served straight to the plate. A quiet, comfortable place that is also suitable for small business gatherings.

■ Opening hours, last orders
Dinner=18:00-23:00 (L.O.)

■ Annual and weekly closing
Closed Golden week, mid-August, late December-early January and Sunday

■ Price
Dinner= menu ¥ 10,500-18,900
carte ¥ 10,000-20,000
Service charge= 10%

**TEL. 03-3455-1407**
Sanrakukan 301,
3-3-7 Azabu-Juban, Minato-ku
www.i-anbai.com/pc/rest6.html

# Tapas Molecular Bar

A surprising and unconventional bar that serves innovative interpretations of traditional dishes from various countries made using liquid nitrogen, carbon-rich gas and alginic acid, among others. Dinner is composed of at least 20 small dishes creatively designed by the head chef, the preparation of which requires highly advanced cooking skills. Exquisite dishes are composed of very fresh foodstuffs and feature a broad range of different textures. As if in conducting a chemistry experiment, the chefs create unique dishes in an entertaining culinary display using cylinders, pipettes and syringes for carrot caviar, crispy beets and strawberry spaghetti. The "dinner show" happens twice nightly at 18:00 and 20:30 for just seven guests each time, who are strongly advised to arrive on time. The second timeslot is recommended for its more relaxed atmosphere. Located in a corner of the Oriental Lounge on the top floor of Mandarin Oriental, the bar introduces guests to a whole new food experience. After the show, diners can relax in a sofa by the window and bask in the afterglow.

■ Opening hours, last orders
Dinner=18:00-20:15 and 20:30-22:45

■ Price
Dinner= menu ¥ 12,000
Service charge= 10%

**TEL. 03-3270-8188**
FAX. 03-3270-8886
Mandarin Oriental Hotel 38F,
2-1-1 Nihonbashi-Muromachi,
Chuo-ku
www.mandarinoriental.co.jp/tokyo

# Tateru Yoshino Shiba

This French restaurant opened in the annex of the Shiba Park Hotel in 2003 and is run by Tateru Yoshino, who shuttles back and forth between Tokyo and Paris -he is also the owner-chef of Stella Maris in Paris. The *carpaccio de chevreau* (*carpaccio* of young goat) made with goat from Kikai Island in Kagoshima, where the chef was born, is a rare speciality. *Duo de foie gras* is a cold hors-d'œuvre of a duck foie gras terrine infused with dried fruits. *Saumon fumé mi-cuit à la Stella Maris* is Yoshino's fish speciality. As for meat, *Tête de cochon sauce tortue,* pork head cuts roasted in a cocotte and served with a *suppon* (soft-shelled turtle) sauce, is a good choice. *Tourte de gibier* (wild game meat pie) is a traditional winter dish using several types of game and foie gras and comes recommended. The wine list is extensive and features some 300 bottles carefully selected by the sommelier.

■ Opening hours, last orders
Lunch=11:30-14:00 (L.O.)
Dinner=18:00-21:00 (L.O.) except Sunday

■ Price
Lunch= menu ¥ 3,675-15,750
carte ¥ 10,000-17,000
Dinner= menu ¥ 6,825-15,750
carte ¥ 10,000-17,000
Service charge= 10%

**TEL. 03–5405–7800**
FAX. 03–5405–7801
Shiba Park Hotel Annex 1F,
1-5-10 Shiba-Koen, Minato-ku
www.tateruyoshino.com

# Tateru Yoshino Shiodome

♿ 🚭 🍷 P 28 ☎🍴

Situated on the 25th floor of the Shiodome Media Tower, together with the Park Hotel Tokyo lobby, this French restaurant was originally opened as "Gastronomie Française Tateru Yoshino" in 2003. Tateru Yoshino, also the owner-chef of its sister restaurants –Stella Maris in Paris and Tateru Yoshino Shiba in Tokyo– had the restaurant's name changed to its current one in July 2008. The compact dining room is sleek and modern with white walls and large windows that overlook the nearby skyscrapers and Tokyo Bay. Décor includes contemporary paintings, crystal glassware and china objets d'art, as well as chestnut-hued seats. The food is creative and flavourful and follows along the lines of contemporary French cuisine; *prix fixe* menus offering customers several choices as well as a chef's choice set menu are available for both lunch and dinner. Bar à vins Tateru Yoshino, the wine bar adjacent to the dining room, offers a well-balanced collection of wines from France and other countries.

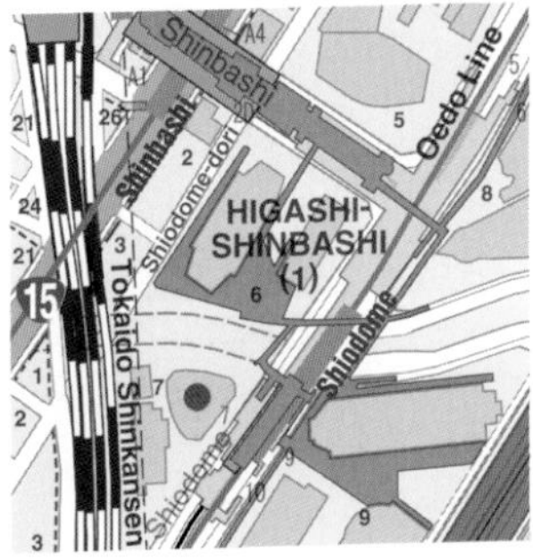

■ Opening hours, last orders
Lunch=11:30-14:00 (L.O.)
Dinner=18:00-21:00 (L.O.)

■ Price
Lunch= menu ¥ 3,675-8,400
Dinner= menu ¥ 7,875-15,750
Private room fee= ¥ 5,250-29,400
Service charge= 10%

**TEL. 03-6252-1155**
FAX. 03-6252-1156
Park Hotel Shiodome Media Tower 25F,
1-7-1 Higashi-Shinbashi, Minato-ku
www.tateruyoshino.com

# Tatsumura
## たつむら

8

A Japanese restaurant run by the owner-chef Masahiko Miyagawa, behind the TBS building. There is only one set menu, consisting of about 10 courses. The chef concentrates on natural flavours and employs various techniques so as not to bore diners' palates: he uses a different soup stock base (bonito flakes, scallops or clams) depending on the dish to add variety. The hors-d'œuvre is a rich-flavoured *mineoka tofu* (milk tofu) with a hint of sesame. The *takikomi-gohan* (rice dish seasoned with broth and boiled with various ingredients) cooked in a traditional *hagama* iron pot changes each season, using such seasonal ingredients as Japanese ice fish and *sakura-ebi* (stardust shrimps) in spring, *samatsudake* mushrooms (similar to *matsutake* mushrooms but harvested in early summer) in summer, and sea bream head in autumn. The interior is simple, with a single counter and three private *tatami* rooms. In spring, one of them offers a lovely view of cherry blossom. The rooms are often used for business entertaining, while the counter is suitable for those who are more concerned with savouring the food.

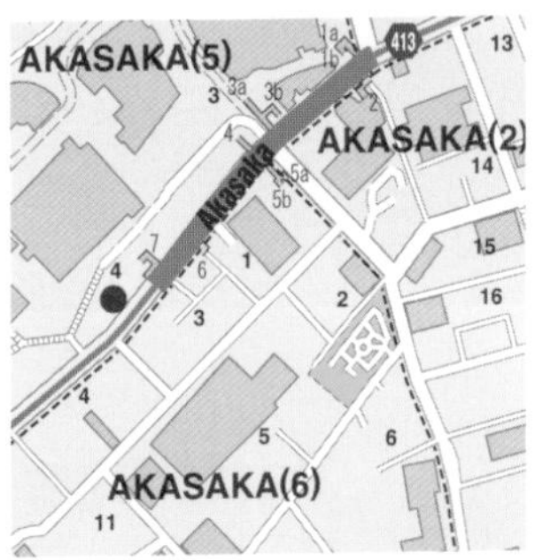

■ Opening hours, last orders
Dinner=17:30-23:00 L.O.21:00

■ Annual and weekly closing
Closed mid-August, late December-early January, Sunday and Bank Holidays

■ Price
Dinner= menu ¥ 12,600
Service charge= 10%

**TEL. 03-3585-7285**
FAX. 03-3585-7285
Trade Akasaka Building 2F,
5-4-14 Akasaka, Minato-ku

# Tensei

## 天青

This *tempura* restaurant works by the motto, "Beginning and ending with prawns and shrimp". *Saimakiebi* (young Japanese tiger prawns) are plucked live from the restaurant's fish tank and are lightly coated and fried. *Kaga-renkon* (lotus root) has a high starch content and resilient texture while *Naruto-kintoki* (sweet potato) from Tokushima is sweet and soft without being mushy. Large ginkgos from Aichi are fried without a coating and are best with a little salt. The *maitake* mushroom is served straight from the frying pan and crackles when dipped in the cold *tentsuyu* sauce. The chef also fries ingredients such as figs and *mukago* (small bulbs on wild yam vines). The last course before dessert is a choice of three types of shrimp *kakiage* (mixed *tempura* with rice): *ten-don* (rice topped with *tempura*), *ten-cha* (*tempura* on rice in a tea broth), or *ten-bara* (rice mixed with salted *tempura*). For the ten-cha, hoji (roasted green tea) is used to aid digestion. The Kyoto-style interior is decorated with antiques from the Edo Period. One of two private rooms has a counter and is suitable for business entertaining.

■ Opening hours, last orders
Lunch=11:30-14:30 L.O.14:00
Dinner=17:00-22:00 L.O.21:30

■ Annual and weekly closing
Closed mid-August, late December-early January, Sunday and Bank Holidays

■ Price
Lunch= menu ¥ 2,700-4,900
Dinner= menu ¥ 7,200-15,000
Service charge= 10% (dinner)

**TEL. 03–5786–2228**
FAX. 03–5786–2229
4-1-3 Minami-Aoyama, Minato-ku
www.four-seeds.co.jp/brand/tensei

# Tetsuan
## 哲庵

Opened in 2000 in Azabu-Juban, this small Japanese restaurant seats just nine people. There are three set menus, each of which has a different number of courses. *Nabe ryori* (hotpot dishes) and *takikomi-gohan* (a rice dish seasoned with broth and boiled with various ingredients) are served year-round. In summer, *nabe* is served as a cold dish containing *yaki-nasu* (baked eggplant), *somen* (fine noodles), abalone and prawns. Frozen cubes of soup stock are added to prevent flavour from being lost. In winter, *mizore-nabe* (hotpot with grated radish) is flavoured with *yuzu* and tilefish; the bones are used to create the tasty stock. Seasoning depends on the season: slightly more salt is used in summer and in winter soy sauce is used for a richer taste. The popular *takikomi-gohan* uses seasonal ingredients like sea bream from Kanagawa and *matsubagani* crab, including its roe and innards. Tetsuzo Goto cooks this dish in an earthenware pot with precise timing. Feel free to ask him for the scorched rice if you prefer. Reservations should be made well in advance as the owner-chef takes care of both cooking and serving.

■ Opening hours, last orders
Dinner=18:00-21:30 (L.O.)

■ Annual and weekly closing
Closed mid-August, late December-early January, Sunday and Bank Holidays

■ Price
Dinner= menu ¥ 10,500-16,800

**TEL. 03-3423-1850**
1-5-26 Azabu-Juban, Minato-ku

# Tofuya Ukai Shiba

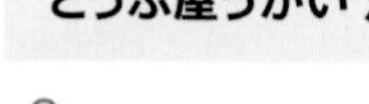

## とうふ屋うかい 芝

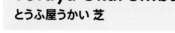

70

This *ryotei* sits in a garden that covers about 6,600 square metres, adjacent to Shiba Park. The garden includes bold and beautiful traditional Japanese design and up this close, Tokyo Tower looms large. Barely a step beyond the front gate and you'll be greeted by a stately atmosphere, thanks to the blend of Edo-style and Art Nouveau furniture. Tofuya Ukai Shiba has 58 *sukiya-zukuri* (tea house-style) private rooms, all of which offer a view of the inner garden. Most rooms have sunken seating but there are some with tables and chairs. Only set menus, combining speciality tofu dishes and seasonal Japanese cuisine, are offered. The tofu, delivered daily from Hachioji, is made by an experienced tofu craftsman using large, high-quality soybeans not normally used for tofu, crystal-clear groundwater from Owada and natural brine from the Izu Peninsula. House specialities are *Tousui-dofu*, tofu lightly boiled in soy milk seasoned with soup stock, and *Age dengaku*, deep-fried tofu coated with flavoured bean paste and charcoal-grilled. There is also a tofu shop and a lounge bar where diners can meet or spend time after dinner.

■ Opening hours, last orders
Lunch=11:00-15:00 (L.O.)
Dinner=15:00-22:00 L.O.20:00

■ Annual and weekly closing
Closed 29 December-2 January

■ Price
Lunch= menu ¥ 5,500-12,600
Dinner= menu ¥ 8,400-12,600
Service charge= 10%

**TEL. 03-3436-1028**
FAX. 03-3436-1029
4-4-13 Shiba-Koen, Minato-ku
www.ukai.co.jp/shiba

JAPANESE　　MAP NO. 9/B-2

# Tomura
## と村

This restaurant serves Kyoto-style cuisine from its new location in Toranomon, having moved from Akasaka in 2007. Owner-chef Kimio Tomura trained in Kyoto for 13 years and he carefully selects ingredients and makes the most of natural tastes. Only an *omakase* set menu is offered. Each dish is carefully prepared and seasonings and temperatures are given the utmost attention. In spring, enjoy *takikomi-gohan* (a rice dish seasoned with broth and cooked with various ingredients) with *takenoko* (bamboo shoots) grown in Kyoto. On the menu in summer: steamed *awabi* (abalone) from Chiba; wild prawns from Saga -fried without batter cooking the surface of the hard shell to seal the taste; and *ayu* (sweetfish) from Aomori. Autumn yields tilefish *sashimi* from Wakasa with salt or *waridashi* (a base stock mixed with soy sauce). In winter the menu has *ebi-imo* (Kyoto yam) from Osaka, which is fried after being gently simmered; the crispy skin seems like it is coated with *mizuame* (viscose malt sugar), giving way to an inside that is moist and tender. The owner-chef is friendly and will gladly answer any questions diners may have.

■ Opening hours, last orders
Dinner=18:00-21:30 (L.O.)

■ Annual and weekly closing
Closed Golden week, mid-August, late December-early January, Sunday and Bank Holiday Mondays

■ Price
Dinner= menu ¥ 26,250-52,500
Service charge= 10%

**TEL. 03-3591-3303**
FAX. 03-3591-3303
1-11-14 Toranomon, Minato-ku

# Totoya Uoshin
## とゝや魚新

6

A fish shop that was founded in 1890 re-opened as this restaurant in 1980. As the restaurant name suggests -*totoya* means 'fish dealer' - dishes revolve around seasonal fish. There are three set menus. Spring is the season for bonito, which is grilled and topped with *wagarashi* (Japanese mustard); this is eaten after dipping it in garlicky *gyoja-nin-niku* soy sauce. In summer, *hamo shabu-shabu* comes with *yuba* (bean curd skin), wax gourd and *samatsudake* mushrooms that you eat with *ponzu* sauce. In autumn, *hamo* takes on a more intense flavour in *dobinmushi* (a clear soup served in an earthenware pot) garnished with *matsutake* mushrooms, ginkgo nuts and wild chervil. In winter, *suppon* (soft-shelled turtle) is served in small pots, and comes with tofu, *negi* (scallion) and grilled rice cakes. There is a large variety of *sake*, chosen by the head chef who visits small breweries all over the country -ask the chefs behind the counter to help you pair your *sake* with the food. For lunch there is a *yakizakana* (grilled fish) set menu and *sumikago bento* (lunch served in a woven basket) that centres on vegetables and fish.

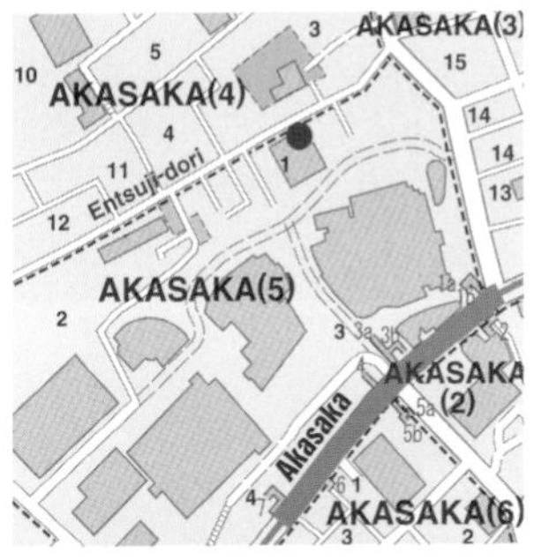

■ Opening hours, last orders
Lunch=11:30-14:00 (L.O.) except Saturday
Dinner=17:30-21:30 (L.O.)

■ Annual and weekly closing
Closed mid-August, late December-early January, Sunday and Bank Holidays

■ Price
Lunch= menu ¥ 5,250-7,350
Dinner= menu ¥ 10,500-15,750
Private room fee= ¥ 3,150 (lunch), ¥ 5,250 (dinner)
Service charge= 10% (dinner)

**TEL. 03–3585–4701**
5-1-34 Akasaka, Minato-ku

# Toyoda
## とよだ

This Japanese restaurant can be found on the second floor of a small building on Ginza Namiki-dori Avenue. Here, only premium, carefully selected seasonal ingredients are used. Thickly cut bamboo shoots grilled over charcoal are popular in spring. In summer, the *ayu* (sweetfish), dried overnight and marinated with *shuto* (salted and fermented bonito gut) before being grilled and served with *honesenbei* (deep-fried or dried fish bones), is a favourite with diners. *Kombu nabe* (kelp hotpot) with pike conger and *matsutake* mushrooms makes an appearance in autumn while *matsubagani* crab grilled over a charcoal fire can be experienced in Japan's coldest months. The last course before dessert is *takikomi-gohan* (a rice dish seasoned with broth and boiled with various ingredients), which can be replaced by plain white rice upon request. The owner-chef welcomes customers at the entrance and the *kimono*-clad waitress is attentive and pleasant. Décor is simple yet sophisticated. This is a restaurant that offers the type of food, hospitality and atmosphere that is always appealing.

■ Opening hours, last orders
Lunch=11:30-14:30 L.O.13:30
Dinner=17:30-22:00 L.O.20:30

■ Annual and weekly closing
Closed mid-August, late December-early January, Sunday and Bank Holidays

■ Price
Lunch= menu ¥ 5,250-10,500
Dinner= menu ¥ 10,500-21,000
Service charge= 10%

TEL. 03-5568-5822
La Vialle Ginza Building 2F,
7-5-4 Ginza, Chuo-ku

JAPANESE MAP NO. 9/B-1

# Tsujitome
## 辻留

20

Tsujitome began life in Kyoto in 1902 as the caterer for Japanese tea ceremonies; the name comes from the founder, Tomejiro Tsuji, grandfather of the current owner-chef. His son, Kaichi Tsuji, opened the Tokyo establishment in 1954 offering *chakaiseki* (simple Japanese cuisine served during tea ceremonies) tradition. The signboard at the entrance has calligraphy by the famous gourmet and ceramicist Rosanjin, who taught the owner-chef, Yoshikazu Tsuji. Making the most of the flavours and nutrition of seasonal ingredients, chef serves *kaiseki* dishes with respect for the *chanoyu* spirit. *Tofu-dengaku* (tofu grilled on skewers dressed with sweetened white soybean paste) is a dish for March. In September, lunar-like *maruage-dofu* (round-shaped deep-fried tofu) is used as the ingredient in a soup to recreate the season inside the bowl. As in *chakaiseki*, *usucha* (thin tea) finishes the meal. Tsujitome, located on the basement level of a white building at the back of Akasaka's Toyokawa Inari Shrine, has four tatami rooms, but chair seating can also be arranged if requested when making the reservation.

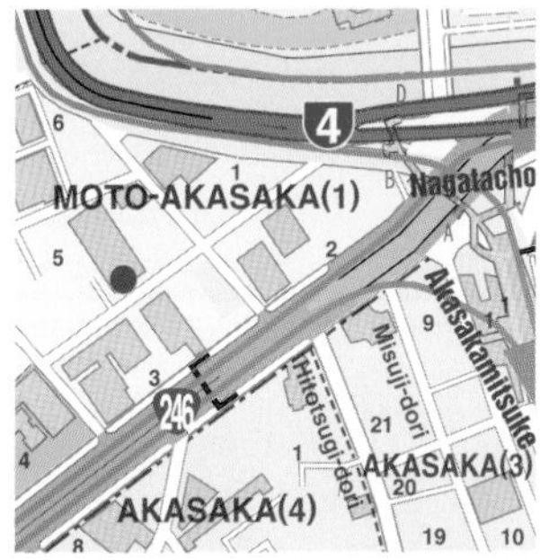

■ Opening hours, last orders
Lunch=12:00-14:00
Dinner=17:00-21:00

■ Annual and weekly closing
Closed Golden week, mid-August, late December-early January and Sunday

■ Price
Lunch= menu ¥ 15,750-36,750
Dinner= menu ¥ 26,250-45,150
Service charge= 10%

**TEL. 03-3403-3984**
FAX. 03-3403-6589
Toraya Daini Building B1F,
1-5-8 Moto-Akasaka, Minato-ku
www.tsujitome.co.jp

# Uchiyama
## うち山

The interior décor features vermilion-lacquered decorations and Tame-nuri lacquer ornaments, which are set off by the mud walls, the stone floor and counters. To owner-chef Hidehito Uchiyama, the spirit of *chakaiseki* (simple Japanese cuisine served during tea ceremonies) holds special importance. This is seen in his devotion to making the most of seasonal ingredients. Giant Pacific octopus eggs are sent directly from Hokkaido and soaked in soy sauce. The Atka mackerel, meanwhile, are delivered raw, and then pickled in *miso* or simmered slowly in a soy broth. *Kasube* (jellied ray fin broth) is a rare dish. *Yaki-goma-dofu* (broiled sesame tofu), which has a fragrant skin and an inner texture that is soft on the tongue, is a speciality of the restaurant. In autumn, enjoy pike conger with *matsutake* mushrooms and potherb mustard produced in Japan which is cooked in individual pots at the table. Boiled rice with raw sea bream and a rich sesame sauce served with green tea is another speciality at the end of the meal. The modesty of the owner and the overall attitude are connected to the "spirit of the tea ceremony."

■ Opening hours, last orders
Lunch=11:30-14:00 (L.O.)
Dinner=17:00-23:00

■ Annual and weekly closing
Closed Golden week, mid-August, late December-early January, Sunday and Bank Holidays

■ Price
Lunch= menu ¥ 5,000-10,000
Dinner= menu ¥ 10,500-21,000
Service charge= 10% (dinner)

**TEL. 03-3541-6720**
FAX. 03-3541-6720
Light Building B1F,
2-12-3 Ginza, Chuo-ku
www.nk-net.jp/uchiyama

# Uemura Honten

## 植むら 本店

15

In this venerable Japanese restaurant fresh seasonal ingredients are sourced from various parts of the country: Kamo eggplants, Manganji chili peppers, Shogoin turnips and Kintoki carrots are grown in Kyoto; white-fleshed fish comes from Nagasaki; *Seki aji* (horse mackerel) and *Seki saba* (chub mackerel), which have a firm texture, are caught in the Bungo Strait in Oita; and sea urchin is harvested in Hokkaido. The sweet tomato soup made with chicken stock and *junsai* (water shield shoots) is a refreshing dish in summer while the *awabi-no iso-mushi* (steamed abalone) is a pleasing winter choice with its unmistakable aroma of *nori* (laver); similar to *chawanmushi* (savoury egg custard), abalone, ginkgo nuts, lily roots and other ingredients are steamed and served in an abalone shell. Each floor (from the second to fifth) offers a different seating option -table seating, Western and Japanese style private rooms and a large room- that customers can choose from to suit the occasion. The counter on the first floor is only open in the evening. Reservations for the lunch *kaiseki* should be made at least a day in advance.

■ Opening hours, last orders
Lunch=11:30-15:00 L.O.14:00
Dinner=17:00-22:00 L.O.20:00

■ Annual and weekly closing
Closed Golden week, mid-August, late December-early January, Sunday and Bank Holidays

■ Price
Lunch= menu ¥ 7,000-20,000
Dinner= menu ¥ 10,000-25,000

**TEL. 03-3541-1351**
FAX. 03-3544-6722
1-13-10 Tsukiji, Chuo-ku
www.tukijiuemura.com/shop/101.html

# Ukai-tei Ginza

The unique spoon and fork figures act as a marker for this *teppan-yaki* restaurant near Higashi-Ginza Station, while inside, a painting of a woman in a red dress grabs your attention. The French Belle Époque-style interior décor fits well with the building which served as the main house of a wealthy farmer, before being relocated from Tokamachi in Niigata. The mosaic near the counter represents the depths of the sea while lamps by Daum Frères, chandeliers by Müller Frères, Baccarat glassware and other adornments create a luxuriant atmosphere. In addition to black-haired cattle bred on a designated farm in Tottori, beef from Miyagi and Iwate is used. As well as meat, a speciality dish of abalone sourced from a small fishing port in Aomori and steamed in rock salt is delicious. There are also options that make the best of seasonal ingredients, such as the truffle course in winter. Lunch orders are taken up to 15:00 on Saturdays, Sundays and public holidays.

■ Opening hours, last orders
Lunch=12:00-14:00 (L.O.)
Dinner=17:00-23:00 L.O.21:00

■ Annual and weekly closing
Closed late December-early January

■ Price
Lunch= menu ¥ 6,830-9,450
carte ¥ 14,000-43,000
Dinner= menu ¥ 16,800-24,150
carte ¥ 14,000-43,000
Service charge= 10%

**TEL. 03-3544-5252**
FAX. 03-3544-6868
Jiji-Tsushin Building,
5-15-8 Ginza, Chuo-ku
www.ukai.co.jp/ginza

# Ukai-tei Omotesando

This *teppanyaki* restaurant may be a relative newcomer to Omote-sando-dori Avenue, opening in 2007, but its interior dates back about 150 years. Its construction centres around a merchant's house from Kanazawa that was in use in the mid 1800s; it was moved and reassembled here. Huge pillars and beams with a *fuki-urushi* lacquer finish provide the background for pieces of Art Nouveau and Art Deco; there is a lamp produced by Emile Gallé and an etched-glass panel by René Lalique. For the cooking, black-haired cattle known as "*ukai-gyu*" come from a designated farm in Tottori as well as others in Saga and Miyazaki. Abalone steamed in rock salt is a speciality. After dinner, you will be invited to take dessert in the Art Nouveau lounge with its antiques. Among the chef's array of desserts are a tasty jelly made of Amakusa oranges from Ehime and a caramel nut millefeuille. There is also terrace seating, where you can dine while taking in the cityscape.

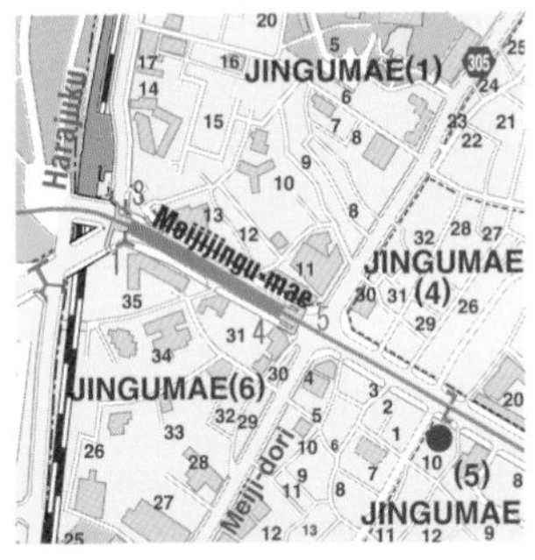

■ Opening hours, last orders
Lunch=12:00-14:30 (L.O.)
Dinner=17:30-23:00 L.O.21:00

■ Annual and weekly closing
Closed 29 December-2 January

■ Price

| | | |
|---|---|---|
| Lunch= | menu | ¥ 6,830-12,600 |
| | carte | ¥ 14,000-43,000 |
| Dinner= | menu | ¥ 16,800-24,150 |
| | carte | ¥ 14,000-43,000 |

Service charge= 10%

**TEL. 03-5467-5252**
FAX. 03-5467-5253
Omotesando Gyre 5F,
5-10-1 Jingumae, Shibuya-ku
www.omotesando-ukaitei.jp

# Umi
海味

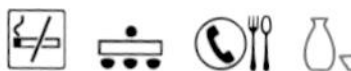

As a practitioner of *kendo*, "Begin and end with courtesy" is the principle by which owner-chef Mitsuyasu Nagano presents himself. Believing that, "A *sushi* restaurant can be judged by its tuna", he is particularly concerned about the quality of this fish, and serves a tuna *nigiri sushi* at the start of meal as a "greeting". Rare fish are sent from Kyushu and Hokkaido and, with *nigiri sushi* and appetisers, up to 30 different types can be sampled. Rice from Niigata is prepared slightly harder and saltier than usual. The mellow-flavoured vinegar is a blend of two red vinegars: one aged for three years with a bouquet of *sake* lees and another, thinner variety. When the restaurant is full, freshly cooked *tamagoyaki* (omelette rolls) containing a generous amount of broth are offered to all guests. The restaurant is located on the right side of Gaiennishi-dori Avenue coming from Aoyama-dori Avenue; look for the black fencing and white curtain. This is a lively *sushi* restaurant with attentive and efficient service, where, as its name -"taste of the sea"- suggests, customers can fully appreciate the bounty of the ocean.

■ Opening hours, last orders
Dinner=18:00-23:00 (L.O.)

■ Annual and weekly closing
Closed mid-August, late December-early January, Sunday and Bank Holidays

■ Price
Dinner= menu ¥ 20,000

**TEL. 03-3401-3368**
3-2-8 Minami-Aoyama, Minato-ku

View from Gaien-Nishi dori

# Uotoku
## うを徳

25

Located on Karukozaka near Iidabashi Station, Uotoku has a history dating back to the beginning of the Meiji Era (1868-1912), when a fish dealer in Hatchobori moved his business to Kagurazaka, changing the trade name to Uotoku. It is said to have inspired a story by Meiji Era novelist Kyoka Izumi. The *ryotei* opened in 1920 and the current owner-chef, Nobuo Hagiwara, is the fifth-generation. The detached building is surrounded by a black fence and inside there is one main dining room and two private rooms. The *ebi-shinjo* (shrimp dumplings) deserve particular mention; shrimps are minced carefully with a knife to maintain their firm texture before being deep-fried. *Tai-no matsukawa-zukuri* (sea bream *sashimi* dowsed with boiling water to cook the skin) is prepared using a technique passed down from the founder. All dishes served here are flavoured in accordance with the *Edomae* tradition. The restaurant is often chosen as a venue for engagement ceremonies, farewell parties and other important occasions as well as business entertaining. Reservations should be made at least a day in advance.

■ Opening hours, last orders
Lunch=11:30-14:30 L.O.13:00
Dinner=17:00-23:00 L.O.20:30

■ Annual and weekly closing
Closed mid-August and late December-early January

■ Price
Lunch= menu ¥ 10,500-15,750
Dinner= menu ¥ 21,000-26,250
Service charge= 10%

**TEL. 03-3269-0360**
FAX. 03-3269-0373
3-1 Kagurazaka, Shinjuku-ku
www.uotoku.com

# Usukifugu Yamadaya
## 臼杵ふぐ山田屋

13

This is a *fugu* (puffer fish) restaurant on Ushizaka in Nishi-Azabu which opened in 2006, a branch of a *ryotei* in Usuki, Oita. The modern dining room makes the most of traditional Japanese architecture and there is certain harmony to the Cassina leather chairs, the *kimono* worn by the waiting staff and in the comforting background music. In season, ocean-caught *tora-fugu* (tiger puffer fish) is delivered daily from Oita. Thick slices of *fugu* are served with homemade *ponzu* dipping sauce made from soy sauce and juicy citrus *kabosu* fruit harvested in Oita. The preparation of fried *fugu* forgoes soy sauce in favour of adding various spices to the batter thus providing a rounded aroma and an enhanced texture. Another speciality is a sushi of the local Usuki dish *o-han* (yellow rice coloured with gardenia fruit) topped with grilled *shi-rako* (fugu milt). *Zosui (*risotto) is offered as the last dish before dessert. Usukifugu Yamadaya offers sophisticated *fugu* dishes, based on traditional Japanese cooking techniques, where the staff are courteous and friendly, making it suitable for both private and business occasions.

■ Opening hours, last orders
Dinner=18:00-24:00 L.O.22:30

■ Annual and weekly closing
Closed Golden week, mid-August, late December-early January, Sunday and Bank Holidays

■ Price
Dinner= menu ¥ 21,000-31,500
carte ¥ 12,000-22,000
Service charge= 10%

TEL. 03-3499-5501
FAX. 03-3499-5502
Fleg Nishi-Azabu Vierge B1F,
4-11-14 Nishi-Azabu, Minato-ku
www.usuki.info/yamadaya

# Waketokuyama
分とく山

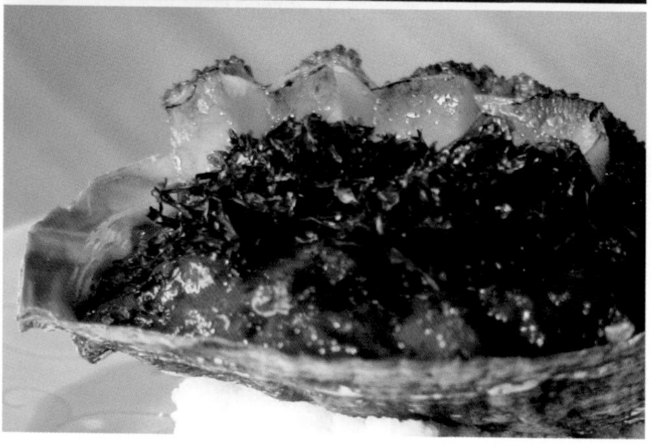

The use of concrete blocks and glass give the building quite a modern feel while inside, both the first and second floors have a certain stylish quality to them. Each floor has a counter and tables, and the annex has a private room that looks onto a garden. Placing great emphasis on palatability, Waketokuyama offers Japanese cuisine that is in touch with the times. The head chef provides a variety of creative dishes, sourcing as many as 80—or sometimes even 100—different ingredients nationwide. The speciality here is *awabi-no-isoyaki* (grilled abalone), which is available year-round. This savoury dish topped with *nori* (laver) sees abalone from Sanriku steamed and covered with a sauce made from puréed viscera and kudzu before it is lightly baked au gratin in its shell. The set menu finishes with a seasonal *takikomi-gohan* (a rice dish seasoned with broth and boiled with various ingredients) cooked in an earthenware pot. The enthusiastic chat between the young chefs as they work echoes pleasingly throughout this busy restaurant and the warm hospitality makes you feel very much at home.

■ Opening hours, last orders
Dinner=17:00-23:00 L.O.21:00

■ Annual and weekly closing
Closed late December-early January and Sunday

■ Price
Dinner= menu ¥ 15,750
Service charge= 10%

**TEL. 03-5789-3838**
5-1-5 Minami-Azabu, Minato-ku

# Wako
## 和幸

"For all to live in harmony and to be grateful to nature for its bounty", this philosophy of owner-chef Ichiro Takahashi is the origin of his restaurant's name. Only wild seafood is used and the tuna comes from Japanese waters. Sea bream from Akashi in Hyogo is served as *kobujime* (fish pressed between two sheets of kelp) and seasoned with soy sauce. *Ayu* (sweetfish) from the Yoshida-gawa river in Gifu is delivered direct to the restaurant to ensure it retains its aroma for which the fish is known. Springtime bamboo shoots and *matsutake* mushrooms used in autumn dishes are from Tanba in Kyoto while kelp from Rishiri in Hokkaido and high-quality *katsuo-bushi* (dried bonito) give the base stock its full flavour. Dishes are prepared adhering to the *kaiseki* tradition and hospitable service adds to the overall comfort. There are four *tatami* rooms, including one for tea ceremonies. The building is located in a residential area in Mejiro and incorporates a style of architecture typical of tea houses. Lunch offers a relaxed and comfortable atmosphere and is particularly pleasant.

■ Opening hours, last orders
Lunch=11:30-13:30 (L.O.)
Dinner=17:30-20:00 (L.O.)

■ Annual and weekly closing
Closed Golden week, mid-August, late December-early January, Sunday and Bank Holidays

■ Price
Lunch= menu ¥ 15,750-52,500
Dinner= menu ¥ 21,000-52,500
Service charge= 10%

**TEL. 03-3982-2251**
FAX. 03-3982-1533
2-16-3 Mejiro, Toshima-ku

# Yamaji
## 山路

This *kappo* (counter style restaurant) was opened in 1990 by Akinobu Yamaji. The speciality here is *tai* (sea bream), freshly shipped every morning from Ehime, the chef's hometown, and delivered in the afternoon. All of the fish is used: the body for *sashimi*, the head is salt-grilled or used for *tsukeyaki* (marinated and grilled) or served in *kotsu-mushi* (steamed with the bones) with *sake* and kelp flavouring. The lean parts are used for *ushiojiru* (fish soup). Another speciality is *tai-chazuke* (rice with sea bream topped with broth) with black sesame sauce aged for six months. Only a set menu is available, but on request the chef can make adjustments. Spring dishes include *tempura* of wild plants as well as *wakatakeni* (boiled bamboo shoots). In summer, *hamo-no-yubiki* (lightly boiled pike conger) is served with apricot pulp sauce; the *aburi* (roasted) dish is served with *wasabi*-soy sauce. In autumn, grilled *matsutake* mushrooms are grilled with *Bincho* charcoal in front of you while in winter, expect *suppon-zosui* (soft-shelled turtle risotto).

■ Opening hours, last orders
Lunch=12:00-14:00 L.O.13:00
Dinner=17:30-22:00 L.O.21:00

■ Annual and weekly closing
Closed mid-August, late December-early January, Sunday and Bank Holidays

■ Price
Lunch= menu ¥ 10,500-13,650
Dinner= menu ¥ 22,050-36,750

**TEL. 03-5565-3639**
Ginza 7 Building B1F,
7-14-14 Ginza,, Chuo-ku

# Yamamoto

## やまもと

12

A *fugu* restaurant near Tsukiji Honganji Temple. This restaurant has been run by the same family for three generations. After 40 years in Nihonbashi, it relocated to Tsukiji about 50 years ago. Housed in a traditional Japanese-style house just off Harumi-dori Avenue, it has homely atmosphere, with antique scrolls and other objects handpicked by the owner-chef, Kuniyoshi Yamamoto. Diners can enjoy the meal either at the counter on the first floor watching the friendly owner-chef at work or upstairs, where each private room has its dedicated *nakai* (server). *Tora-fugu* caught in the Genkai-nada sea or Iyo-nada sea in the southwestern part of Japan is featured on the set menu, including traditional *fugu* dishes such as *kiku-zukuri* (paper thin centre cuts arranged in the shape of a chrysanthemum accompanied by skin and tailfin centrepiece) and *nikogori* (skin jelly) alongside original dishes like whisky-infused grilled *nakaochi*, flavoursome milt crêpes and clear soup made with *fugu* skin. English menus, with drawings of *fugu* done by the chef, are also available so it is a good place to entertain foreign nationals.

■ Opening hours, last orders
Dinner=17:00-22:30

■ Annual and weekly closing
Closed April-September, Sunday and Bank Holidays

■ Price
Dinner= menu ¥ 36,750
Service charge= 10%

**TEL. 03-3541-7730**
FAX. 03-3541-7697
2-15-4 Tsukiji, Chuo-ku
www8.plala.or.jp/tsukijiyamamoto

# Yamane
## やま祢

12

A long-established restaurant that has been serving *fugu* (puffer fish) since 1954. The founder of Yamane trained at a *fugu* restaurant in Shimonoseki which was frequented by Hirobumi Ito (1841-1909), Japan's first prime minister. Atsushi Yamane, the present owner-chef, after refining his skills in Osaka, succeeded his father to become the third-generation chef. Renovated in 2004, the restaurant is a fine example of Showa-style modernism with its high ceiling. Here, only wild *fugu* flown in directly from Shimonoseki is used. The *sashimi* comes highly recommended as the *nimaibiki* cutting technique used at this restaurant ensures thicker slices to add firmness. *Karaage* (deep-fried *fugu*), a speciality, boasts a unique flavour credited to the restaurant's use of homemade *miso* before the frying. For the *miso nabe* hotpot, white *miso* is used to lighten the fish's distinctive aroma. The hotpot is prepared in the kitchen and the food is served in bowls, rather than in a pot, which is the norm for this style of dish. Off-season, the restaurant offers a variety of high-quality fish, shellfish and seasonal vegetables sourced nationwide.

■ Opening hours, last orders
Dinner=17:30-19:30 (L.O.)

■ Annual and weekly closing
Closed Golden week, mid-August, late December-early January and Sunday

■ Price
Dinner= menu ¥ 26,250-36,750
Service charge= 10% (tatami room 15%)

TEL. 03-3541-1383
FAX. 03-3541-1384
7-15-7 Ginza, Chuo-ku

# Yamanochaya
## 山の茶屋

An *unagi* (eel) restaurant in the grounds of Sanno Hie Shrine. The entrance is diagonally opposite the rear gate of Hibiya High School. Greenery and a quaint garden gate add to the inviting look of Yamanochaya, originally a *kashiseki* renting rooms for private parties. Present owner-chef Tsuneo Endo has kept with tradition; *kabayaki* (*unagi* broiled and basted with a sweet sauce) -the house speciality- is in the Edo style. *Unagi* from areas such as Shizuoka and Kagoshima are broiled without any seasoning; after being steamed slowly until tender, it is then broiled over a *Bincho* charcoal fire with a sweet sauce -kept for years and continually added to ensure the original taste. Lunchtime and Saturday evening set menus are more reasonable. All dining rooms are private; the main house has 2 rooms and a hall that accommodates up to 30 people while the newly built annex has a room with *horigotatsu*-style sunken seating; recommended when making reservations. Prices are rather high, but worth it for the Japanese-style fine dining experience. This is an ideal venue for business entertaining in small groups.

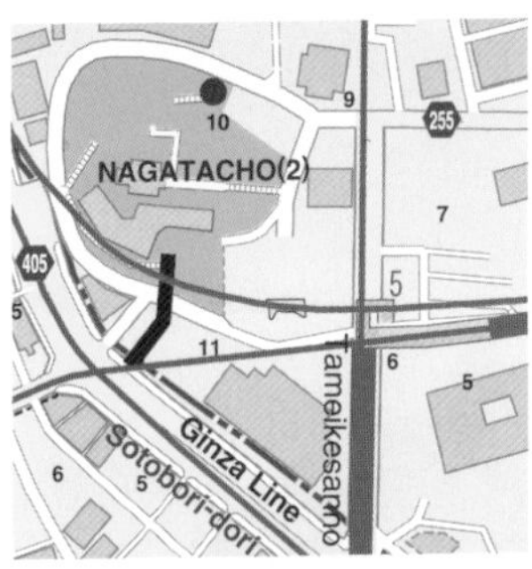

■ Opening hours, last orders
Lunch=11:30-13:00 (L.O.)
Dinner=17:00-19:00 (L.O.)

■ Annual and weekly closing
Closed mid-August, late December-early January, Sunday and Bank Holidays

■ Price
Lunch= menu ¥ 9,450-16,170
Dinner= menu ¥ 18,270
Service charge= 10%

**TEL. 03-3581-0585**
FAX. 03-3581-0667
2-10-6 Nagatacho, Chiyoda-ku

# Yamasaki
## 山さき

Yamasaki is located on the second floor of a building in front of Bishamonten Zenkokuji Temple but because the entrance of the building is not on Kagurazaka-dori Avenue, it is slightly difficult to spot. This homely restaurant, with its simple interior consisting of only four tables, was established in 2002 by the owner-chef Mika Yamasaki after she had spent eight years training in Japanese cuisine. One of her specialities is *negima nabe*; tasty *setoro* (fatty back flesh of tuna) is dipped into a soup before being eaten and goes nicely with *negi* (scallion) and also with *wakame* (seaweed), watercress and Japanese parsley. Dishes with scallops, clams, trough shells, pen shells and other early spring shellfish, offered only in February and March, are also available. Popular summer fare includes refreshing *ainame* greenling from Joban cooked with bonito stock, *sake* and salt-pickled Kishu *ume* (Japanese apricot). *Moryo nabe* uses Awaodori chicken or Shamo gamecock, boiled whole before the meat is removed, giant white radish, *myoga* ginger and winter melon. Prices are modest considering the quality of the offerings.

■ Opening hours, last orders
Dinner=18:00-22:00 L.O.20:00

■ Annual and weekly closing
Closed mid-August, late December-early January, Sunday and Bank Holidays

■ Price
Dinner= menu ¥ 7,350-15,750
Service charge= 5%

TEL. 03-3267-2310
Fukuya Building 2F,
4-2 Kagurazaka, Shinjuku-ku

# Yebisu
## 恵比寿

10

This *teppanyaki* restaurant -refurbished in August 2008- is on the 22nd floor of The Westin. At each counter, chefs skilfully grill Japanese and Western ingredients right in front of diners. A wide variety of set menus based around, for example, Miyazaki or Maezawa beefsteak, spiny lobster or seafood, are available. The house speciality is salt-baked abalone served with rock laver sauce with a Japanese-style soup stock base. The head chef pays particular attention to colour, composing dishes in tempting colours. For business entertaining and family dining, there are three private rooms, each with a different feel -"Sazanka", "Shakunage" and "Ajisai" and are available for parties of 2 to 10. After dinner, guests can move from the *teppanyaki* counter to the sofas for dessert. The wine list offers choices from around the world, although the prices are generally high. Guests can enjoy panoramic views on a clear day or glittering city lights in the evening.

■ Opening hours, last orders
Lunch=11:30-15:00 (L.O.)
Dinner=17:30-22:00 (L.O.)

■ Price
Lunch= menu ¥ 4,000-22,000
carte ¥ 8,200-39,400
Dinner= menu ¥ 15,000-50,000
carte ¥ 15,700-39,400
Private room fee= ¥ 6,930 (lunch), ¥11,550 (dinner)

**TEL. 03–5423–7790**
FAX. 03–5423–1470
Westin Hotel 22F,
1-4-1 Mita, Meguro-ku
www.westin-tokyo.co.jp

# Yokota
## よこ田

The sign outside this Toriizaka restaurant simply reads "*tempura.*" Owner-chef Tsuneo Yokota trained in a well-known *tempura* restaurant in Ginza before opening this restaurant in 1981, which he runs with the help of his wife and their son. Yokota offers only an *omakase* (chef's choice) set menu. The son prepares the ingredients, leaving the cooking to his father. The *tempura* here is not oily and the flavour of ingredients is kept intact. The light-tasting oil is a mix of sesame and corn oils, and the chef varies the amount of batter used and the heat depending on the ingredient. All pieces, which are precisely timed, come with *tentsuyu* (dipping sauce), salt, lemon juice and curry powder—the chef will teach you which to use for each ingredient. Eating *tempura* with curry powder is a totally new concept and, according to the chef, it is best with *megochi* (a kind of flathead) and *anago* (conger eel) caught in Tokyo Bay. At Yokota, local seafood and a variety of seasonal vegetables can be enjoyed.

■ Opening hours, last orders
Dinner=17:30-20:00 (L.O.)

■ Annual and weekly closing
Closed Golden week, mid-August, late December-early January and Wednesday

■ Price
Dinner= menu ¥ 10,500

**TEL. 03-3408-4238**
Hatano Building 2F,
1-5-11 Azabu-Juban, Minato-ku

# Yokoyama
## よこやま

Owner-chef Tadashi Yokoyama trained for five years at a premier *tempura* restaurant in Kyoto before gaining several more years' experience at its Tokyo branch. Popular ingredients include *megochi* (big-eyed flathead) from Takeoka, available year-round, white asparagus from Kagawa and young *ayu* (sweetfish) from Lake Biwa in spring and corn from Okinawa in May. In summer, *hamo* (pike conger) from Awaji is good as are the domestic *matsutake* mushrooms in autumn. Ordered by size, *makiebi* (Japanese tiger prawns) come from Kyushu. Yokoyama's *tempura* is gently deep-fried and has a light colour. No dipping sauce is served; you will just have finely crushed salt and lemon juice. Seasoned *daikon-oroshi* (grated Japanese radish) is for refreshing the palate. *Tencha* (bowl of rice steeped in green tea and topped with *kakiage*), a house speciality, is a must to finish with. Take the Keiyo Road towards Ryogoku from the front of the department store outside JR Kinshicho Station and turn left at the Kotobashi 2-chome intersection. Walk three blocks until you see the *noren* curtain, diagonally opposite a small park.

■ Opening hours, last orders
Dinner=17:30-22:00 L.O.20:00

■ Annual and weekly closing
Closed mid-August, late December-early January, Wednesday, Sunday and Bank Holidays

■ Price
Dinner= menu ¥ 13,125

**TEL. 03-3631-3927**
2-7-10 Kotobashi, Sumida-ku

# Yonemura
## よねむら

A branch of a restaurant located in Kyoto's historical Gion quarter opened in Ginza in 2004 -look out for the wall painting of rice plant ears that marks the entrance to this establishment. Owner-chef Masayasu Yonemura started his career specialising in French cuisine. "Not so concerned about the categories of cuisine, I have established my own style by responding to my customer's requests and always being on the lookout for new ideas", he says, and so his restaurant serves "Yonemura-style" dishes, rich in creativity. A small toasted rice ball placed on a spoon and topped with a layer of sautéed foie gras and another of roasted duck breast are two good examples. Both Japanese and Western ingredients are used and culinary traditions from various countries are deliberately fused to create this unique cuisine. All dishes come as part of a set menu that changes each month; lunchtime represents particularly good value and is recommended. The wide counter in this modern space seats 12, while tables are placed in small rooms divided by partitions.

■ Opening hours, last orders
Lunch=12:00-15:30 L.O.14:00
Dinner=17:30-23:00 L.O.21:00

■ Annual and weekly closing
Closed mid-August, late December-early January and Monday

■ Price
Lunch= menu ¥ 6,000-10,000
Dinner= menu ¥ 14,000

TEL. 03-5537-6699
Kojun Building 4F,
6-8-7 Ginza, Chuo-ku

# Yoneyama
## よねやま

A small *kappo* (counter style restaurant) located halfway up Tsunokamizaka-dori Avenue. Five seats at the counter and two tables in this cosy, quiet space create a relaxed atmosphere. Owner Mitsuo Yoneyama may have had no specific experience in big-name restaurants, but he has established himself by developing his skill using his innate culinary sense. Spring dishes include giant clams of nearly 10cm from Kashimanada while abalone from Boshu on the southern tip of the Boso Peninsula in Chiba is a summer speciality - the abalone is slightly moistened in hot bonito soup stock, sliced and served with strained liver sauce. High quality sea bream is the chef's pick while *Akamutsu* (red big-eye) from Choshi, also in Chiba, is char-grilled with salt. The typical winter dish is *matsuba* crab from Sakaiminato in Tottori; shredded crab meat is dressed in crab innards in the shell and mixed with sweet white *miso*. The meal ends with typical Japanese sweets: *kudzukiri* (kudzu jelly with syrup) and *mitarashi dango* (rice dumplings with sugar and soy sauce). A good spot for a relaxed meal with family or friends.

■ Opening hours, last orders
Dinner=18:00-21:30 (L.O.)

■ Annual and weekly closing
Closed mid-August, late December-early January and Sunday

■ Price
Dinner= menu ¥ 10,500-15,750

**TEL. 03-3341-3117**
FAX. 03-3341-3117
15 Arakicho, Shinjuku-ku

# Yoshihashi
## よしはし

A *sukiyaki* restaurant serving high-quality, marbled *wagyu* beef expertly selected by a connoisseur. Thickly cut meat is coated with comparatively dense *sukiyaki* sauce and pan roasted to the preferred tenderness. To create a raw egg dipping sauce, the white is beaten quickly with chopsticks into a meringue-like foam, while the yolk is left whole. Three *sukiyaki* set menus are available; the quality of meat is the same, but its quantity and the number of courses differ. Meat aficionados may prefer to request a set menu with fewer courses and add a separate order of meat. *Shabu-shabu* and steak set menus are also on offer, along with wine and *sake*. The restaurant is decorated with a Hiroshi Senju lithograph and has one counter with 12 seats and a private room with sunken seating. To find it, from the intersection in front of the Akasaka Police Station on Aoyama-dori Avenue, proceed towards Yotsuya alongside the Akasaka Gosho Palace, turn right at the second signalled intersection and then right again into a small street. Visitors are advised not to wear strong perfume.

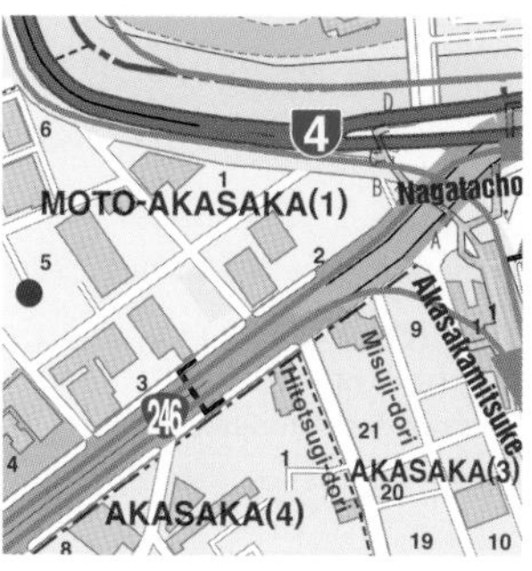


■ Opening hours, last orders
Lunch=11:30-14:30 L.O.13:30
Dinner=17:30-22:30 L.O.20:30

■ Annual and weekly closing
Closed mid-August, late December-early January, Sunday and Bank Holidays

■ Price
Lunch= menu ¥ 2,100-3,700
Dinner= menu ¥ 12,000-17,000
carte ¥ 10,000-20,000
Private room fee= less than 4 persons ¥ 5,000/hour
Service charge= 15% (dinner)

**TEL. 03-3401-3129**
FAX. 03-3401-4135
1-5-25 Moto-Akasaka, Minato-ku

Toyokawa Inari Shrine

# Yotaro
## 与太呂

This speciality *tai* (sea bream) and *tempura* restaurant has been in business since 1981. Located in Roppongi, it is run by owner-chef Motohiro Kawaguchi and his son, who trained at a Japanese restaurant in Kyoto. With black marble-coated walls, it has a relaxed atmosphere where customers enjoy counter-style dining. The sea bream comes from various ports throughout Japan; wild sea bream with an exquisitely firm texture, such as those caught near Matsuwa on the Miura Peninsula, are used for the raw *otsukuri* dish, while sea bream from Tokushima are used for *tai meshi* (sea bream with rice). It is said that the regional variations of the fish complement different dishes. The sea bream from Tokushima, for example, is said to be perfect for the *tai meshi*—a Roppongi Yotaro speciality—as the tender and tasty flesh mixes well with rice. *Tempura* made with *saimakiebi* (young Japanese tiger prawns) from Amakusa in Kumamoto is cooked to make the most of their firm texture, while *tempura* using seasonal vegetables highlights the natural fragrance of each ingredient. Even dessert is prepared with the same precision.

■ Opening hours, last orders
Dinner=17:30-22:00 (L.O.)

■ Annual and weekly closing
Closed Golden week, mid-August, late December-early January and Sunday

■ Price
Dinner= menu ¥ 13,650

**TEL. 03-3405-5866**
FAX. 03-3746-2727
4-11-4 Roppongi, Minato-ku
www.roppongi-yotaro.com

# Yotsuha
## 四つ葉

Located in a quiet residential area, this restaurant specialises in *suppon* (soft shelled turtle). The proprietress runs the restaurant with the chef who is also a qualified tea ceremony instructor. Classical music plays in this small establishment with counter seats for eight and a tatami room that can hold up to four. *Suppon mushi*, soft savoury egg custard containing *suppon* broth is one of house specialities. *Ayu-no-shioyaki* (salt-grilled sweetfish) is cooked to release aroma and retain the softness. *Takikomi-gohan* (a rice dish seasoned with broth and boiled with various ingredients) and pickles, served at the end of the meal, are prepared by the proprietress. There are two set menus, offering *kaiseki* (simple Japanese cuisine served during tea ceremonies) and *suppon* dishes, but wild *shiro tora-fugu* (white-finned puffer fish) is also available in January and February. From Ogikubo station, go along the railway towards Nishi-Ogikubo; turn right on Route 311 and cross the road at the first traffic light; turn right again at the petrol station and you'll see the white sign and purple *noren*.

■ Opening hours, last orders
Dinner=18:30-20:30 (L.O.)

■ Annual and weekly closing
Closed mid-August, late December-early January, Sunday and Bank Holidays

■ Price
Dinner= menu ¥ 14,700-15,750

**TEL. 03–3398–7093**
2-20-7 Kamiogi, Suginami-ku

Ogikubo Hakusan Shrine

# Yukicho
## 有季銚

8

The head chef of this Japanese restaurant on Hanatsubaki-dori Avenue in Ginza once worked at a well-known *fugu* restaurant, and this is evident in the *kaiseki* set menus which are served from October to March. These include ocean-caught *tora-fugu* (tiger puffer fish) from the Bungo Strait. Summer is the time for *okoze* (stonefish); in addition to serving it as *sashimi*, the lightly boiled head is good with *ponzu* dipping sauce. *Iwa-gaki* (oysters that come into season in summer) from Ishikawa are fried after being char-grilled with *kombu* (kelp). In spring, *hanabira-take* (cauliflower mushrooms) from Niigata, sautéed in sesame oil and seasoned with *shiroshoyu* (light-coloured soy sauce), has a nice texture. Dessert brings *shiruko* (red bean paste soup) with black tapioca sweetened with *wasanbon* (a traditional Japanese refined sugar). All dishes are beautifully presented on an exquisite range of tableware, including Kyoyaki, Wajimanuri lacquer ware and Baccarat glass. Private rooms are the only option and some have a counter. As Yukicho may move, check the address when reserving.

■ Opening hours, last orders
Lunch=11:30-14:30 L.O.13:30
Dinner=17:30-22:00 L.O.21:00

■ Annual and weekly closing
Closed Golden week, mid-August, late December-early January, Sunday and Bank Holidays

■ Price
Lunch= menu ¥ 5,000-35,000
Dinner= menu ¥ 16,000-35,000
Service charge= 15% (lunch 10%)

**TEL. 03-3544-2700**
FAX. 03-3541-6814
Success Ginza 7 Building B1F,
7-13-10 Ginza, Chuo-ku
www.four-seeds.co.jp/brand/yukicho

# Yukimura
## 幸村

This Japanese restaurant is full night after night and reservations are difficult to get. It has no sign, so look for the blue board with the address on the wall and the four steps; then take the red lift. Here, seasonal specialities that boldly use Kyoto ingredients as well as other selected seasonal ingredients deserve a mention. The *shabu-shabu*, (thinly sliced beef briefly dipped into a soup stock) with *hanasansho* (Japanese pepper flowers) from Tanba is good in spring, as is the *ayu* (sweetfish) from Miyama in summer. Charcoal-grilled *matsutake* mushrooms wrapped in *hamo* (pike conger) feature in autumn and, in winter, *taizagani* (snow crab from the Tango Peninsula) are not to be missed. As well as the claws and legs, carefully grilled over charcoal, *kanimiso* (crab innards) grilled in the shells are very flavoursome. Only an *omakase* (chef's choice) set menu is available, where the final dish of the meal consists of rice boiled with broth and seasonal ingredients in an earthenware pot. Kyoto cuisine with an added touch of creativity is what draws the customers here.

■ Opening hours, last orders
Dinner=17:30-20:00 (L.O.)

■ Annual and weekly closing
Closed Golden week, mid-August and late December-early January

■ Price
Dinner= menu ¥ 23,100-31,500
Service charge= 10%

**TEL. 03-5772-1610**
Yuken Azabujuban Building 3F,
1-5-5 Azabu-Juban, Minato-ku

# Yuta
## ゆう田

6

Right next to the Embassy of Romania, this little *sushi* restaurant is a five-minute walk from Roppongi Hills -look out for the doorknob that carries a handprint of owner-chef Fumio Shimada, who opened this restaurant in 2001. Dishes make use of the natural flavours of ingredients without resorting to excessive elaboration. The speciality appetiser is large *sazae-no-tsuboyaki* (turban shell broiled in the shell) from Ohara in Chiba. In summer, *mizunasu* (eggplant) from Osaka is served *asazuke* style (lightly pickled) with a subtle touch of salt; juicy *shime-saba* (raw chub mackerel soaked in vinegar) from Matsuwa in Kanagawa is an autumnal treat. Homemade *karasumi* (salted and dried grey mullet roe) made with large roe is on offer from late November. Select high-quality *uni* (sea urchin) from areas like Yagishiri or the Tsugaru Strait is good for both *gunkan-maki* (*sushi* with a strip of *nori* wrapped around the perimeter) and standard-type *nigiri sushi*. The modern interior adopts elements of traditional tearoom design; there is only counter seating for six on the first floor and a private room in the basement.

■ Opening hours, last orders
Dinner=18:00-22:00 (L.O.)

■ Annual and weekly closing
Closed late December-early January, Sunday and Bank Holidays

■ Price
Dinner= menu ¥ 21,000

**TEL. 03-3423-2885**
FAX. 03-3423-2885
3-13-1 Nishi-Azabu, Minato-ku

# HOTELS

# HOTELS BY ORDER OF COMFORT

| | | |
|---|---|---|
| Mandarin Oriental | 428 | MAP NO. 5/A-1 |
| The Ritz-Carlton | 456 | MAP NO. 9/B-2 |
| Four Seasons Chinzan-so | 410 | MAP NO. 1/A-2 |
| The Peninsula | 452 | MAP NO. 4/C-3 |
| Conrad | 408 | MAP NO. 9/C-1 |
| Grand Hyatt | 414 | MAP NO. 10/A-4 |
| Park Hyatt | 442 | MAP NO. 19/A-3 |
| Four Seasons Marunouchi | 412 | MAP NO. 4/C-3 |

| | | |
|---|---|---|
| Okura | 440 | MAP NO. 9/B-2 |
| Seiyo Ginza | 448 | MAP NO. 6/D-1 |

| | | |
|---|---|---|
| Westin | 460 | MAP NO. 7/C-2 |
| New Otani (The Main) | 436 | MAP NO. 3/A-2 |

# ANA Intercontinental

A 37-storey hotel that opened in 1986, at the same time as Akasaka Ark Hills. The entrance to the banquet rooms is on the 1st floor while the front lobby is on the 2nd. The 7th to 35th floors, on which the guest rooms are located, are divided into Regular, Upper and Club Intercontinental Floors, with the latter at the top. Standard non-suite rooms are from 28 to 32m², with white walls and brown carpets giving each room a comfortable, chic ambience. Separate views of the Imperial Palace Outer Garden, Tokyo Tower and Roppongi Hills can be seen from the three sides of the triangular-shaped hotel. Those rooms on the Upper Floors with a view of Tokyo Tower are particularly popular. There is also a variety of restaurants and bars, including the stately main bar with its wide selection of cigars. Another bar on the 36th floor has spectacular views and the casual Champagne Bar is something a little different. Offering a stylish urban stay, the hotel has a good reputation among domestic and international guests alike. Tariffs vary depending on the occupancy rate and date of reservation.

■ Price
Single = ¥ 30,450-52,500
Double = ¥ 42,000-52,500
Suite = ¥ 73,500-299,250
Breakfast = ¥ 2,100

Rooms=798
Suites=48
Restaurants=8

**TEL. 03–3505–1111**
FAX. 03–3505–1155
1-12-33 Akasaka, Minato-ku
www.anaintercontinental-tokyo.jp

# Century Southern Tower

This hotel occupies the 19th to 35th floors of the Odakyu Southern Tower. There are two entrances: the one on the second floor is accessible from the Southern Terrace pedestrian mall near the South Exit of Shinjuku Station; the other, on the first floor, is just a short walk towards Shinjuku from the West Exit of Yoyogi Station. The main lobby is on the 20th floor; the neighbouring lounge and bar offer fine views across Tokyo. Although the hotel is next to a busy railway, the guest rooms are soundproofed with double-glazed windows and are quite comfortable. Standard rooms range in size from 19 to $34m^2$ and all rooms are suitable for business or leisure guests. Those on the eastern side command views of Shinjuku Gyoen, giving guests a sense of the season; guest rooms on the west look onto the Shinjuku skyscraper district and Yoyogi Park - each room is equipped with a panoramic map so guests can place the important landmarks. Despite cutting out conventional hotel services, such as bell and room services, the hotel manages to cater to guest needs through luggage carts, vending machines and a small convenience store.

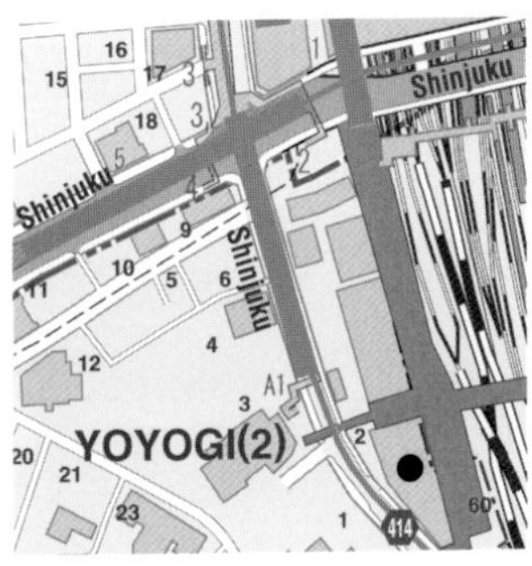

■ Price
🚹 = ¥ 18,480-57,750
🚹🚹 = ¥ 27,720-63,525
☕ = ¥ 2,194

Rooms=375
Restaurants=3

TEL. 03-5354-0111
FAX. 03-5354-0100
2-2-1 Yoyogi, Shibuya-ku
www.southerntower.co.jp

# Cerulean Tower Tokyu

A hotel conveniently located in the 40-storey Cerulean Tower building near Shibuya Station. Guest rooms occupy floors 19 to 37 and all command a view across the capital. The 33rd to 37th floors are Executive Floors and guests in these rooms have exclusive access to the spacious Executive Salon on the 35th floor. All rooms are quiet and feature soothing décor with Japanese design elements. On the top floor, Coucagno offers French-Mediterranean cuisine while Bellovisto bar provides a night view of Shinjuku. There are also restaurants and bars near the main lobby on the first floor, and on the second the jazz club has live music (except Sundays or public holidays). To relax the mind and body, head for the fitness club which has a 20m indoor pool and a resort-style salon. For those interested in traditional Japanese performing arts, take in a *Noh* or *Kyogen* performance at the Cerulean Tower Noh Theatre. The hotel has 11 banquet rooms with varying capacities, including the large Cerulean Tower Ballroom. The hotel is more about functionality and convenience than any "wow" factor.

■ Price
🚹 = ¥ 32,340-78,540
🚹🚹 = ¥ 42,735-80,850
Suite = ¥ 98,175-485,100
☕ = ¥ 3,003

Rooms=402
Suites=9
Restaurants=5

**TEL. 03–3476–3000**
FAX. 03–3476–3001
26-1 Sakuragaokacho, Shibuya-ku
www.ceruleantower-hotel.com

# Conrad

The front desk of this hotel, which opened in 2005, is located on the 28th floor of the Tokyo Shiodome Building, while the guest rooms and facilities occupy the floors up to the 37th. On the 1st floor, where an original sculpture greets visitors, you will find a hotel porter; on the 28th floor, there's the main lobby, bar & lounge Twenty Eight, a brasserie and other restaurants. Mizuki Spa and the fitness centre with a 25m indoor pool have floor-to-ceiling windows; the spa offers various relaxation facilities and treatments. Guest rooms are spacious -the smallest being 48m²- and divide into two types: City Rooms facing the Shiodome area and Garden Rooms facing Hamarikyu Gardens. *Sumie* (ink brush) paintings of cherry trees on the walls of the bedrooms make for a sophisticated space, which uses natural stone and wood. All bathrooms have a view and different colours are used to reflect it: natural green in the Garden Rooms with black, symbolising an urban feel, for the City Rooms. The hotel not only provides excellent access for those here for business or sightseeing, it is also at the forefront of the latest trends.

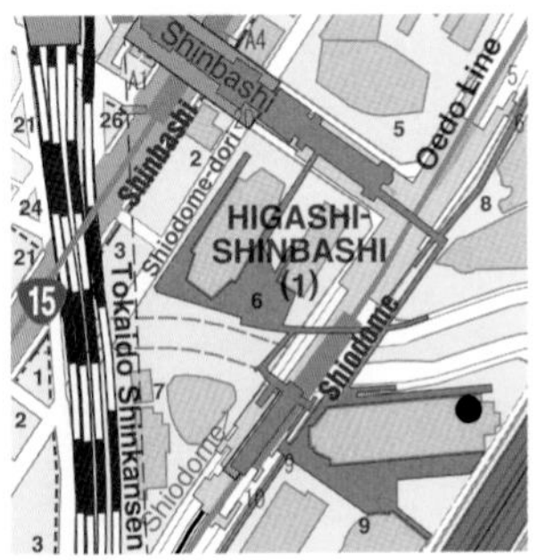

■ Price
† = ¥ 74,000-91,000
†† = ¥ 79,000-96,000
Suite = ¥ 102,000-620,000
☕ = ¥ 2,800

Rooms=222
Suites=68
Restaurants=4

**TEL. 03–6388–8000**
FAX. 03–6388–8001
1-9-1 Higashi-Shinbashi, Minato-ku
www.conradtokyo.co.jp

# Four Seasons Chinzan-so

Chinzan-so was originally built by Aritomo Yamagata, a military leader and politician of the Meiji Era, in the scenic surrounds of Mejirodai. Located inside this garden, the Four Seasons Hotel at Chinzan-so opened in 1992. As well as streams flowing along gentle natural slopes and the abundant greenery, the gardens -about 66,000m$^2$- are dotted with three-storey pagodas and stone lanterns reminiscent of those at Hannyaji Temple. In summer, fireflies could be seen, adding to the fantasy. The main lobby features a European décor of green marble flooring and beautiful wooden walls. Each guest room is at least 45m$^2$. Western-style rooms are in the gracious style of the 19th century, while Japanese-style rooms are both exquisite and restful. Elegantly decorated and luxurious suites encourage total relaxation, with views either of the Chinzan-so Gardens or the cityscape. There are a number of restaurants and shops, including a lobby lounge with a garden view. Guests can use the hot spring baths, pool or Guerlain Paris at Yu, the Spa. This hotel is a smart, tranquil oasis.

■ Price
= ¥ 52,500-65,100
= ¥ 63,000-70,350
Suite = ¥ 84,000-577,500
= ¥ 2,700
Service charge= 10%

Rooms=259
Suites=24
Restaurants=4

**TEL. 03-3943-2222**
FAX. 03-3943-2300
2-10-8 Sekiguchi, Bunkyo-ku
www.fourseasons-tokyo.com

# Four Seasons Marunouchi

This hotel opened in 2002 and is adjacent to Tokyo Station. It occupies the 3rd to 7th floors of the 31-storey Pacific Century Place Marunouchi building; is within easy reach of the Tokyo International Forum and all its exterior walls are glass, providing guests with views of Tokyo Station and the surrounding cityscape. The vibe is one of urban sophistication: guest rooms have a contemporary, elegant feel, with walls and floors in tones of beige and grey, leather bed canopies and furnishings in polished natural materials. There are only 57 bedrooms, including the suites, but all are spacious, with the smallest being 44m². Triple-glazed windows ensure soundproofing. Relative to the hotel's size, staff numbers are high and they provide attentive service. A greetings service is also available and can be arranged for those guests arriving at Narita Airport or Tokyo Station. There is the ekki BAR & GRILL which offers contemporary grilled fare in a stylish setting, with a relaxing bar area. A spa and fitness centre is amongst the variety of facilities. This is a chic and elegant boutique hotel.

■ Price
🚹 = ¥ 65,100-75,600
🚹🚹 = ¥ 65,100-75,600
Suite = ¥ 115,500-525,000
☕ = ¥ 2,900
Service charge= 10%

Rooms=48
Suites=9
Restaurants=1

**TEL. 03–5222–7222**
FAX. 03–5222–1255
Pacific Century Place Building,
1-11-1 Marunouchi, Chiyoda-ku
www.fourseasons.com/jp/
marunouchi

# Grand Hyatt

Opened in 2003, Roppongi Hills is a commercial complex with a range of diverse functions -it is a business centre, a cultural centre and also a major shopping and dining destination. Positioned next to the Mori Tower, which is the core of the complex, is the Grand Hyatt. This contemporary hotel marks a clear departure from competitors in terms of its design, comfort and size. Guests can enjoy a contemporary ambience created with materials and flavours unique to Japan by touring the hotel's facilities like Nagomi Spa & Fitness, which features a stone pool and uses natural materials. The hotel is home to a wide variety of cosmopolitan restaurants that attract a range of guests beyond those staying at the hotel. There are 389 guest rooms and a wide array of luxury suites. Rooms on the east lie adjacent to the Mori Tower and even standard rooms have a spacious 42m$^2$ floor area. The hotel offers an extensive list of amenities expected by hotel guests in today's world, such as sophisticated interior design, fully-fledged facilities and state-of-the-art telecommunications.

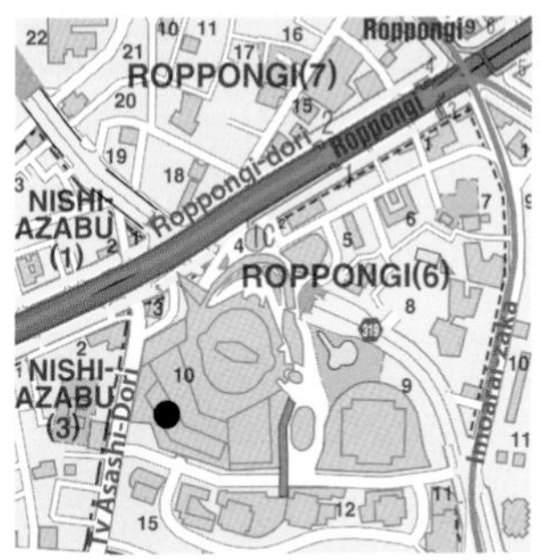

■ Price
† = ¥ 60,060-83,160
†† = ¥ 65,900-88,940
Suite = ¥ 112,100-808,500
☕ = ¥ 2,860

Rooms=361
Suites=28
Restaurants=7

**TEL. 03-4333-1234**
FAX. 03-4333-8123
6-10-3 Roppongi, Minato-ku
www.tokyo.grand.hyatt.jp

# Grand Pacific Le Daiba

A 30-storey hotel that connects directly to Daiba Station on the Yurikamome Line. The hotel adopted its current name in June 2008. Centred around an impressive large dome, the entrance hall on the 2nd floor opens expansively up to the 3rd. Standard guest rooms are on the 6th to 28th floors and each has a different panoramic view; the Rainbow Bridge, central Tokyo, Tokyo Bay or Haneda Airport. Standard rooms range from 30 to 50m² and are decorated in an 18th century European style. Marble is used for the floor of the spacious and comfortable bathrooms. Rooms on the executive floors (27th and 28th) are even more luxurious. Dining options range widely from Japanese cuisine -including a *soba* restaurant- to buffet style. A *teppanyaki* restaurant and a sky lounge on the 30th floor offer commanding vistas of the Tokyo Bay area. Indoor and outdoor swimming pools, a fitness club, beauty salons and other facilities are on the 1st to 6th floors. Due to its proximity to Tokyo Disneyland and leisure facilities in Daiba, the hotel is often used by families. On weekends it buzzes with wedding guests.

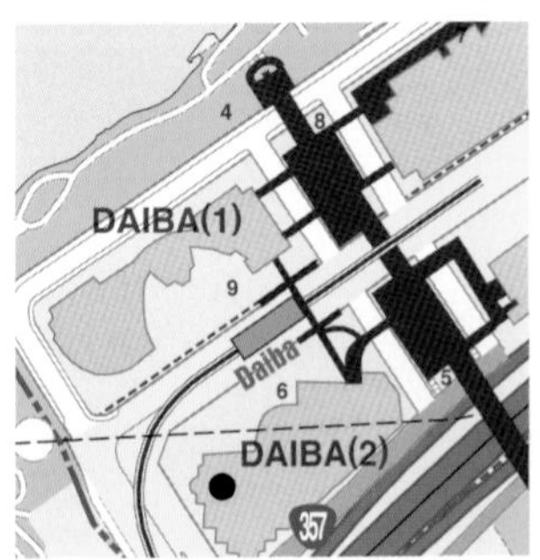

■ Price
🚹 = ¥ 36,000-58,000
🚹🚹 = ¥ 36,000-58,000
Suite = ¥ 90,000-460,000
☕ = ¥ 1,850

Rooms=860
Suites=24
Restaurants=9

**TEL. 03–5500–6711**
FAX. 03–5500–4507
2-6-1 Daiba, Minato-ku
www.grandpacific.jp

# Hilton

This 38-storey hotel, with its distinctive S-shaped wave, is located in Nishi-Shinjuku. Marble Lounge in the first-floor lobby offers a buffet and an à la carte menu and is open 24 hours a day, which is rare for hotels in Tokyo. Five restaurants are located on the second floor, including a French restaurant, a Japanese restaurant as well as *teppan-yaki*. The 815 guest rooms take on a simple and modern style with Japanese touches: including *shoji* and *fusuma* (sliding screens) window furnishings. The 12 Gallery Suite guest rooms (66m$^2$) feature fine art by 12 young artists -each room by a different artist- creating the feeling of being in an art gallery. In addition to regular stays, they are also available for small meetings between 10:00 and 18:00. The 32nd to 38th floors are Executive Floors with spacious rooms offering a high level of comfort for both business and leisure guests. Guests staying on these floors can check-in and out at the exclusive lounge on the 37th floor. There is a fitness centre, and the gym is open round the clock.

■ Price
🚹 = ¥ 22,900-48,900
🚹🚹 = ¥ 25,900-51,900
Suite = ¥ 30,900-186,900
☕ = ¥ 2,600

Rooms=688
Suites=127
Restaurants=6

**TEL. 03–3344–5111**
FAX. 03–3342–6094
6-6-2 Nishi-Shinjuku, Shinjuku-ku
www.hilton.co.jp/tokyo

# Hyatt Regency

Opened in 1980 as the Century Hyatt, the hotel changed its name to Hyatt Regency in 2007. A full-scale renovation started in 2004 is due for completion in February 2009 so when making reservations make sure you book one of the "new" rooms. The lobby soars from the 2nd to 8th floors and has a gorgeous chandelier lavishly decorated with Strass beads from Austria which serves as a symbol of the hotel. Guest rooms are classified into Regency Floor rooms located on the 6th to 9th floors and Standard Floor rooms from 10th to 26th. They are further classified according to their view so choose from a cityscape of high-rises or an outlook across Shinjuku Chuo Park. Guests staying on the Regency Floor can check in and out in the executive lounge. On the top floor there is a pleasant spa, pool facilities and a fitness gym open from 5am. You also have French restaurant Cuisine[s] Michel Troisgros and a relaxing, intimate bar. The hotel is next to the Tokyo Metropolitan Government Office and has easy access to public transportation. There is a complimentary shuttle bus service from Shinjuku Station.

■ Price
🚹 = ¥ 29,400-57,750
🚹🚹 = ¥ 38,850-60,900
Suite = ¥ 73,500-178,500
☕ = ¥ 1,900
Service charge= 10%

Rooms=726
Suites=18
Restaurants=6

**TEL. 03–3348–1234**
FAX. 03–3344–5575
2-7-2 Nishi-Shinjuku, Shinjuku-ku
www.hyattregencytokyo.com

# Imperial

This hotel, which sits across from Hibiya Park, has been in operation since 1890. Well-known for its Japanese-style hospitality, it has hosted overseas dignitaries and its history reflects the ebb and flow of Japan's modernisation. The Wright building, designed by American architect Frank Lloyd Wright and opened in 1923, was replaced by the current Main Building in 1970. More than a decade later the hotel was expanded with the completion of the 31-story Imperial Hotel and Tower. There are a number of options when it comes to bars and restaurants. The Rendezvous Lounge and Bar is a handy place to wait for your dinner guests. The Old Imperial Bar features décor from the 1923 Wright Imperial. French restaurant Les Saisons is on the 2nd floor mezzanine. The suite on the 14th floor of the Main Building incorporates elements of Wright's design. Upon the completion of an extensive renovation project started in 2003, all floors will have a security entrance that can only be opened with the guest's key card. Walk in and feel the dignity of a time-honoured hotel.

■ Price
🚹 = ¥ 37,800-63,000
🚹🚹 = ¥ 43,050-68,250
Suite = ¥ 78,750-262,500
☕ = ¥ 2,730
Service charge= 10%

Rooms=936
Suites=69
Restaurants=13

TEL. 03–3504–1111
FAX. 03–3581–9146
1-1-1 Uchisaiwaicho, Chiyoda-ku
www.imperialhotel.co.jp

# Intercontinental Tokyo Bay

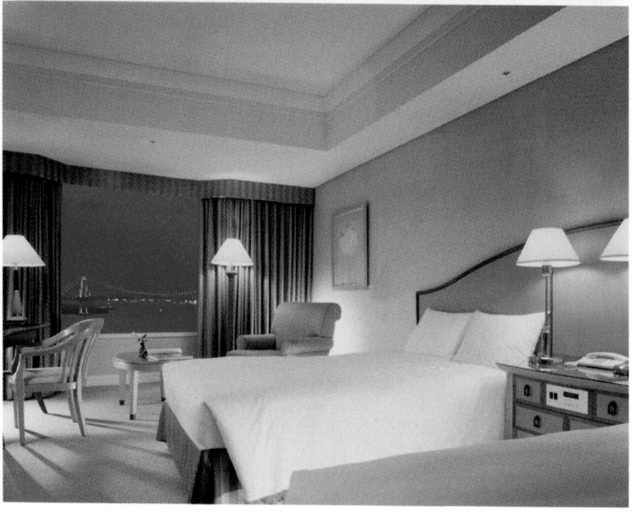

This white, 24-storey building with guest rooms located on the 8th to the top floor opened in 1995 in the New Pier Takeshiba complex is on the Tokyo Bay waterfront. Guests staying on the Club Intercontinental Floors (20th to top) can check-in and out at a dedicated desk. Guest rooms range from 34 to 52m² and are positioned either bay side or river side. All rooms offer commanding views: from the former, of the Rainbow Bridge and Ferris wheel in Odaiba and, from the latter, of the Sumida-gawa river threading among high-rise buildings. Guest rooms are quiet and comfortable with a décor of light beige tones and wooden furnishings. The large windows can be opened to let in the pleasant sea breeze. Room service and the business centre are available around the clock. The 3rd floor, where some of the restaurants such as Japanese and French with a romantic atmosphere are located, directly connects to Takeshiba Station on the Yurikamome Line; an easy access to Shiodome and Odaiba. Combining convenient functionality with the feel of a resort, this hotel is popular with both businesspeople and holiday-makers.

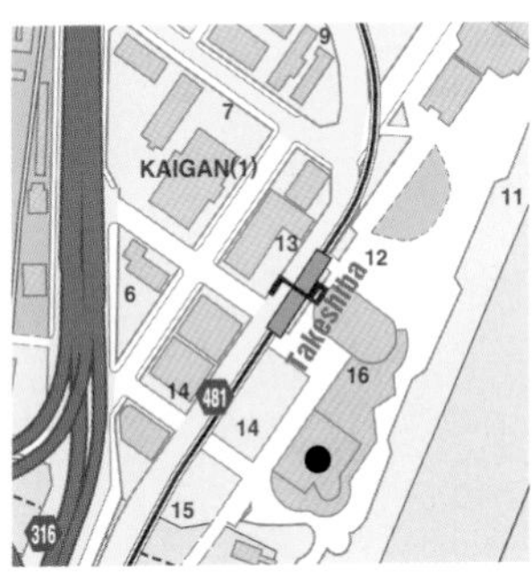

■ Price
= ¥ 41,780-71,810
= ¥ 41,980-72,010
Suite = ¥ 115,700-346,700
= ¥ 1,848

Rooms=331
Suites=8
Restaurants=5

TEL. 03–5404–2222
FAX. 03–5404–2111
1-16-2 Kaigan, Minato-ku
www.interconti-tokyo.com

## Keio Plaza

This hotel has 1,440 guest rooms spread over two buildings and is opposite the Tokyo Metropolitan Government Office, not far from Shinjuku Station. The 45-storey Main Tower was opened in 1971 and the 34-storey South Tower in 1980. About half of the hotel's rooms have been upgraded as part of a renovation program started several years ago. Contemporary décor and comprehensive facilities offer particular good comfort levels in the Plaza Premier rooms, for which refurbishment work has been completed. Guests in these rooms have their own exclusive check-in counter. Rooms that have yet to be renovated have a 1980s feel. For overseas guests keen to experience a Japanese tradition, there are older Japanese-style rooms with a *hinoki* (Japanese cypress) bathtub. All rooms command panoramic views of the city. The outdoor swimming pool on the seventh floor of the Main Tower is open between June and September. Conveniently located in Shinjuku, a major transportation hub, the hotel also has a shopping arcade, a clinic and a variety of other facilities and amenities.

■ Price
♦ = ¥ 26,250-58,800
♦♦ = ¥ 34,650-58,800
Suite = ¥ 97,650-378,000
☕ = ¥ 2,310
Service charge= 10%

Rooms=1413
Suites=27
Restaurants=13

**TEL. 03–3344–0111**
FAX. 03–3345–8269
2-2-1 Nishi-Shinjuku, Shinjuku-ku
www.keioplaza.co.jp

MAP NO. 5/A-1

# Mandarin Oriental

The hotel occupies the first three and top nine floors of Nihonbashi Mitsui Tower. The walls and flooring of the guest rooms use bamboo and other natural materials, while the fabrics carry a nature motif. Features include Japanese-inspired decorative adornments that add an air of elegance and tranquility. The west side offers view of the gardens of the Imperial Palace and to the east you can see Odaiba in Tokyo Bay and the Sumida-gawa river. The main reception is on the 38th floor, and the Oriental Lounge located off the main lobby is the place to try new-style "molecular cuisine." Go to the 37th floor to dine at Sense, a Cantonese restaurant or the French eatery, Signature. These restaurants also command spectacular views of the city. The spacious fitness gym is on the 38th floor while the nine treatment rooms -including five Spa Suites- on the 37th floor offer guests high levels of comfort and relaxation. In addition to the refined interior and design concept, the high-quality service adds to the attraction of this hotel.

■ Price
= ¥ 71,400-81,900
= ¥ 71,400-81,900
Suite = ¥ 136,500-945,000
= ¥ 2,800
Service charge= 10%

Rooms=157
Suites=22
Restaurants=5

**TEL. 03-3270-8800**
FAX. 03-3270-8828
2-1-1 Nihonbashi-Muromachi, Chuo-ku
www.mandarinoriental.co.jp/tokyo

# Marunouchi

Located in front of Tokyo Station's Marunouchi North Exit, this hotel is convenient for both businesspeople and tourists visiting the centre of Tokyo. The ultra-modern building was constructed in 2004 and the vast atrium extending up to the top floor gives it an airy feel. The elegant, contemporary lobby is on the 7th floor, with a garden that can be seen through plate glass. On the same floor are also a Japanese and *teppan-yaki* restaurant and a cigar bar; a French restaurant is located on the floor above. Guest rooms are on the 9th to 17th floors - those on the east side overlook the busy, red brick Tokyo Station, while those on the west face the Marunouchi business district. Rooms on both sides, however, are very quiet. The 81 single rooms are not especially large, but their coved or arched ceilings add a feeling of spaciousness and the rooms feature Italian furniture and subtle lighting, giving them a relaxed ambience. A range of different kinds of larger rooms are also available, all of which are comfortable. A refined hotel with all the 21st century modern conveniences.

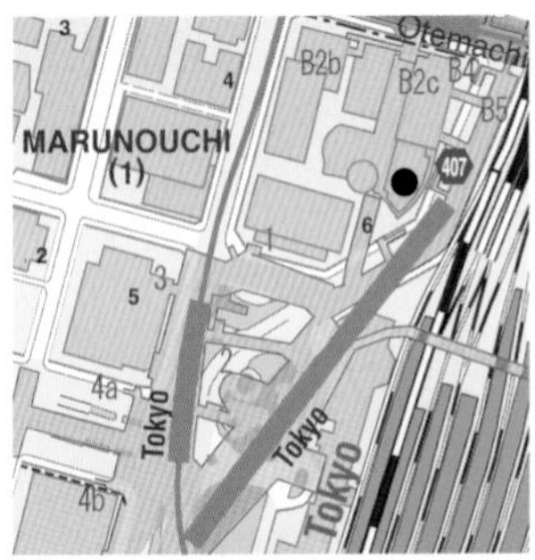

■ Price
= ¥ 23,300-52,175
= ¥ 31,385-52,375
Suite = ¥ 115,700-115,900
= ¥ 1,900

Rooms=204
Suites=1
Restaurants=3

**TEL. 03–3217–1111**
FAX. 03–3217–1115
1-6-3 Marunouchi, Chiyoda-ku
www.marunouchi-hotel.co.jp

# Meguro Gajoen

Meguro Gajoen, well known as a wedding venue, was first opened in 1931 and is situated at the foot of Gyoninzaka near Meguro Station. The Japanese-style house, known as Hyakudan Kaidan, that lies within the premises was built in 1935 and is a registered cultural property; it served as the inspiration for the building of Yuya in the famed movie *Spirited away*. The eight-storey main building was constructed in 1991. Guest rooms are situated on the sixth floor and provide a tranquil space, in contrast to the lavishly decorated public areas which incorporate wooden beams, paintings and carvings from the former building. Central hallway is a division point for Western-style and Japanese-style rooms and all have floor space of at least 80m². The Western rooms include *Ryukyu tatami* mats in the corner and can accommodate up to four guests. Rooms on the west overlook the Meguro-gawa River and offer beautiful views of cherry blossoms in spring. Mt. Fuji can sometimes be seen in the distance. On days considered auspicious in Japan, Meguro Gajoen bustles with wedding activity.

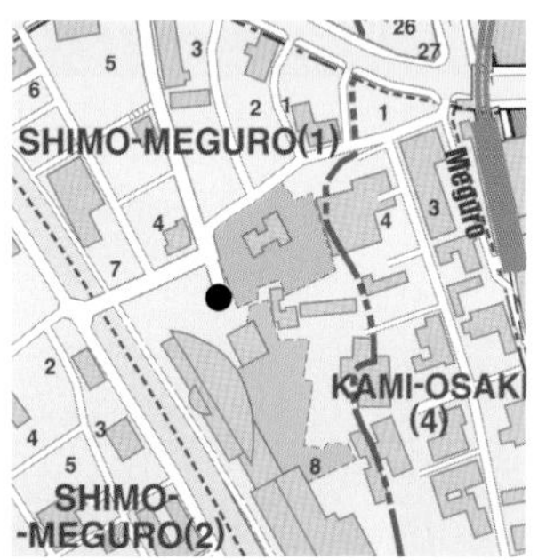

■ Price
🚹 = ¥ 70,000-116,000
🚹🚹 = ¥ 70,000-116,000
☕ = ¥ 2,400

Rooms=23
Restaurants=4

**TEL. 03–3491–4111**
FAX. 03–5434–3931
1-8-1 Shimo-Meguro, Meguro-ku
www.megurogajoen.co.jp

# Mitsui Garden Ginza

The reception desk of this Ginza 8-chome hotel, which opened in 2005, is located on the 16th floor and its spacious glass-walled lobby features contemporary lounge seating, tables and light fittings. A salon bar and a restaurant offering modern Italian cuisine are on the same floor, which overlooks the Tokyo Tower, Shiodome skyline and Tsukiji market. Guest rooms, which occupy the 17th to 25th floors, have good views of Tokyo Bay on the southwest side and Ginza on the northwest. The hotel has a large number of compact rooms in stylish brown and white basic tones: 100 rooms measuring 18.5$m^2$ (Moderate) and 122 rooms at 20.4$m^2$ (Superior). Guests choosing the View Bath Double or View Bath Twin rooms can luxuriate in the bathtub against the backdrop of Tokyo at night. For an even higher level of comfort, the 25th or Executive Floor have bedrooms measuring 40$m^2$. Catering to the needs of businesspeople requiring overnight accommodation only, the hotel has card-key equipped lifts for extra security. The hotel is impressive in its functional yet contemporary design.

■ Price
= ¥ 18,900-44,100
= ¥ 25,200-44,100
= ¥ 2,100

Rooms=360
Restaurants=1

**TEL. 03–3543–1131**
FAX. 03–3543–5531
8-13-1 Ginza, Chuo-ku
www.gardenhotels.co.jp

# New Otani (The Main)

This hotel faces a huge 40,000m² Japanese garden that dates back four centuries. Opened in 1964, the hotel consists of the Main Building and the Garden Tower. This guide covers only the Main Building, which underwent major renovations completed in 2007. Guest rooms feature modern interior décor in muted colours that include elements of Japanese design. For greater levels of comfort, try the Executive House Zen rooms: these recently refurbished rooms are based on the concept of Zen, are well equipped and feature a contemporary black and white design. At the top of the hotel, a revolving buffet restaurant that goes full circle every 70 minutes offers panoramic views. Other restaurants include La Tour d'Argent. There is even an art museum in the Garden Court and shops can be found throughout the hotel. In a rarity for Tokyo hotels, guests have access to 3 tennis courts and a golf range.

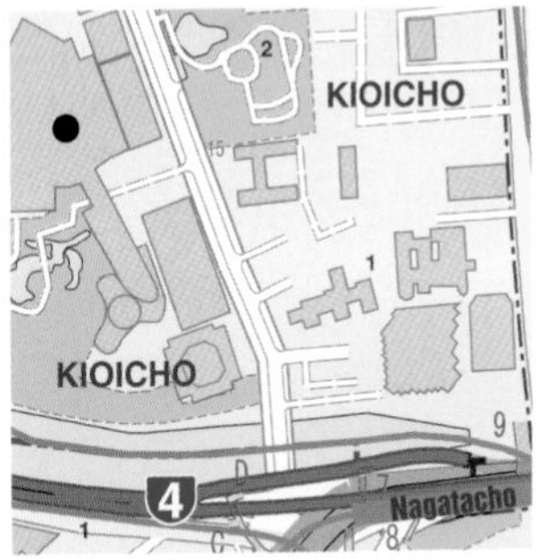

■ Price
♦ = ¥ 31,500-73,500
♦♦ = ¥ 39,900-73,500
Suite = ¥ 126,000-273,000
☕ = ¥ 1,890
Service charge= 10%

Rooms=614
Suites=29
Restaurants=29

**TEL. 03-3265-1111**
FAX. 03-3221-2619
4-1 Kioicho, Chiyoda-ku
www.newotani.co.jp/tokyo

# Nikko

A hotel with the outward appearance of a luxury cruise ship anchored at Odaiba. It describes itself as "the balcony of Tokyo", so every room has one. The lobby on the 2nd floor, with its atrium and high columns, offers a view of Rainbow Bridge. Guest rooms on the 5th to 8th floors were completely renovated and reopened in summer 2008; designed with the theme of "Tokyo Resort", these rooms, with their contemporary, chic tones, are particularly stylish. Guest rooms on the 9th to 15th floors will be renovated in 2009. For even higher levels of comfort, the suites with their own garden are recommended. The hotel's relaxation space -also recently refurbished and relaunched as Spa Zen Tokyo- comes complete with a bar; the view from the outdoor spa pool overlooking Tokyo Bay is breathtaking. (One of the 5th floor guest rooms also has a private spa.) There are a variety of restaurants and some have a terrace where diners can eat while enjoying the refreshing sea breezes. An urban resort hotel with a relaxing, leisurely feel in the heart of Tokyo.

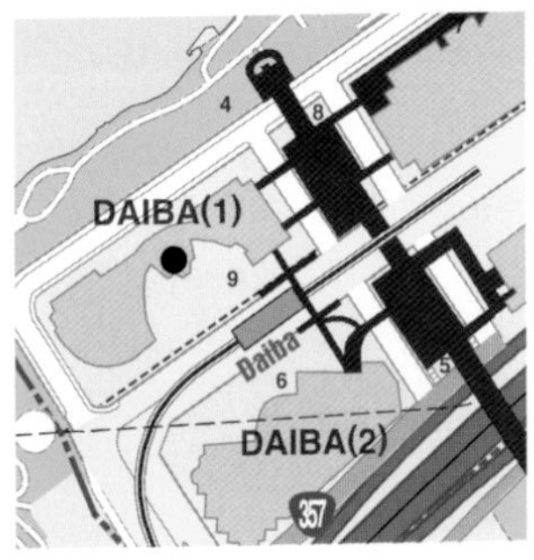

■ Price
Single = ¥ 34,000-62,000
Double = ¥ 40,000-68,000
Suite = ¥ 150,000-330,000
Breakfast = ¥ 2,287

Rooms=434
Suites=18
Restaurants=8

TEL. 03-5500-5500
FAX. 03-5500-2525
1-9-1 Daiba, Minato-ku
www.hnt.co.jp

# Okura

The Hotel Okura was opened in 1962, two years before the Tokyo Olympics, and its regal atmosphere has not changed since. Visitors are drawn into the Main Building's Lobby by the soft glow of lantern-like lights suspended from the ceiling. Its designers deliberately avoided the use of metals in favour of a chic all-wood décor. A shopping arcade lined with boutiques connects the Main Building with the South Wing, which was added in the 1970s and is home to another spacious lobby. Guest rooms vary in size, style and the view on offer, but all are sophisticated, comfortable and well equipped. There is also an Executive Service Salon, fitness facilities with dedicated staff and the relaxation Nature Court. A wide choice of Japanese, Western and Chinese restaurants are available, including wine restaurant Baron Okura with its impressive wine list. Across from the entrance to the Main Building is the Okura Shukokan Museum of Fine Arts, established by the hotel's founder. This is a hotel with a proud tradition and impeccable service.

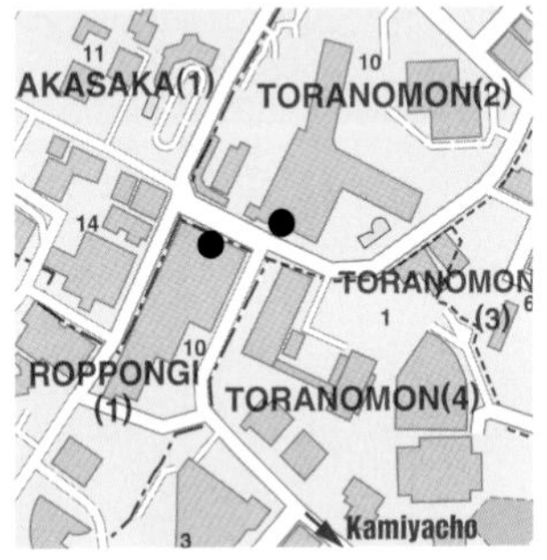

■ Price
🚹 = ¥ 36,750-66,150
🚹🚹 = ¥ 42,000-105,000
Suite = ¥ 94,500-577,500
☕ = ¥ 1,890
Service charge= 10%

Rooms=773
Suites=60
Restaurants=10

TEL. 03-3582-0111
FAX. 03-3582-3707
2-10-4 Toranomon, Minato-ku
www.hotelokura.co.jp/tokyo

# Park Hyatt

A hotel occupying the 39th to 52nd floors of the Shinjuku Park Tower, a high-rise building opened in 1994. Guest rooms are on the 42nd to 51st floors and offer panoramic views of the city. On a clear day Mt. Fuji can be seen from the rooms on the west side. Guest bedrooms are decorated in tones of beige and green, with comfort taking priority over extravagance. One of the most notable features is the Club on The Park spa and fitness centre, which has the same spectacular views as the guest rooms which and makes the pool and gym seem even larger. The hotel also has a number of restaurants and bars, including a Japanese restaurant and a European brasserie, both with stylish interiors and the Peak Lounge bar. Drawings by Federico Fellini, the Italian film director, are on display around the hotel, along with other works by contemporary artists. The hotel was used as the setting for the Sofia Coppola film, *Lost in Translation*. A regular shuttle bus service is available between the hotel and Shinjuku Station's West Exit.

■ Price
= ¥ 68,200-86,700
= ¥ 68,200-86,700
Suite = ¥ 165,200-898,200
= ¥ 2,420

Rooms=154
Suites=23
Restaurants=4

**TEL. 03-5322-1234**
FAX. 03-5322-1288
3-7-1-2 Nishi-Shinjuku, Shinjuku-ku
www.parkhyatttokyo.com

# Royal Park

This hotel opened in 1989 at a convenient location close to the Tokyo City Air Terminal, a major bus terminal with regular services to and from Narita and Haneda airports. The spacious and well-designed lobby with marble flooring and a chandelier that stretches across the ceiling like a scaled-down Milky Way includes, as well as the ordinary reception area, a second "woman travellers' desk" offering check-in, reservations, information and personal services exclusively for female guests. With bright-coloured walls and chic modern interiors, the rooms in various sizes have panoramic views and come equipped with modern conveniences such as a computer. The private salon, swimming pool, fitness club and meeting rooms are free of charge for guests on the Executive Floors. There are various restaurants and bars, such as a French restaurant with a panorama of Tokyo, a relaxing Japanese restaurant overlooking a garden and a Chinese restaurant with modern stylish décor; the main bar has a British theme and there is also a sky lounge. On a fine day, guests can enjoy a pleasant stroll in the beautiful 5th-floor garden.

■ Price
👤 = ¥ 27,300-53,550
👥 = ¥ 35,700-57,750
Suite = ¥ 84,000-262,500
☕ = ¥ 1,365
Service charge= 10%

Rooms=395
Suites=11
Restaurants=7

**TEL. 03-3667-1111**
FAX. 03-3667-1115
2-1-1 Nihonbashi-Kakigaracho,
Chuo-ku
www.rph.co.jp

# Royal Park Shiodome Tower

This hotel, which occupies the 24th to 38th floors of Shiodome Tower, opened in 2003 and is handily placed for sightseeing and good for business purposes. Guest rooms are equipped with multifunctional personal computers with high-speed Internet access, TV and a Cyber-Concierge. The latter answers queries related to hotel facilities and delivery services. Each room on the uppermost Tower Floor has a fax machine & printer, a trouser press, an automatic massage chair and an air cleaning & humidifying system. The hotel also has a coin laundry, convenient for those on long stays. Guest rooms are varied, ranging from single rooms (20m$^2$) to corner deluxe double rooms equipped with a sitting room (57m$^2$). Interior décor is modern and simple. While most rooms offer splendid views of the Hamarikyu Gardens, Tokyo Tower or the Imperial Palace, there is one side of the hotel that's obstructed so request a room with a view. To ease fatigue, head for the Balinese-style Mandara Spa or the British reflexology salon Grande Refle on the 2nd-basement level. Some of the restaurants are open until 1am.

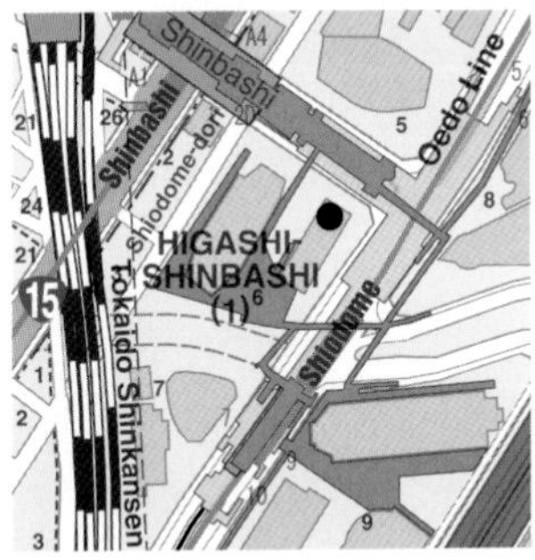

■ Price
= ¥ 23,100-43,890
= ¥ 33,495-69,300
Suite = ¥ 103,950
= ¥ 1,386

Rooms=488
Suites=2
Restaurants=3

**TEL. 03–6253–1111**
FAX. 03–6253–1115
1-6-3 Higashi-Shinbashi, Minato-ku
www.rps-tower.co.jp

# Seiyo Ginza

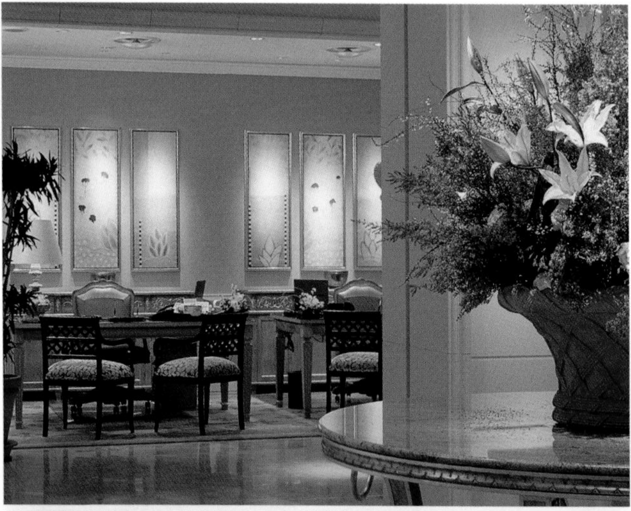

A 12-storey hotel opened in Ginza in 1987. Located on the bustling Chuo-dori Avenue, the hotel nonetheless exudes an air of serenity and comfort. Although small -with only 77 guest rooms, occupying the 7th to 12th floors- there are 60 different types of room, each a different size. The hotel concept is to provide high-level hotel services and relaxation in the ambience of a private residence. In line with this, a butler in a tailcoat is assigned to every guest room to take care of guests' daily needs. Seiyo Ginza was the first hotel in Tokyo to offer this personal butler service, which, along with a concierge service, is available 24 hours a day. The guest rooms are designed in 18th-century European style, with beige walls and light brown carpets creating a refined atmosphere. The spacious bathrooms are bright with sunlight and particularly pleasant in the morning. On the 2nd floor is an elegant French restaurant and a bar and lounge with well-spaced sofas. A *sushi* restaurant is on the 1st floor, and Japanese and Italian restaurants are located on the basement floor.

■ Price
🚹 = ¥ 63,525-78,540
🚹🚹 = ¥ 63,525-78,540
Suite = ¥ 92,400-219,450
Breakfast = ¥ 2,772

Rooms=51
Suites=26
Restaurants=4

TEL. 03–3535–1111
FAX. 03–3535–1110
1-11-2 Ginza, Chuo-ku
www.seiyo-ginza.co.jp

# The Agnes

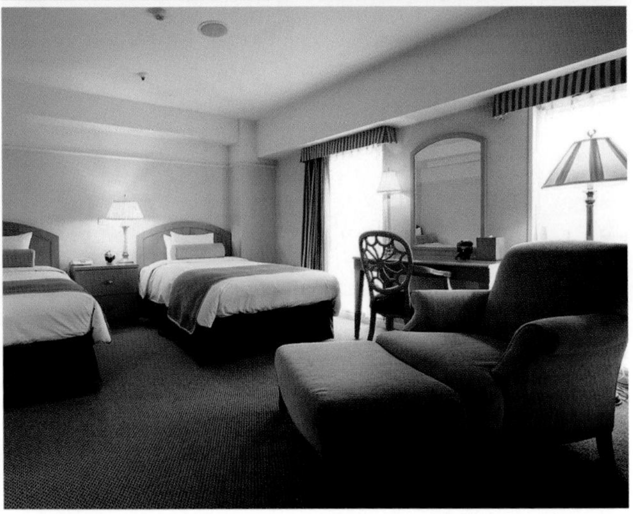

From Iidabashi Station head along Sotobori-dori Avenue towards Ichigaya and go past the Tokyo University of Science; this hotel, opened in 2000, is on a quiet backstreet close to the university. Based on a beige colour scheme, the hotel's accommodation is comfortable and relaxing. With only 56 rooms -all are equipped with Jacuzzi and most have a balcony- and a large number of staff on hand to take care of each guest's every need, the hotel will be particularly appreciated by those seeking a peaceful environment to provide a respite from the demands of urban life. All bathrooms are fitted with a spa bath and separate shower. For longer-term guests, there are apartments equipped with a refrigerator, microwave, washing machine, dryer and so on. As special rates apply to these apartments, it is advisable to inquire in advance. There is a restaurant serving traditional French cuisine and, for an extra charge, a private-dining space on the top-level fifth floor. Both the tea lounge and bar are good spots to meet friends or just relax. This hotel has many repeat guests, so make reservations well in advance.

■ Price
🚹 = ¥ 22,000-35,000
🚹🚹 = ¥ 27,000-40,000
Suite = ¥ 50,000-80,000
☕ = ¥ 2,100

Rooms=51
Suites=5
Restaurants=1

**TEL. 03-3267-5505**
FAX. 03-3267-5513
2-20-1 Kagurazaka, Shinjuku-ku
www.agneshotel.com

# The Peninsula

A 24-storey hotel that opened in 2007 in an enviable location opposite the Imperial Palace Outer Garden and Hibiya Park. The Lobby lounge found on the first-floor is a lively space from breakfast through to cocktail hour. You'll find the front desk behind the eye-catching bamboo creation. Guest rooms, which occupy the 8th to 23rd floors, are described as "contemporary with Japanese-inspired accents". Doors made of Japanese horse chestnut; vermillion-lacquered counters and other design elements blend together well and demonstrate the hotel's commitment to design elegance. Guest bathrooms are equipped with the latest technology so that the telephone, TV and lights can be operated from the bathtub. The Deluxe Park View Rooms offering impressive views are particularly recommended. Restaurants include the elegant Hei Fung Terrace on the 2nd floor. On the first basement floor, Boutique & Café sells Peninsula brand wines and chocolates.

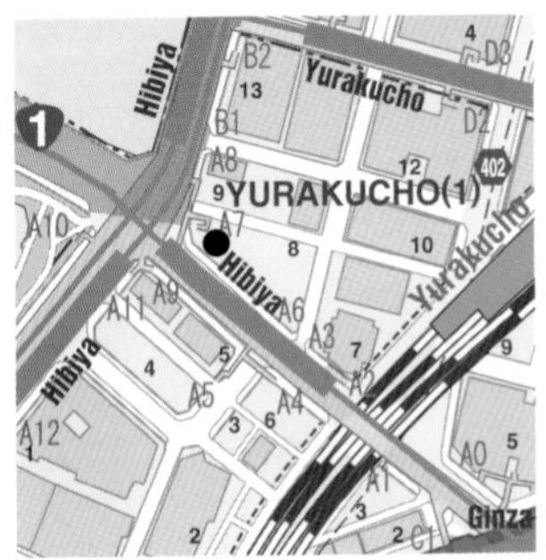

■ Price
= ¥ 69,300-92,400
= ¥ 69,300-92,400
Suite = ¥ 115,500-981,750
= ¥ 2,800

Rooms=267
Suites=47
Restaurants=4

**TEL. 03-6270-2888**
FAX. 03-6270-2000
1-8-1 Yurakucho, Chiyoda-ku
www.tokyo.jp.peninsula.com

# The Prince Park Tower

Amid the greenery of Shiba Park, this hotel emphasises the importance of comfort through a range of relaxation facilities. Its 33 storeys are divided into two sections: the Park Floors on the 3rd to 18th floors, and the Executive and Executive Premium Floors, which consist of the second and 19th to 31st floors. Personal butler services are available for guests staying in any of the comfortable and unique Royal Suites -choose from among British, French, Italian and Japanese styles. 400 guest rooms come with their own small balcony and those on the northeast side have a view of the nearby Tokyo Tower. In addition to the bar lounge on the top floor, which also commands a view of the tower, the hotel offers a wide choice of restaurants and bars. A visit to the wine -and *sake*- tasting corner on the first basement floor can help diners choose a bottle to suit their meal from the list of 100 *sakes* and 200 wines. There are also spa and fitness facilities, banquet rooms that can also be used for wedding ceremonies, a beautiful swimming pool and a bowling alley.

■ Price
♦ = ¥ 34,000-70,000
♦♦ = ¥ 34,000-70,000
Suite = ¥ 104,000-980,000
☕ = ¥ 2,000

Rooms=639
Suites=34
Restaurants=13

**TEL. 03–5400–1111**
FAX. 03–5400–1110
4-8-1 Shiba-Koen, Minato-ku
www.princehotels.co.jp/parktower

# The Ritz-Carlton

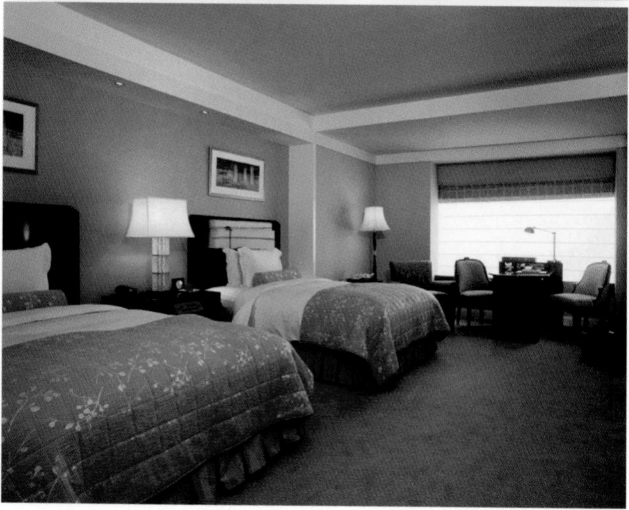

This hotel is located in the 53-storey Midtown Tower that soars 248m above the rest of the Tokyo Midtown complex which opened in 2007. It occupies from the 1st -level basement to the 2nd floor as well as from the 45th to the top. The front desk is in the spacious entrance lobby on the 45th floor, which has an 8m ceiling, large contemporary paintings and objets d'art and where the welcoming atmosphere is enhanced by the sound of flowing water. Enjoy afternoon tea in The Lobby Lounge and take in the live piano and string performances. There are also restaurants on this floor, including Hinokizaka. The interior décor of the 248 guestrooms, which have a floor space of at least 52m$^2$, is elegant and sophisticated. In addition to Asian-inspired Art Deco furniture, the well-appointed rooms are fitted with a large-screen TV and a CD & DVD players. The sleek bathrooms have a second TV. On the 46th floor you'll find the 20m swimming pool, a well-equipped fitness centre and a relaxing spa. Stunning panoramic views take in Mt. Fuji and Tokyo Tower.

■ Price
† = ¥ 70,350-94,500
†† = ¥ 70,350-94,500
Suite = ¥ 115,500-2,100,000
☕ = ¥ 2,850
Service charge= 10%

Rooms=212
Suites=36
Restaurants=3

**TEL. 03-3423-8000**
FAX. 03-3423-8001
Tokyo Midtown,
9-7-1 Akasaka, Minato-ku
www.ritzcarlton.com/ja/tokyo

# The Strings by Intercontinental

Connected directly by the Skyway pedestrian overpass, this hotel is within a two-minute walk of Shinagawa Station's Konan Exit. It occupies the 26th to the top floor of a 32-storey high-rise; the reception desk -where a large atrium provides natural light during the day, and a comfortable ambience at night- is also on the 26th. The view of the water feature and glass walkway is particularly impressive; beyond the bridge you will find a French fusion restaurant and bar and a Chinese restaurant. The guest rooms are stylishly decorated in brown and beige tones and large windows allow guests to take in views of the city while relaxing in modern surroundings. The bathrooms' attractive design incorporates wood and marble floorings. Guest rooms come in a variety of sizes, from $24m^2$ to $40m^2$ and facilities include a 24 hour business centre and a fitness centre with the same spectacular panoramic views as the bedrooms. Guests opting to stay in the Club Intercontinental rooms –which all face Tokyo Bay- can take advantage of the extra services on offer. A hotel equally suitable for leisure and business travellers.

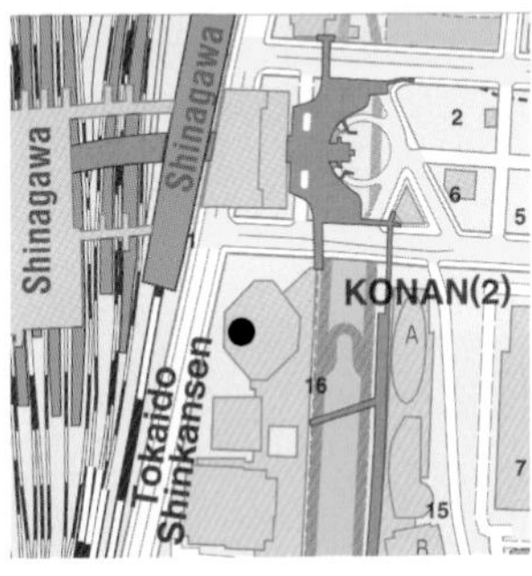

■ Price
† = ¥ 50,000-65,000
†† = ¥ 56,000-71,000
Suite = ¥ 162,000-237,000
☕ = ¥ 2,656

Rooms=200
Suites=6
Restaurants=2

**TEL. 03–5783–1111**
FAX. 03–5783–1112
Shinagawa East One Tower,
2-16-1 Konan, Minato-ku
www.intercontinental-strings.jp

# Westin

This 22-storey building is part of Yebisu Garden Place. The interior décor takes inspiration from early 19th-century French style. The imported Italian marble used for the floors and pillars fits well with the Japanese design elements like the prints and folding screens and helps create an elegant feel throughout the hotel. The spacious 1st-floor lobby leads to The Lounge and The Terrace, where you can have afternoon tea overlooking the well-tended garden. Chinese and Japanese restaurants can be found on the 2nd floor. For *teppanyaki*, there is Yebisu on the top floor. The guest rooms are also decorated in an early 19th-century European style with a Japanese sensibility. All guest rooms are well-equipped and offer good views. Choose from two room types: Deluxe or Westin Executive Club. Those in executive rooms can check in at the exclusive lounge on the 17th floor and have access to exclusive services, including a complimentary breakfast. The 5th floor is for women only and offers rooms with some unique features such as yoga mats and humidifiers. There is also a gym which is open 24 hours and a spa.

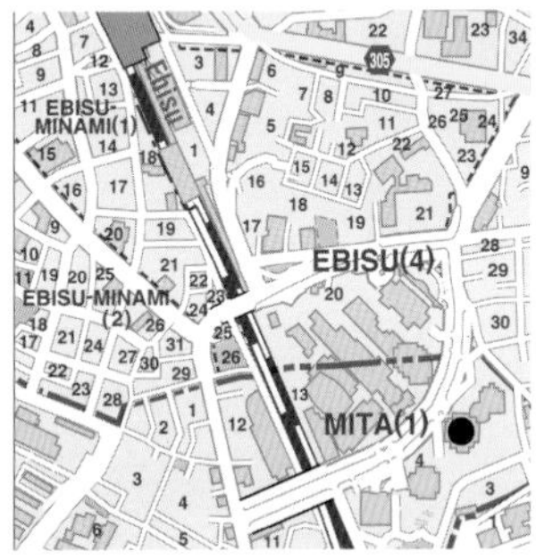

■ Price
= ¥ 61,950-79,800
= ¥ 61,950-79,800
Suite = ¥ 157,500-525,000
= ¥ 2,182
Service charge= 10%

Rooms=398
Suites=40
Restaurants=5

**TEL. 03–5423–7000**
FAX. 03–5423–7600
1-4-1 Mita, Meguro-ku
www.westin-tokyo.co.jp

# MAPS

# Tokyo in 28 maps

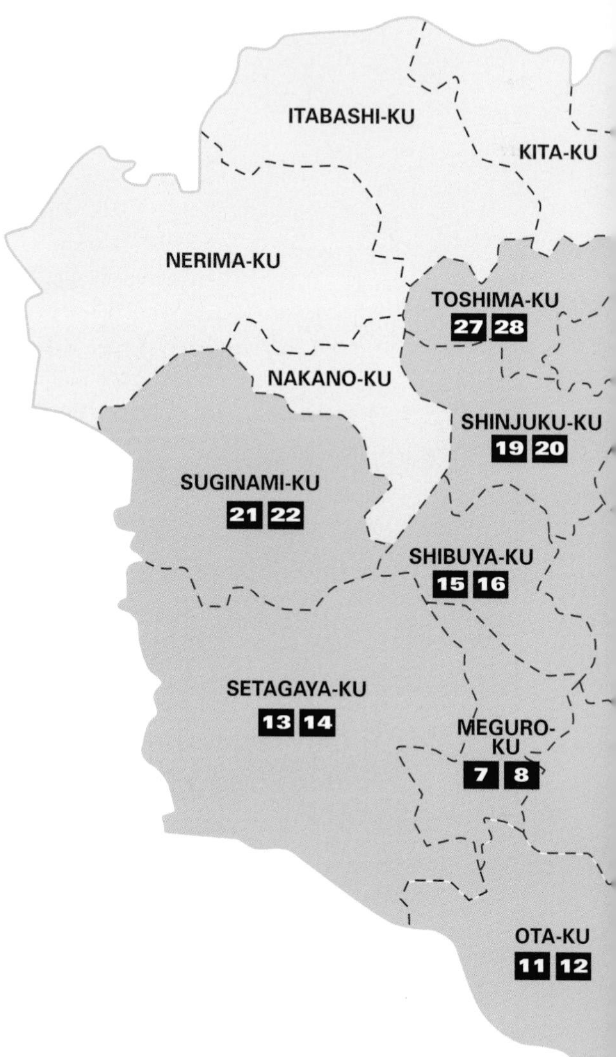

ADACHI-KU
KATSUSHIKA-KU
ARAKAWA-KU
SUMIDA-KU
23 24
BUNKYO-KU
1 2
TAITO-KU
25 26
EDOGAWA-KU
CHIYODA-KU
3 4
CHUO-KU
5 6
KOTO-KU
MINATO-KU
9 10
SHINAGAWA-KU
17 18

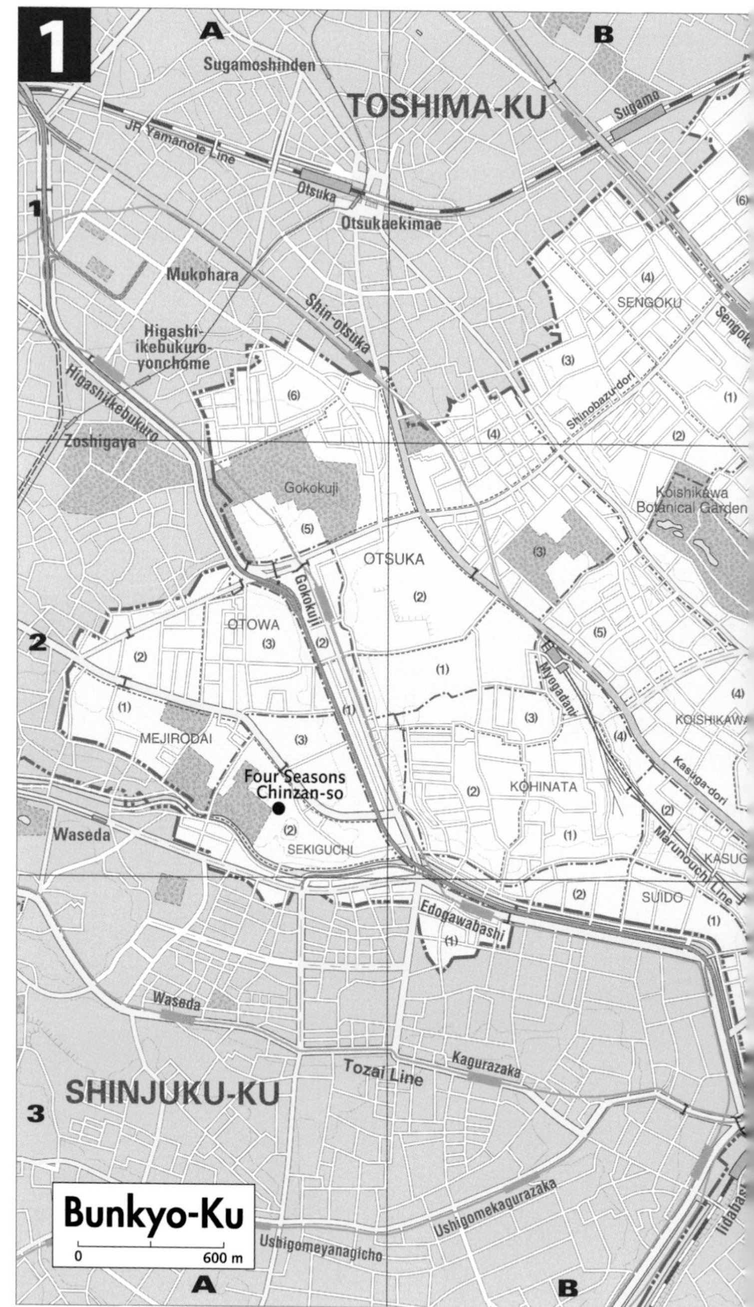
1
A
B
Sugamoshinden
TOSHIMA-KU
Sugamo
JR Yamanote Line
Otsuka
Otsukaekimae
Mukohara
Shin-otsuka
Higashi-ikebukuro-yonchome
Higashiikebukuro
Zoshigaya
SENGOKU
Sengoku
Shinobazu-dori
Gokokuji
Koishikawa Botanical Garden
OTSUKA
OTOWA
Gokokuji
Myogadani
KOISHIKAWA
MEJIRODAI
KOHINATA
Kasuga-dori
Four Seasons Chinzan-so
Waseda
SEKIGUCHI
Marunouchi Line
KASUG
SUIDO
Edogawabashi
Waseda
Tozai Line
Kagurazaka
SHINJUKU-KU
Ushigomekagurazaka
Ushigomeyanagicho
Iidabash
Bunkyo-Ku
0
600 m
2
3

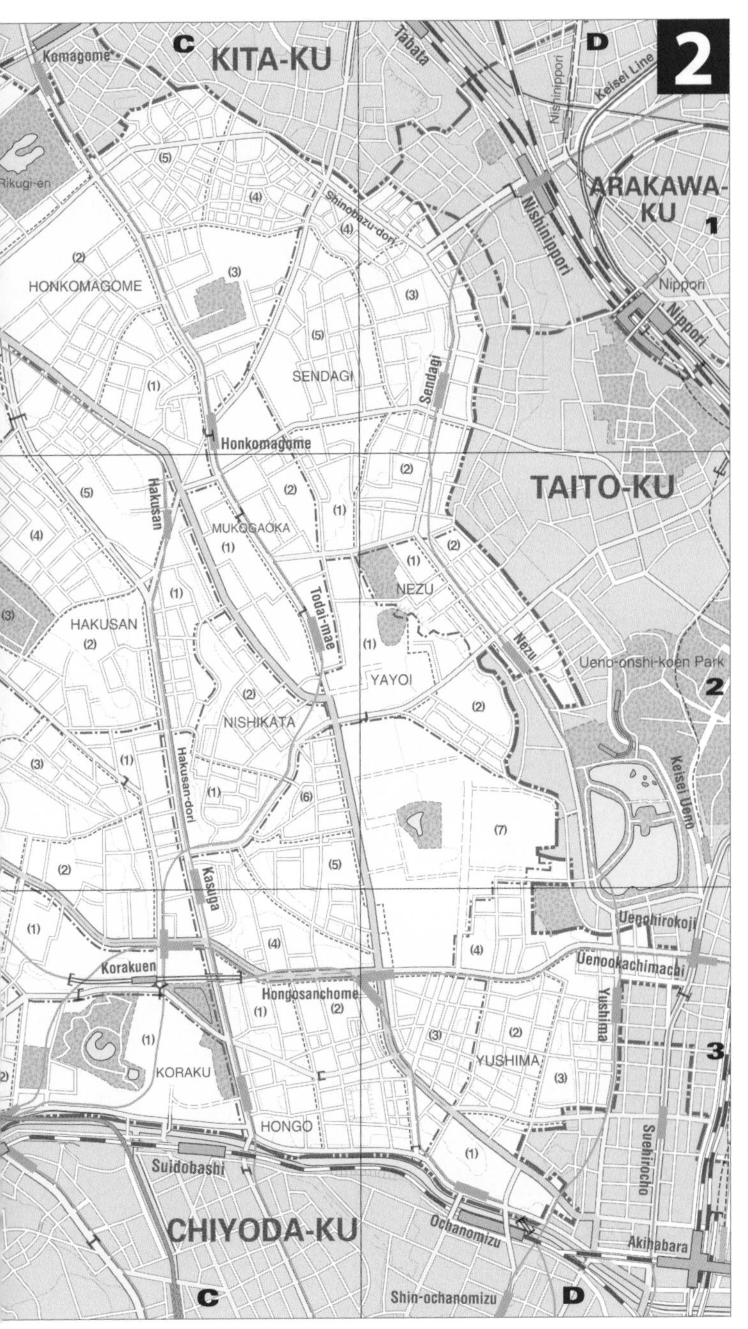
2
C
D
KITA-KU
Komagome
Tabata
Nishinippori
Keisei Line
Rikugi-en
Shinobazu-dori
ARAKAWA-KU
1
Nishinippori
HONKOMAGOME
Nippori
Nippori
SENDAGI
Sendagi
Honkomagome
TAITO-KU
Hakusan
MUKOGAOKA
NEZU
Todai-mae
HAKUSAN
Nezu
Ueno-onshi-koen Park
2
YAYOI
NISHIKATA
Hakusan-dori
Keisei Ueno
Kasuga
Uenohirokoji
Korakuen
Uenookachimachi
Hongosanchome
Yushima
3
KORAKU
YUSHIMA
HONGO
Suehirocho
Suidobashi
CHIYODA-KU
Ochanomizu
Akihabara
Shin-ochanomizu
C
D

3
A
B
1
2
3
SHINJUKU-KU
MINATO-KU
Chiyoda-Ku
0
500 m
Ushigomekagurazaka
Iidabashi
IIDABASHI
Suidobashi
MISAKICHO
NISHIKAND
FUJIMI
Kudanshita
KUDANKITA
KUDANMINAMI
Science Museum
KITANOMARUKOEN
National Museum of Modern Art Tokyo
Ichigaya
GOBANCHO
SANBANCHO
YONBANCHO
ROKUBANCHO
ICHIBANCHO
Aimée Vibert
Kojimachi
Hanzomon
NIBANCHO
Yotsuya
Imperial Palace
CHIYODA
KOJIMACHI
Fukudaya
La Tour d'Argent
KIOICHO
HAYABUSA CHO
HIRAKAWACHO
New Otani (The Main)
Nadaman Honten Sazanka-so
Nagatacho
Yurakucho Line
Sakuradamon
Yurakucho Line
NAGATACHO
Akasakamitsuke
Hanzomon Line
Marunouchi Line
Yamanochaya
Kokkaigijido-mae
KASUMIGASEKI
Tameikesanno
Kasumigaseki
Hibiya-koen Park
Akasaka
UCHISAIWAI CHO
Toranomon
Uchisaiwaicho

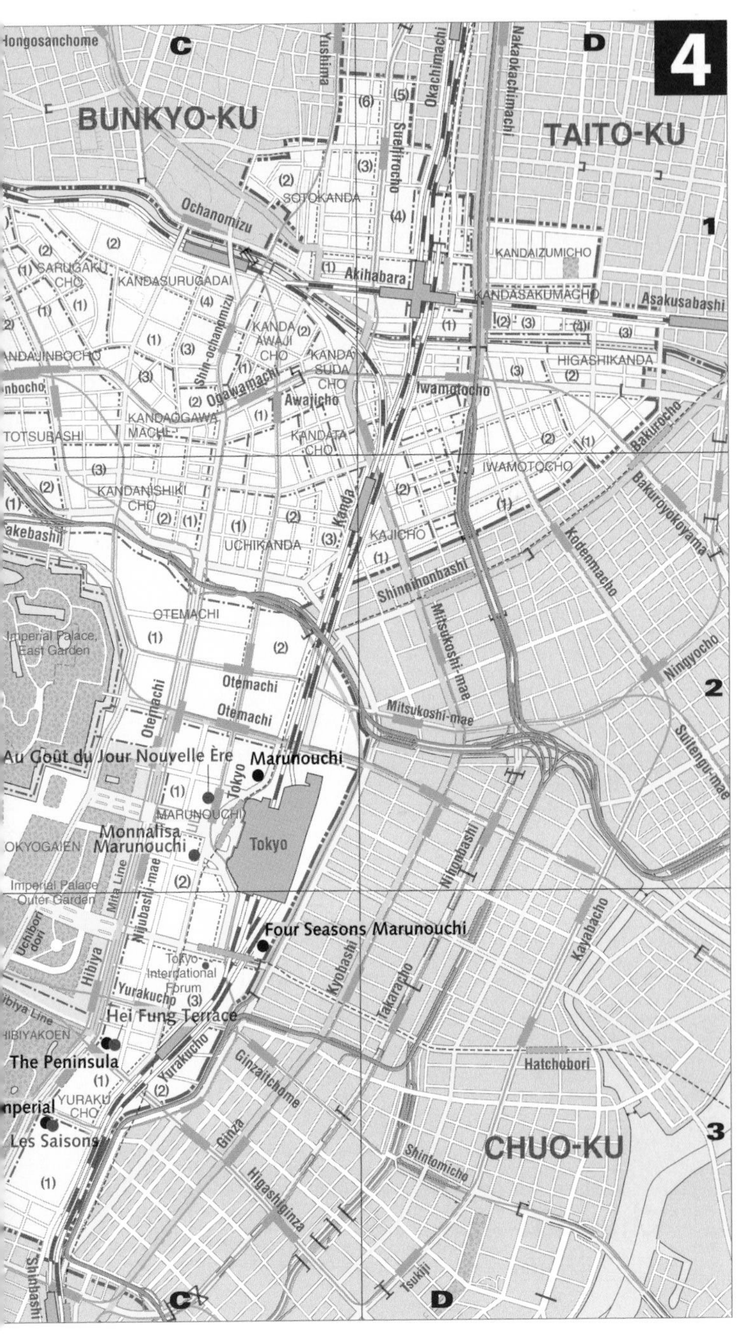
4
C
D
BUNKYO-KU
TAITO-KU
CHUO-KU
Hongosanchome
Yushima
Okachimachi
Nakaokachimachi
Suehirocho
SOTOKANDA
Ochanomizu
KANDAIZUMICHO
SARUGAKU CHO
KANDASURUGADAI
Akihabara
KANDASAKUMACHO
Asakusabashi
Shin-ochanomizu
KANDA AWAJI CHO
KANDA SUDA CHO
HIGASHIKANDA
KANDAJINBOCHO
Jinbocho
Ogawamachi
Awajicho
Iwamotocho
KANDAOGAWA MACHI
KANDATA CHO
Bakurocho
TOTSUBASHI
IWAMOTOCHO
Bakuroyokoyama
KANDANISHIKI CHO
Kanda
Takebashi
UCHIKANDA
KAJICHO
Kodenmacho
Shinnihonbashi
OTEMACHI
Mitsukoshi-mae
Imperial Palace, East Garden
Otemachi
Ningyocho
Otemachi
Otemachi
Mitsukoshi-mae
Suitengu-mae
Au Goût du Jour Nouvelle Ère
Marunouchi
Tokyo
MARUNOUCHI
Tokyo
Monnalisa Marunouchi
KOKYOGAIEN
Nihonbashi
Nijubashi-mae
Imperial Palace Outer Garden
Mita Line
Uchibori dori
Four Seasons Marunouchi
Kayabacho
Hibiya
Tokyo International Forum
Kyobashi
Takaracho
Yurakucho
Hibiya Line
Hei Fung Terrace
HIBIYAKOEN
The Peninsula
Yurakucho
Ginzaitchome
Hatchobori
YURAKU CHO
Imperial
Les Saisons
Ginza
Shintomicho
Higashiginza
Tsukiji
Shinbashi
1
2
3

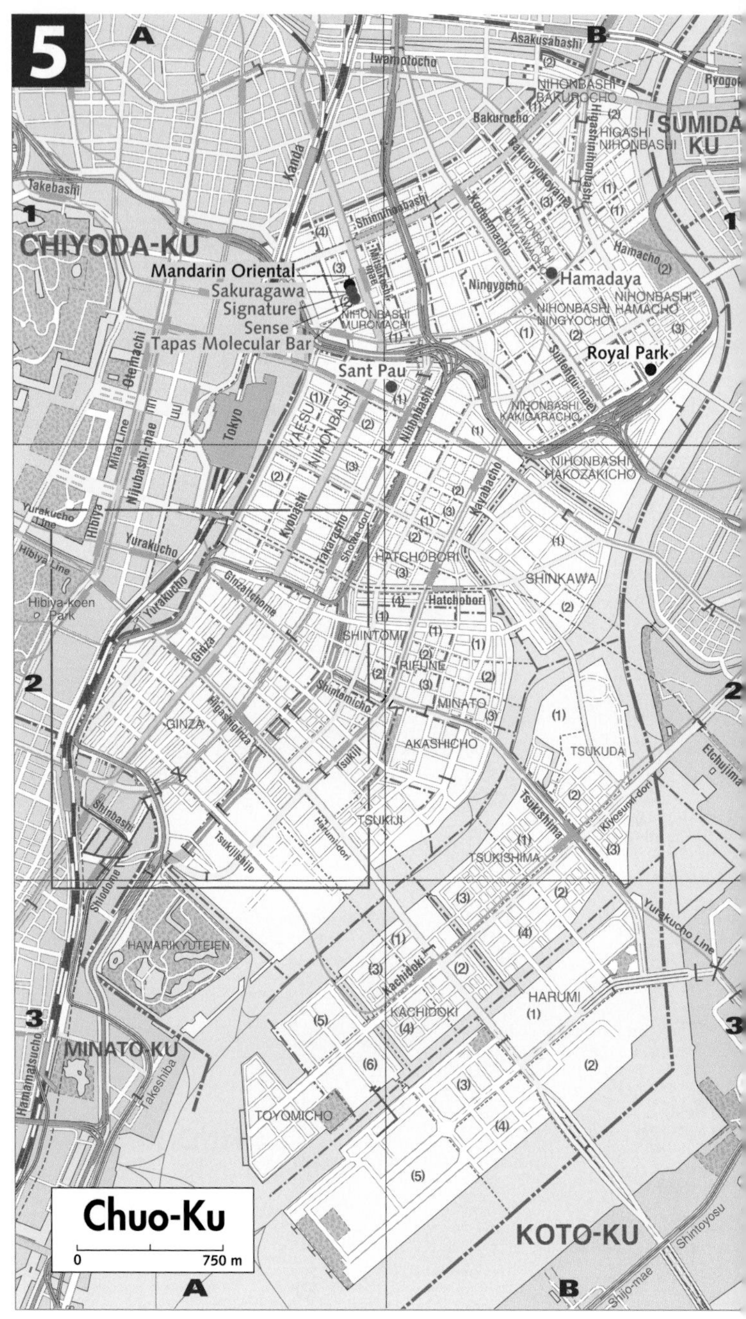
5
A
B
1
2
3
Chuo-Ku
0
750 m
CHIYODA-KU
SUMIDA KU
MINATO-KU
KOTO-KU
Mandarin Oriental
Sakuragawa
Signature
Sense
Tapas Molecular Bar
Sant Pau
Hamadaya
Royal Park
Asakusabashi
Iwamotocho
Bakurocho
Takebashi
Kanda
Otemachi
Tokyo
Mita Line
Nijubashi-mae
Hibiya
Yurakucho Line
Hibiya Line
Yurakucho
Hibiya-koen Park
Kyobashi
Takaracho
Ginza
Ginzaitchome
Higashiginza
Shinbashi
Shiodome
Tsukijishijo
Tsukiji
Shintomicho
Hatchobori
Kayabacho
Ningyocho
Nihonbashi
Mitsukoshi mae
Shinnihonbashi
Kodenmacho
Bakuroyokoyama
Higashinihonbashi
Hamacho
Suitengu-mae
Tsukishima
Kiyosumi-dori
Kachidoki
Harumi-dori
Showa-dori
Etchujima
Hamamatsucho
Takeshiba
Shijo-mae
Shintoyosu
Ryogoku
NIHONBASHI BAKUROCHO
HIGASHI NIHONBASHI
NIHONBASHI KOMAZAWACHO
NIHONBASHI HAMACHO
NIHONBASHI NINGYOCHO
NIHONBASHI MUROMACHI
NIHONBASHI KAKIGARACHO
NIHONBASHI HAKOZAKICHO
YAESU
NIHONBASHI
HATCHOBORI
SHINKAWA
SHINTOMI
IRIFUNE
MINATO
AKASHICHO
GINZA
TSUKIJI
TSUKUDA
TSUKISHIMA
HAMARIKYUTEIEN
HARUMI
KACHIDOKI
TOYOMICHO

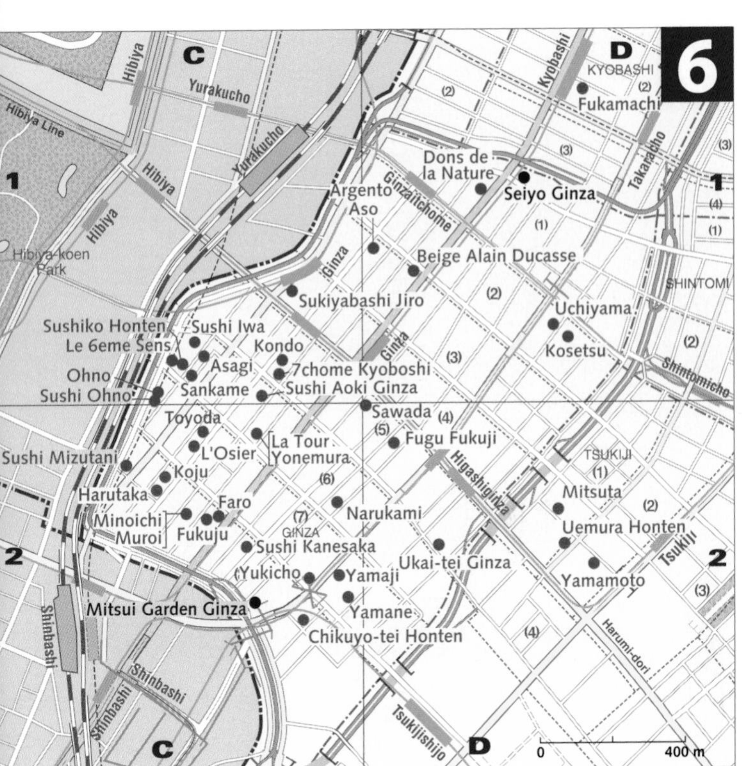
6
C
D
Yurakucho
Hibiya
Hibiya Line
Hibiya-koen Park
Kyobashi
KYOBASHI
Fukamachi
Takaracho
Dons de la Nature
Seiyo Ginza
Argento Aso
Ginzaitchome
Beige Alain Ducasse
Ginza
Sukiyabashi Jiro
SHINTOMI
Uchiyama
Kosetsu
Shintomicho
Sushiko Honten
Le 6eme Sens
Sushi Iwa
Kondo
Asagi
7chome Kyoboshi
Ohno
Sushi Ohno
Sankame
Sushi Aoki Ginza
Sawada
Toyoda
La Tour
Yonemura
Fugu Fukuji
L'Osier
Sushi Mizutani
Koju
Higashiginza
TSUKIJI
Harutaka
Faro
Mitsuta
Narukami
Minoichi
Muroi
Fukuju
GINZA
Uemura Honten
Sushi Kanesaka
Ukai-tei Ginza
Tsukiji
Yukicho
Yamaji
Yamamoto
Mitsui Garden Ginza
Yamane
Chikuyo-tei Honten
Harumi-dori
Shinbashi
Tsukijishijo
0
400 m

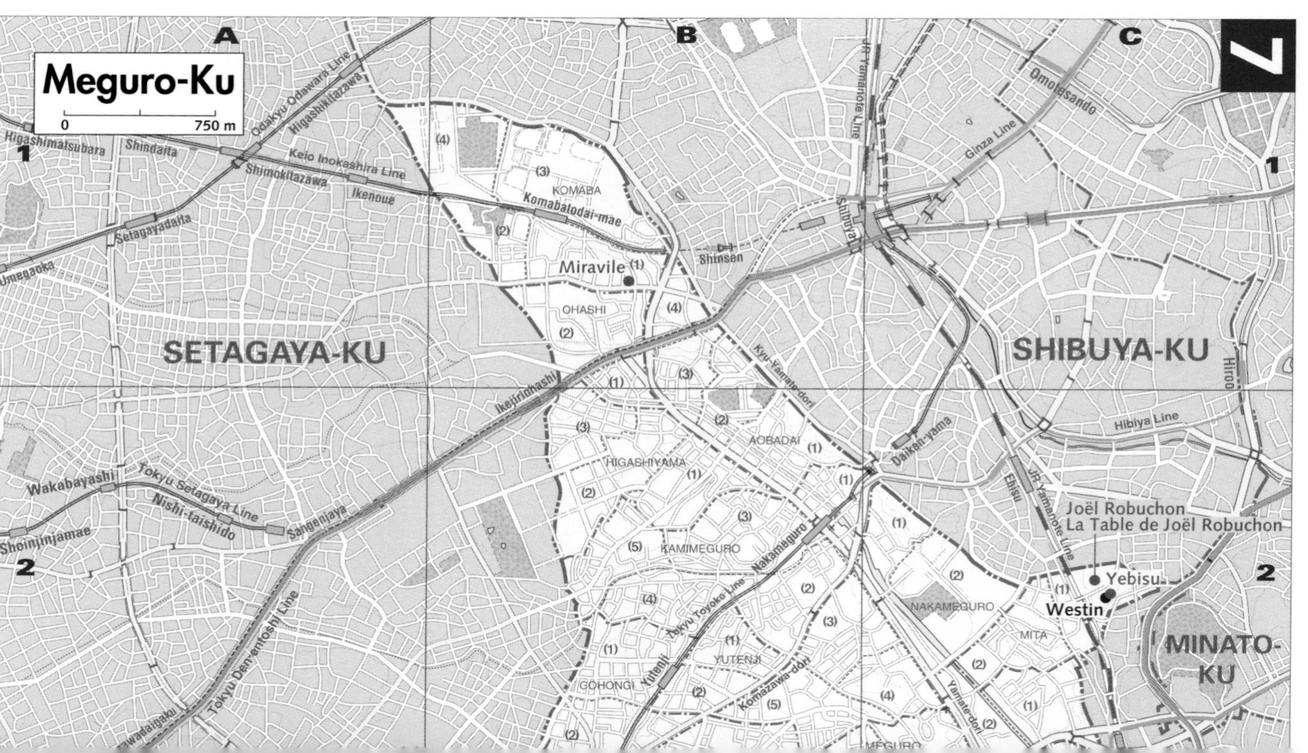
7
Meguro-Ku
0
750 m
A
B
C
1
2
SETAGAYA-KU
SHIBUYA-KU
MINATO-KU
Higashimatsubara
Shindaita
Odakyu Odawara Line
Higashikitazawa
Keio Inokashira Line
Shimokitazawa
Ikenoue
Setagayadaita
Umegaoka
KOMABA
Komabatodai-mae
Miravile
OHASHI
Shinsen
Shibuya
JR Yamanote Line
Omotesando
Ginza Line
Kyu-Yamate-dori
Ikejiriohashi
AOBADAI
HIGASHIYAMA
Daikan-yama
Ebisu
Hibiya Line
Hiroo
Wakabayashi
Tokyu Setagaya Line
Nishi-taishido
Sangenjaya
Shoinjinjamae
KAMIMEGURO
Nakameguro
Tokyu Toyoko Line
Tokyu Den-entoshi Line
NAKAMEGURO
Joël Robuchon
La Table de Joël Robuchon
Yebisu
Westin
MITA
YUTENJI
Yutenji
GOHONGI
Komazawa-dori
Yamate-dori

8
Meguro Gajoen
Meguro
Gotanda
Osakihirokoji
Togoshi
Togoshiginza
Tokyu Oimachi Line
Togoshikoen
Nakanobu
Asakusa Line
Ebaranakanobu
Tokyu Ikegami Line
Ebaramachi
Hatanodai
NISHI GOTANDA
Fudomae
Tokyu Meguro Line
Musashikoyama
SHINAGAWA-KU
KOYAMADAI
SHIMOMEGURO
Meguro-dori
NAKACHO
MEGURO HONCHO
Nishikoyama
HARAMACHI
Senzoku
SENZOKU
Nagahara
Kitasenzoku
OTA-KU
Senzokuike-koen Park
Senzokuike
CHUOCHO
Suzuki
TAKABAN
Gakugeidaigaku
HIMON-YA
MINAMI
OOKAYAMA
Ookayama
TAIRAMACHI
Toritsudaigaku
Kannana-dori
KAKINOKIZAKA
YAKUMO
NAKANE
MIDORIGAOKA
Midorigaoka
Tokyu Toyoko Line
Okusawa
HIGASHIGAOKA
Jiyu-dori
JIYUGAOKA
Jiyugaoka
Komazawa Olympic Park
Kuhonbutsu
Oyamadai
A
B
C
3
4

Minato-Ku
0
870 m
A
B
C
1
2
9
CHIYODA-KU
SHINJUKU-KU
SHIBUYA-KU
CHUO-KU
Tsujitome
Yoshihashi
Sushisho Saito
Totoya Uoshin
Les Créations de Narisawa
Tatsumura
Chemins
Kikumi
Ristorante Honda
Kikunoi
Kamiya Nogizaka
Raku-tei
Sushi Saito
Tomura
Umi
Tensei
Hinokizaka
Abe
Okura
The Ritz-Carlton
ANA Intercontinental
L'Embellir
Yotaro
Edition Koji Shimomura
Kikuchi
Pierre Gagnaire
Daigo
La Bombance
Taku
Kodama
Sushi Musashi
Maison d'Umemoto Shang-hai
Sushi Aoki Nishiazabu
Usukifugu Yamadaya
Yuta
Shin
Tofuya Ukai Shiba
Tateru Yoshino Shiba
Banrekiryukodo
Crescent
The Prince Park Tower
Waketokuyama
Hiramatsu
Sasada
Hirosaku
Aragawa
Ayumasa
Tateru Yoshino Shiodome
Conrad
Bice
Royal Park Shiodome Tower
China Blue
Gordon Ramsay
Hamarikyu Garden
0
250 m

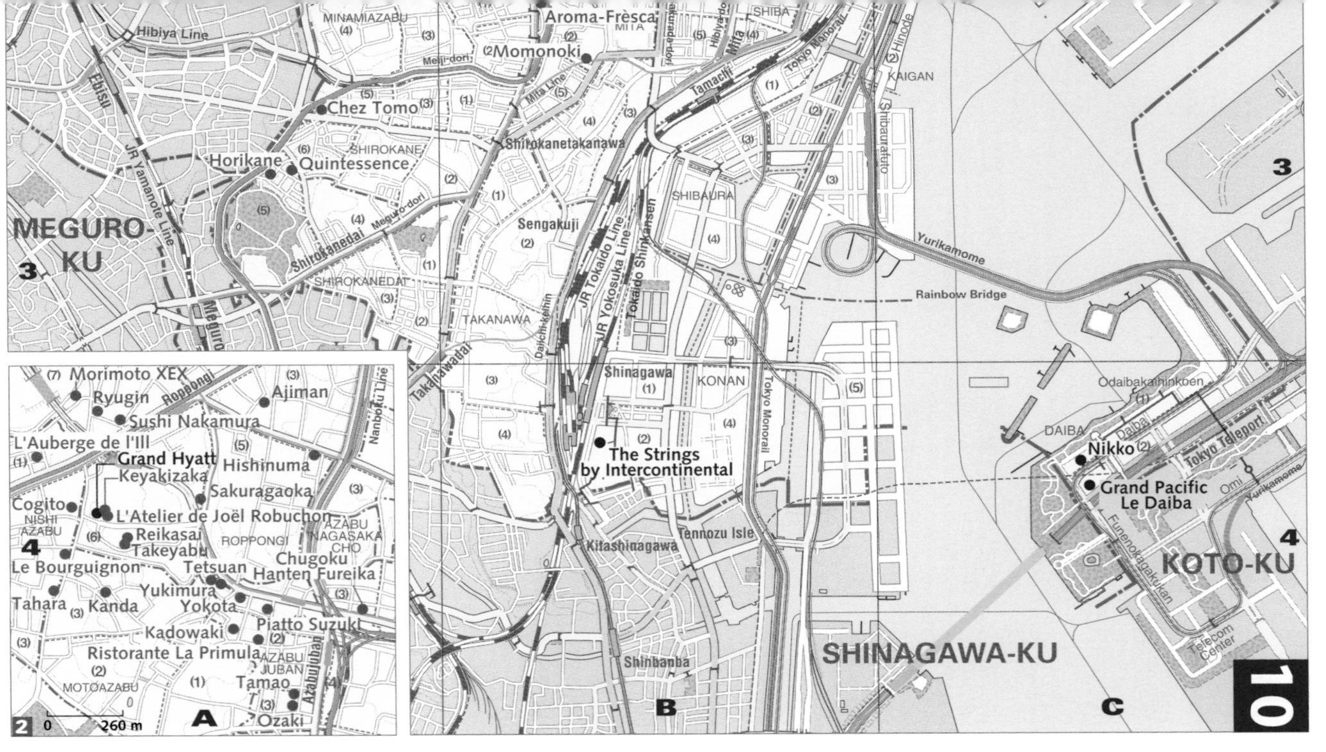

10
MEGURO-KU
KOTO-KU
SHINAGAWA-KU
Aroma-Frèsca
Momonoki
Chez Tomo
Horikane
Quintessence
Nikko
Grand Pacific Le Daiba
The Strings by Intercontinental
Hibiya Line
JR Yamanote Line
Mita Line
Nanboku Line
JR Tokaido Line
JR Yokosuka Line
Tokaido Shinkansen
Tokyo Monorail
Yurikamome
Rainbow Bridge
Ebisu
Meguro
Shirokanedai
Shirokanetakanawa
Sengakuji
Tamachi
Shinagawa
Kitashinagawa
Shinbanba
Tennozu Isle
Takanawadai
Shibaurafuto
Hinode
Odaibakaihinkoen
Daiba
Tokyo Teleport
Funenokagakukan
Telecom Center
Omi
MINAMIAZABU
MITA
SHIBA
KAIGAN
SHIROKANE
SHIROKANEDAI
SHIBAURA
TAKANAWA
KONAN
DAIBA
Meiji-dori
Meguro-dori
Sakurada-dori
Daiichi-keihin
Morimoto XEX
Ryugin
Sushi Nakamura
Ajiman
L'Auberge de l'Ill
Grand Hyatt
Keyakizaka
Hishinuma
Sakuragaoka
Cogito
L'Atelier de Joël Robuchon
Reikasai
Takeyabu
Le Bourguignon
Tetsuan
Chugoku Hanten Fureika
Yukimura
Yokota
Tahara
Kanda
Kadowaki
Piatto Suzuki
Ristorante La Primula
Tamao
Ozaki
Roppongi
Azabujuban
NISHI AZABU
ROPPONGI
AZABU NAGASAKA CHO
AZABU JUBAN
MOTOAZABU
0 260 m
A
B
C

11
A
B
MEGURO-KU
SHINAGAWA-KU
NAKAHARA-KU
SAIWAI-KU
KAWASAKI-KU
1
2
3
Tokyu Toyoko Line
Tokyu Oimachi Line
Tokyu Meguro Line
Tokyu Ikegami Line
Asakusa Line
JR Yamanote Line
Tokaido Shinkansen
JR Yokosuka Line
JR Tokaido Line
Keikyu Kamata
JR Nambu Line
Musashikoyama
Togoshiginza
Togoshi
Oyamadai
Jiyugaoka
Midorigaoka
Ookayama
Kitasenzoku
Hatanodai
Kuhonbutsu
Okusawa
Senzokuike
Nagahara
Ebaramachi
Den-enchofu
Tamagawa
Ikegami
Kamata
Hatsunezushi
Yaguchinowatashi
Shimomaruko
Musashinitta
Unoki
Chidoricho
Kawasaki
Hatchonawate
Minatocho
Suzukicho
Ota-Ku
0
1,4 km

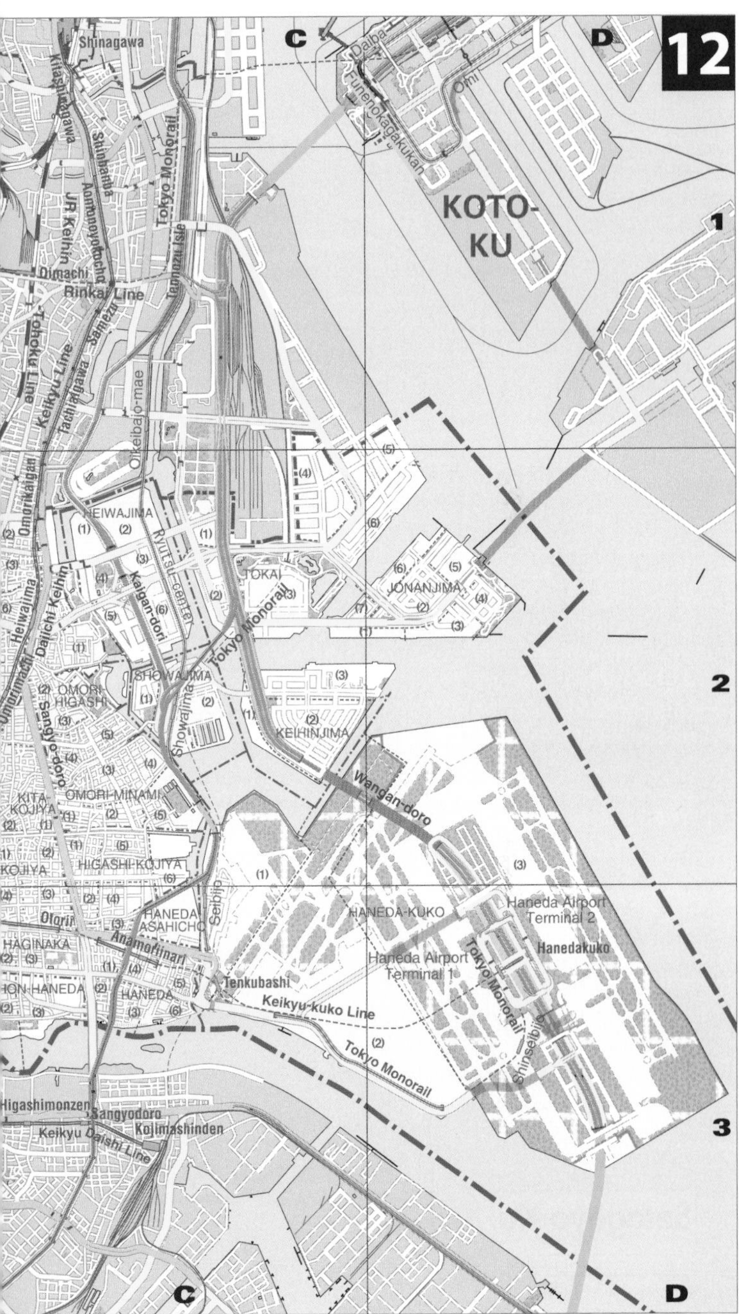
12
C
D
1
2
3
Shinagawa
Kitashinagawa
Shinbanba
Aomonoyokocho
JR Keihin
Tokyo Monorail
Tennozu Isle
Daiba
Fune-no-kagakukan
Omi
KOTO-KU
Oimachi
Rinkai Line
Tohoku Line
Keikyu Line
Samezu
Tachiaigawa
Oikeibajo-mae
Omorikaigan
HEIWAJIMA
Ryutsu-center
TOKAI
JONANJIMA
Kaigan-dori
Heiwajima
Daiichi Keihin
Umorimachi
Sangyo-doro
OMORI-HIGASHI
SHOWAJIMA
Showajima
KEIHINJIMA
Wangan-doro
KITA-KOJIYA
OMORI-MINAMI
KOJIYA
HIGASHI-KOJIYA
Seibijo
HANEDA-KUKO
Haneda Airport Terminal 2
Hanedakuko
Haneda Airport Terminal 1
Otorii
HANEDA ASAHICHO
HAGINAKA
Anamoriinari
Tenkubashi
HANEDA
Keikyu-kuko Line
Shinseibijo
Tokyo Monorail
Higashimonzen
Sangyodoro
Kojimashinden
Keikyu Daishi Line

13
A
B
1
2
3
Hamadayama
KITA-KARASUYAMA
Rokakoen
Hachiman-yama
Keio Line
MINAMI-KARASUYAMA
Chitosekarasuyama
Kamikitazawa
Sakurajosui
Kanpachi-dori
KAMI-KITAZAWA
KASUYA
KAMI-SOSHIGAYA
KYUDEN
HACHIMAN-YAMA
Sengawa
Tsutsujigaoka
SAKURAJOSUI
FUNABASHI
CHITOSEDAI
Chitosefunabashi
SOSHIGAYA
SEIJO
KOMAE-SHI
Soshigayaokura
Seijogakuen-mae
Kitami
Odakyu Odawara Line
KINUTA
Setagaya-dori
SAKURAGAOKA
OKURA
KITAMI
Komae
KINUTA-KOEN
KAMI-YOGA
Izumitamagawa
OKAMOTO
TAMAGAWADAI
Noborito
UNANE
KAMATA
SETA
Shukugawara
JR Nanbu Line
Futakotamagawa
TAMAGAWA
Kuji
Futakoshinchi
Tsudayama
Takatsu
Mizonokuchi
Musashimizonokuchi
Setagaya-Ku
0
1,2 km
TAKATSU-KU
Kajigaya
JR Nanbu Line

14
C
D
SHIBUYA-KU
MEGURO-KU
OTA-KU
Keio Line
Keio Inokashira Line
Odakyu Odawara Line
Chiyoda Line
Tokyu Setagaya Line
Tokyu Den-entoshi Line
Tokyu Toyoko Line
Tokyu Oimachi Line
Tokyu Meguro Line
Meiji-jingu Shrine
Yoyogi-koen Park
Yoyogikoen
Yoyogiuehara
Hatagaya
Hatsudai
Sangubashi
Sasazuka
Meidai-mae
Daitabashi
OHARA
KITAZAWA
HANEGI
Higashikitazawa
Shindaita
Shimokitazawa
MATSUBARA
Higashimatsubara
Matsubara
Shimotakaido
Eifukucho
KATSUTSUMI
Yamashita
Gotokuji
Umegaoka
Setagayadaita
Sushi Fukumoto
Ikenoue
Komabatodai-mae
Shinsen
DAIZAWA
DAITA
Kannana-dori
UMEGAOKA
GOTOKUJI
MISHUKU
Ikejiribashi
IKEJIRI
TAISHIDO
MIYASAKA
Miyanosaka
Wakabayashi
WAKABAYASHI
SAKURA
Setagaya
Nishitaishido
Sangenjaya
Kamimachi
Shoinjinja-mae
SANGENJAYA
Setagaya-dori
SETAGAYA
Nakameguro
KAMIUMA
Yutenji
SHIMOUMA
TSURUMAKI
Sakurashinmachi
Komazawadaigaku
Tamagawa-dori
NOZAWA
SAKURA SHINMACHI
KOMAZAWA
Gakugeidaigaku
Komazawa Olympic Park
KOMAZAWA-KOEN
SHINMACHI
YOGA
Komazawa-dori
FUKASAWA
Toritsudaigaku
Nishikoyama
NAKAMACHI
Kampachi-dori
Meguro-dori
Kaminoge
Todoroki
TODOROKI
Oyamadai
Senzoku
Jiyugaoka
Midorigaoka
Ookayama
Kitasenzoku
Okusawa
Kuhonbutsu
Kanpachi-dori
Senzokuike-koen Park
Nagahara
NOGE
Tamatsutsumi-dori
Jiyu-dori
OKUSAWA
OYAMADAI
TAMAGAWA-DEN-ENCHOFU
Den-enchofu
Senzokuike
HIGASHI-TAMAGAWA
Ishikawadai
TAMAZUTSUMI
Yukigayaotsuka
1
2
3

15
Shibuya-Ku
0
460 m
A
B
1
2
3
WADA
Nakanofujimicho
Nakanoshinbashi
Nishishinjukugochome
Shinjukuchuo-koen Park
SHINJUKU-KU
NAKANO-KU
SUGINAMI-KU
SETAGAYA-KU
MEGURO-KU
Honancho
Honan-dori
Yamate-dori
HONMACHI
Koshu-Kaido
Hatsudai
HATAGAYA
Hatagaya
HATSUDAI
Keio Line
SASAZUKA
Sasazuka
NISHIHARA
MOTOYOYOGI CHO
Odakyu Odawara Line
Yoyogihachiman
Yoyogiuehara
OYAMACHO
Daitabashi
UEHARA
TOMIGAYA
KAMIYAMA
Higashikitazawa
Shimokitazawa
Higashimatsubara
Shindaita
Ikenoue
Komabatodai-mae
Keio Inokashira Line
Setagayadaita
Umegaoka
Ikejiriohashi
Wakabayashi
Tokyu Setagaya Line
Sangenjaya

16
C
D
Shinjuku
Shinjukusanchome
Shinjukugyoen-mae
Yotsuyasanchome
Marunouchi Line
Century Southern Tower
Shinjuku Gyoen National Garden
YOYOGI
Minamishinjuku
Yoyogi
Sendagaya
Oedo Line
Shinanomachi
Kokuritsukyogijo
SENDAGAYA
Meiji-jingu
Meiji-jingu-gaien
Fukutoshin Line
YOYOGIKAMIZONO CHO
Higuchi
Hanzomon Line
Aoyamaitchome
Harajuku
Esaki
Gaien-mae
Chiyoda Line
Meijijingu-mae
Sekiho-tei
Shigeyoshi
Ukai-tei Omotesando
Inokashira-dori
JINNAN
JR Yamanote Line
Meiji-dori
Omotesando
Nogizaka
2
JINGUMAE
Kogetsu
UDAGAWA CHO
Chez Matsuo
SHIBUYA
Ginza Line
MINATO-KU
DOGENZAKA
Shibuya
Cerulean Tower Tokyu
Coucagno
SAKURAGAOKA CHO
Les Enfants Gâtes
HIGASHI
NANPEIDAI CHO
UGUISUDANI CHO
Hiroo
HACHIYAMA CHO
SARUGAKU CHO
HIROO
Maison Paul Bocuse
Le Jeu de l'Assiette
Okina
Hibiya Line
Ristorante Aso
Daikan-yama
Monnalisa Ebisu
3
EBISUNISHI
EBISU
Nasubi-tei
Ebisu
EBISUMINAMI
Sugawara
Tokyu Toyoko Line
Nakameguro
JR Yamanote Line

17
A
B
1
2
3
MEGURO-KU
MINATO-KU
OTA-KU
Shinagawa-Ku
0
750 m
Meguro
Gotanda
Osaki
Fudomae
Musashikoyama
Nishikoyama
Senzoku
Kitasenzoku
Hatanodai
Ebaramachi
Nagahara
Nakanobu
Ebara nakanobu
Togoshiginza
Togoshi
Togoshikoen
Shimoshinmei
Oimachi
Nishioi
Omori
Magome
Shirokanedai
Takanawadai
KAMIOSAKI
HIGASHI GOTANDA
NISHI GOTANDA
KOYAMADAI
OSAKI
NISHI SHINAGAWA
KOYAMA
EBARA
HIRATSUKA
NAKANOBU
NISHI NAKANOBU
HIGASHI NAKANOBU
TOGOSHI
HATANODAI
YUTAKACHO
FUTABA
NISHIOI
OI
Ohara's
Makimura
Tokyu Meguro Line
Tokyu Ikegami Line
Tokyu Oimachi Line
JR Yamanote Line
Asakusa Line
Rinkai Line
JR Tokaido Line
Tokaido Shinkansen
JR Yokosuka Line
Sakurada-dori
Yamate dori
Osakihirokoji
Nakahara Kaido
Daini-keihin
Sangen-dori

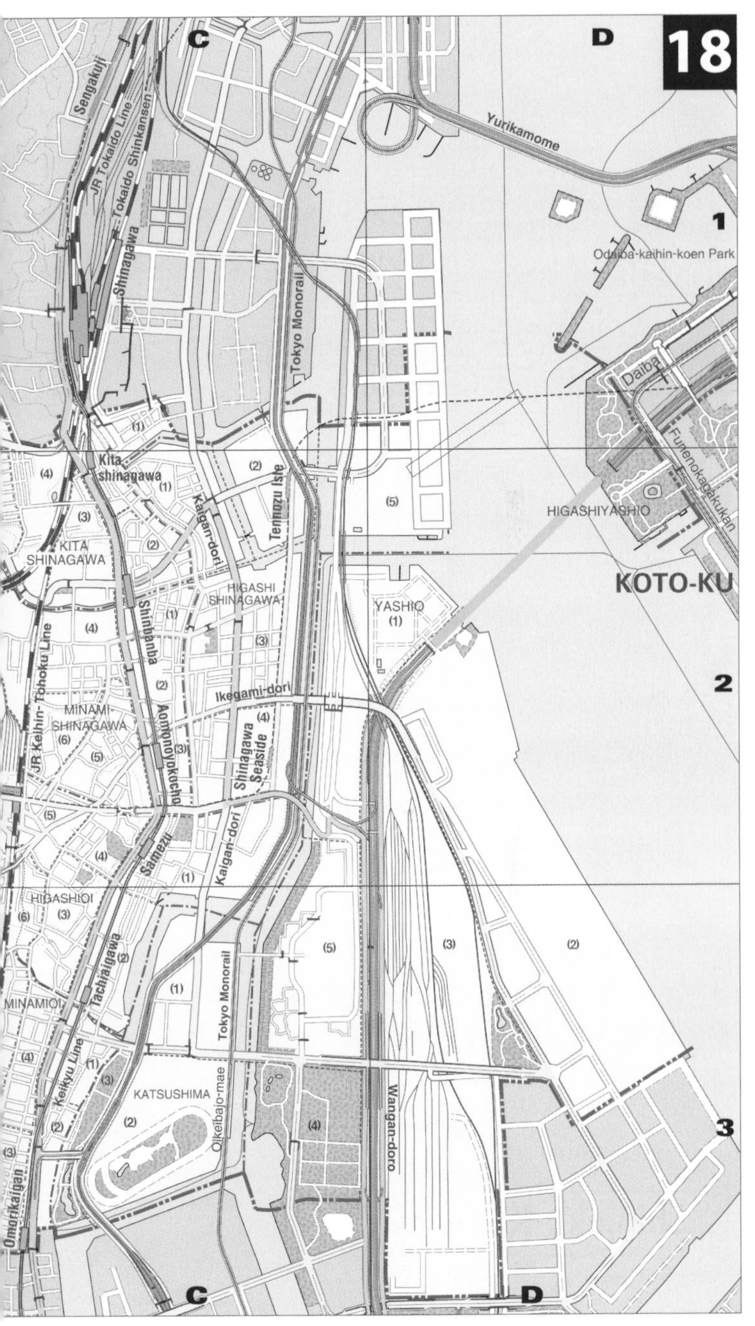
18
C
D
Sengakuji
JR Tokaido Line
Tokaido Shinkansen
Shinagawa
Yurikamome
1
Odaiba-kaihin-koen Park
Tokyo Monorail
Daiba
Funenokagakukan
HIGASHIYASHIO
Kita shinagawa
KITA SHINAGAWA
Kaigan-dori
Tennozu Isle
HIGASHI SHINAGAWA
Shinbanba
YASHIO
KOTO-KU
JR Keihin-Tohoku Line
MINAMI SHINAGAWA
Ikegami-dori
Aomonoyokocho
Shinagawa Seaside
2
Samezu
Kaigan-dori
HIGASHIOI
Tachiaigawa
Tokyo Monorail
MINAMIOI
Keikyu Line
KATSUSHIMA
Oikeibajo-mae
Wangan-doro
3
Omorikaigan
C
D

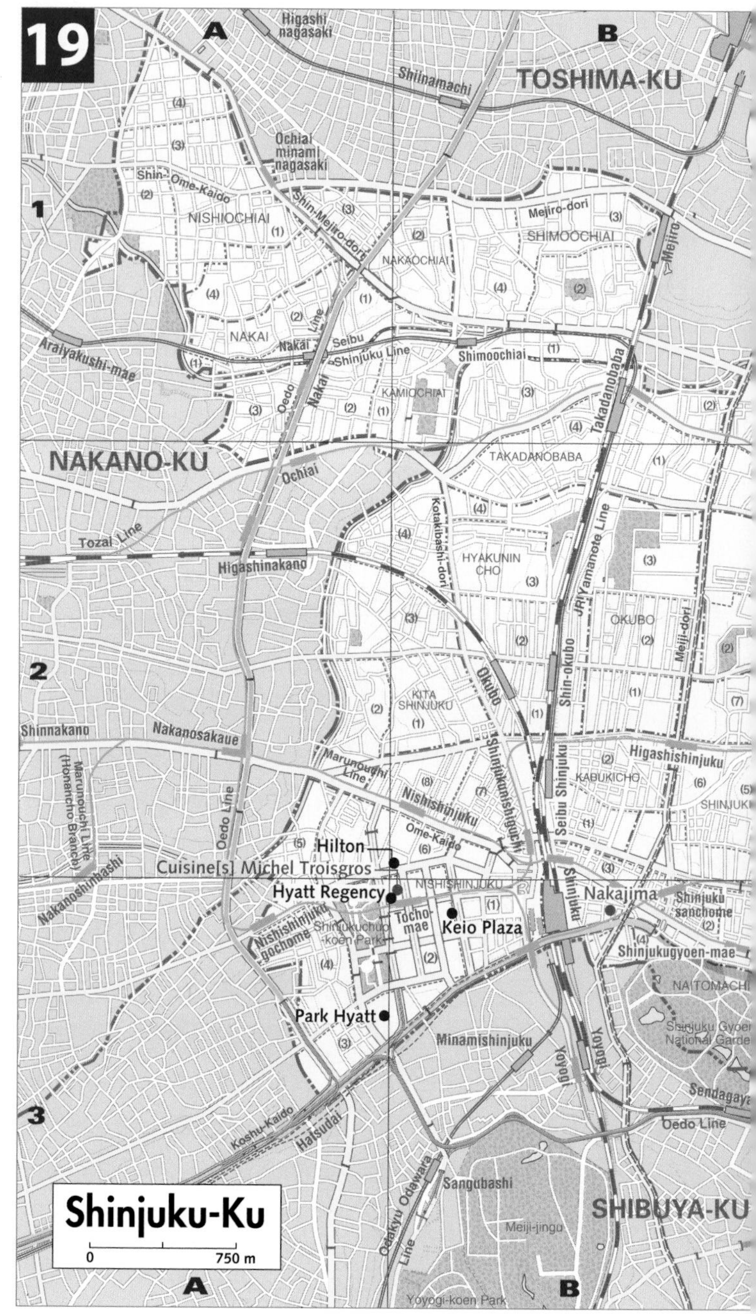
19
Shinjuku-Ku
0
750 m
A
B
1
2
3
TOSHIMA-KU
NAKANO-KU
SHIBUYA-KU
Higashi nagasaki
Shiinamachi
Ochiai minami nagasaki
Shin-Ome-Kaido
Shin-Mejiro-dori
Mejiro-dori
Mejiro
NISHIOCHIAI
NAKAOCHIAI
SHIMOOCHIAI
NAKAI
Nakai
Seibu Shinjuku Line
Shimoochiai
Araiyakushi-mae
KAMIOCHIAI
Oedo
Nakai Line
Takadanobaba
TAKADANOBABA
Ochiai
Tozai Line
Higashinakano
Kotakibashi-dori
HYAKUNIN CHO
JR Yamanote Line
OKUBO
Meiji-dori
Shin-okubo
Okubo
KITA SHINJUKU
Shinnakano
Nakanosakaue
Marunouchi Line (Honancho Branch)
Marunouchi Line
Nishishinjuku
Shinjukunishiguchi
Seibu Shinjuku
Higashishinjuku
KABUKICHO
Oedo Line
Ome-Kaido
Hilton
Cuisine[s] Michel Troisgros
Hyatt Regency
NISHISHINJUKU
Nakanoshinbashi
Nishishinjuku gochome
Shinjukuchuo-koen Park
Tocho-mae
Keio Plaza
Shinjuku
Nakajima
Shinjuku sanchome
Shinjukugyoen-mae
NAITOMACHI
Park Hyatt
Minamishinjuku
Yoyogi
Shinjuku Gyoen National Garden
Sendagaya
Oedo Line
Koshu-Kaido
Hatsudai
Odakyu Odawara Line
Sangubashi
Meiji-jingu
Yoyogi-koen Park

20
C
D
AKAGISHITA MACHI
AKAGIMOTO MACHI
Kagurazaka
SHIROGANE CHO
TSUKUDO HACHIMANCHO
YARAICHO
SHIMOBIYABI CHO
TSUKUDO CHO
Uotoku
AGEBA CHO
YOKODERA CHO
KAGURAZAKA
Yamasaki
Ichimonji
IWATOCHO
Iidabashi
Ishikawa
FUKURO MACHI
L'Alliance
TANSU MACHI
Ushigome kagurazaka
Komuro
The Agnes
KITAMACHI
WAKAMIYACHO
NAKACHO
MINAMICHO
ICHIGAYA FUNAGAWARA MACHI
HARAIKATA MACHI
0 145 m
Mukohara
Higashiikebukuro
Zoshigaya
Gokokuji
Toden Arakawa Line
Kishibojinmae
Gakushuinshita
Omokagebashi
Waseda
NISHIWASEDA
Waseda-dori
WASEDA TSURUMAKI CHO
YAMABUKI CHO
Edogawabashi
NISHIGOKEN CHO
HIGASHI GOKEN CHO
SHIN OGAWAMACHI
Korakuen
Koishikawa-korakuen Garden
ENOKICHO
TOYAMA
KIKUICHO
Tozai Line
YARAICHO
BENTEN CHO
MINAMI ENOKICHO
Suidobashi
HARAMACHI
WAKAMATSUCHO
Wakamatsu kawada
Ushigome yanagicho
Le Mange-Tout
Ogasawara Hakushaku-tei
Kudanshita
YOCHOMACHI
KAWADACHO
ICHIGAYA KAGACHO
ICHIGAYA NAKANOCHO
ICHIGAYA HONMURACHO
Akebonobashi
TOMIHISACHO
Yasukuni-dori
Yoneyama
SAKAMACHI
Ichigaya
AIZUMICHO
ARAKICHO
SAN-EICHO
HONSHIO CHO
Gaien-nishi-dori
Yotsuyasanchome
Marunouchi Line
Yotsuya
L'Anneau d'Or
SUGACHO
YOTSUYA
Kojimachi
Hanzomon
CHIYODA-KU
DAIKYOCHO
WAKABA
SHINANO MACHI
Sotobori-dori
Shinanomachi
MINAMI MOTOMACHI
Kokuritsukyogijo
Gaien-higashi-dori
Yurakucho Line
Nagatacho
Sakuradamon
KASUMIGAOKA MACHI
Akasaka mitsuke
Kokkai gijido-mae
Kasumigaseki
MINATO-KU
Marunouchi Line
Aoyamaitchome
Hanzomon Line
Tameikesanno

21
A
B
NERIMA-KU
MUSASHINO-SHI
MITAKA-SHI
SETAGAYA-KU
Musashiseki
Kamishakujii
Seibu Shinjuku Line
Kamiigusa
Iogi
IGUSA
Shimoigusa
KAMIIGUSA
SHIMOIGUSA
Kanpachi-dori
ZENPUKUJI
IMAGAWA
Ome-Kaido
SHIMIZU
MOMOI
HON-AMANUMA
Zenpukuji-koen Park
NISHIOGIKITA
KAMIOGI
AMANUMA
Yotsuha
Kichijoji
Nishiogikubo
Ogikubo
NISHIOGIMINAMI
SHOAN
MINAMIOGIKUBO
Inokashirakoen
Itsukaichi-Kaido
Inokashira-dori
OGIKUBO
Mitakadai
Keio Inokashira Line
MIYAMAE
Kugayama
Hitomi-Kaido
Fujimigaoka
KUGAYAMA
Takaido
TAKAIDONISHI
TAKAIDOHIGASHI
KAMITAKAIDO
Keio Line
Rokakoen
Hachiman-yama
Kamikitazawa
Chitosekarasuyama
Suginami-Ku
0
875 m
1
2
3

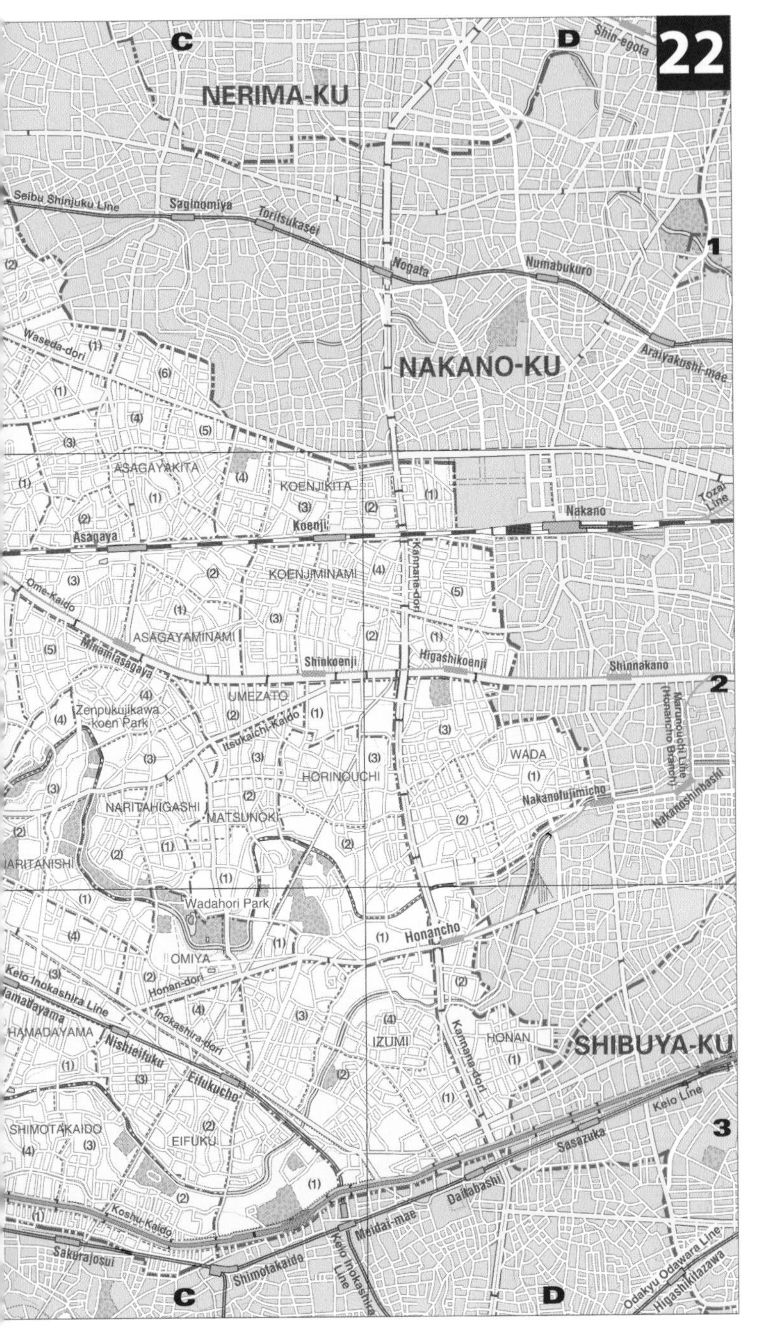
22
C
D
NERIMA-KU
NAKANO-KU
SHIBUYA-KU
Seibu Shinjuku Line
Saginomiya
Toritsukasei
Nogata
Numabukuro
Araiyakushi-mae
Shin-egota
Waseda-dori
ASAGAYAKITA
KOENJIKITA
Asagaya
Koenji
Nakano
Tozai Line
KOENJIMINAMI
Kannana-dori
Ome-Kaido
ASAGAYAMINAMI
Minamiasagaya
Shinkoenji
Higashikoenji
Shinnakano
UMEZATO
Zenpukujikawa
-koen Park
Itsukaichi-Kaido
Marunouchi Line
(Honancho Branch)
HORINOUCHI
WADA
Nakanofujimicho
Nakanoshinbashi
NARITAHIGASHI
MATSUNOKI
NARITANISHI
Wadahori Park
Honancho
OMIYA
Keio Inokashira Line
Hamadayama
Honan-dori
Inokashira-dori
HAMADAYAMA
Nishieifuku
Eifukucho
IZUMI
HONAN
Kannana-dori
Keio Line
SHIMOTAKAIDO
EIFUKU
Sasazuka
Daitabashi
Koshu-Kaido
Meidai-mae
Keio Inokashira Line
Sakurajosui
Shimotakaido
Odakyu Odawara Line
Higashikitazawa
1
2
3

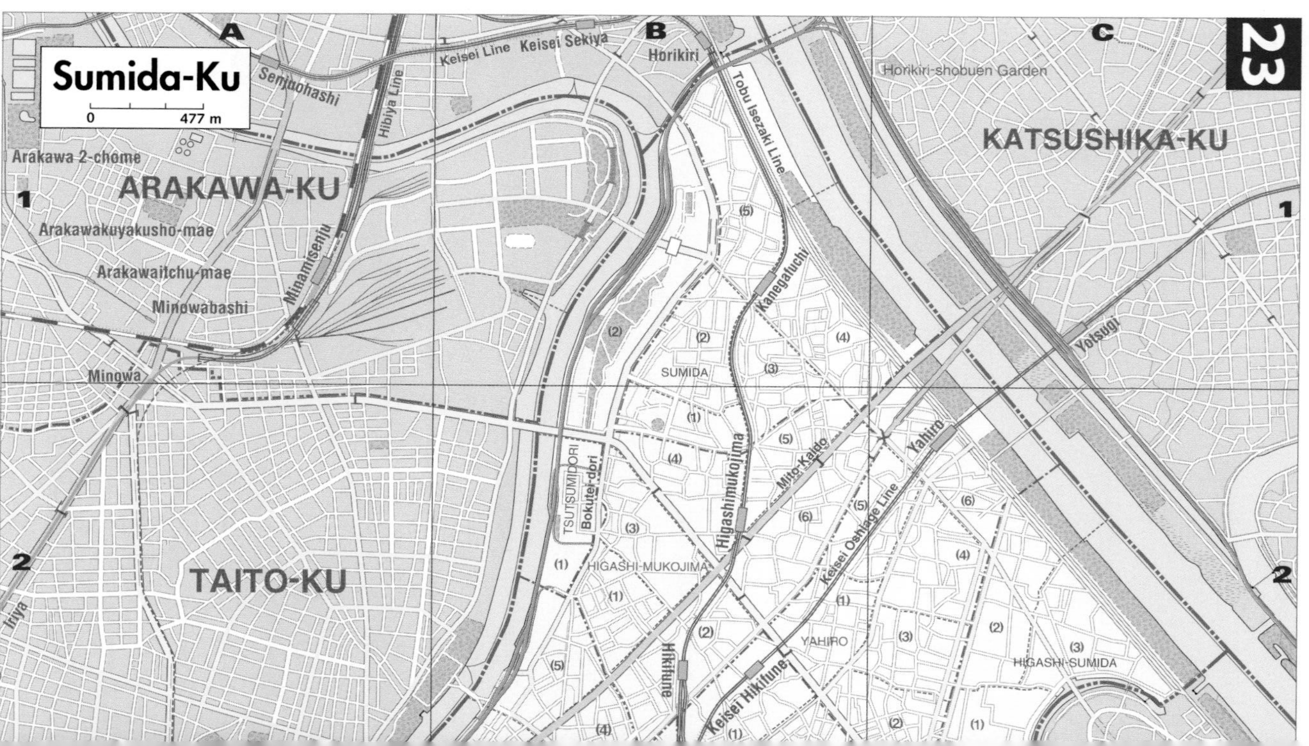

23
Sumida-Ku
0
477 m
A
B
C
1
2
Keisei Line
Keisei Sekiya
Horikiri
Horikiri-shobuen Garden
KATSUSHIKA-KU
Senjuohashi
Hibiya Line
Tobu Isezaki Line
Arakawa 2-chome
ARAKAWA-KU
Arakawakuyakusho-mae
Arakawaitchu-mae
Minowabashi
Minamisenju
Kanegafuchi
Yotsugi
SUMIDA
Minowa
Yahiro
Mito-kaido
TSUTSUMIDORI
Bokutei-dori
Higashimukojima
Keisei Oshiage Line
HIGASHI-MUKOJIMA
TAITO-KU
YAHIRO
HIGASHI-SUMIDA
Iriya
Hikifune
Keisei Hikifune

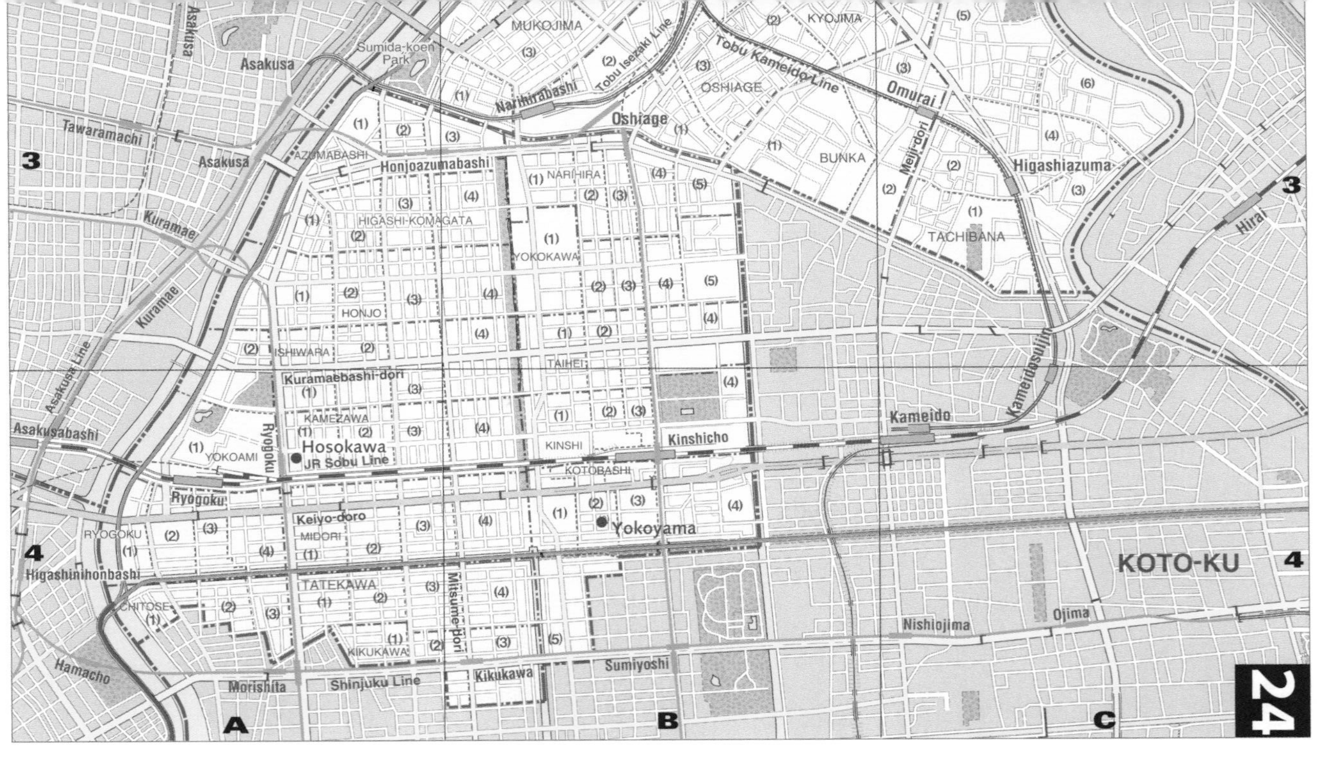
Asakusa
Sumida-koen Park
MUKOJIMA
KYOJIMA
Tobu Isezaki Line
Tobu Kameido Line
OSHIAGE
Omurai
Narihirabashi
Oshiage
Tawaramachi
3
Asakusa
AZUMABASHI
Honjoazumabashi
BUNKA
Meiji-dori
Higashiazuma
NARIHIRA
TACHIBANA
Hirai
Kuramae
HIGASHI-KOMAGATA
YOKOKAWA
HONJO
ISHIWARA
TAIHEI
Kuramaebashi-dori
KAMEZAWA
Kameidosuijin
Kameido
Asakusa Line
Asakusabashi
YOKOAMI
Ryogoku
Hosokawa
JR Sobu Line
KINSHI
Kinshicho
KOTOBASHI
Keiyo-doro
MIDORI
Yokoyama
RYOGOKU
4
Higashinihonbashi
TATEKAWA
Mitsume-dori
KOTO-KU
CHITOSE
KIKUKAWA
Nishiojima
Ojima
Hamacho
Sumiyoshi
Kikukawa
Morishita
Shinjuku Line
A
B
C
24

25
A
B
ARAKAWA-KU
BUNKYO-KU
CHIYODA-KU
Taito-Ku
0
502 m
1
2
3
Nishinippori
Nippori
Sendagi
Uguisudani
Nezu
Todai-mae
Iriya
Ueno
Keisei Ueno
Inaricho
Uenohirokoji
Uenookachimachi
Okachimachi
Nakaokachimachi
Shin-okachimachi
Oedo Line
Hongosanchome
Yushima
Suehirocho
Ochanomizu
Akihabara
Asakusabash
Iwamotocho
Awajicho
YANAKA
NEGISHI
SHITAYA
UENO-SAKURAGI
上野公園
UENO-KOEN
Ueno-onshi-koen Park
KITA-UENO
IKENOHATA
HIGASHI-UENO
MOTO-ASAKUS
UENO
TAITO
KOJIMA
MISU
TORIGOE
ASAKUSABASH
神田岩本町
神田佐久間河岸

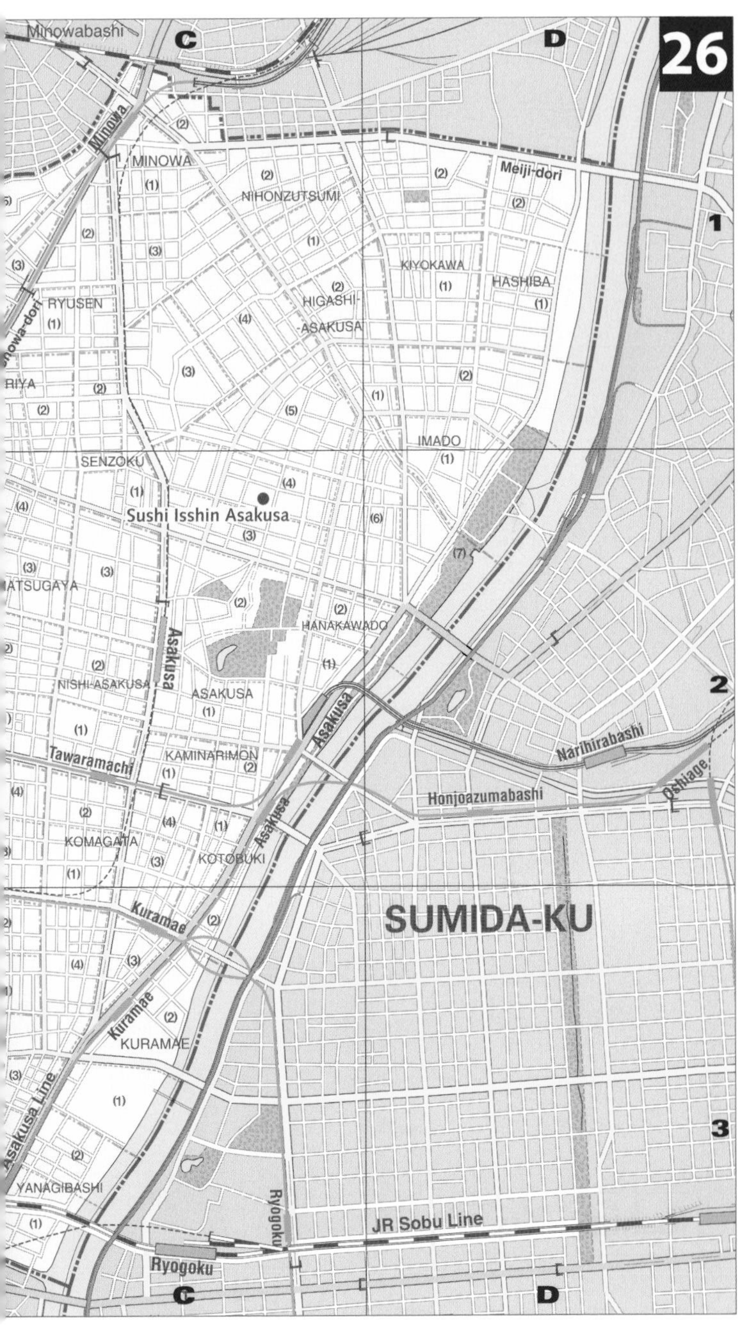
26
C
D
1
2
3
Minowabashi
Minowa
MINOWA
NIHONZUTSUMI
Meiji-dori
KIYOKAWA
HASHIBA
RYUSEN
HIGASHI-
-ASAKUSA
Minowa-dori
IRIYA
IMADO
SENZOKU
Sushi Isshin Asakusa
MATSUGAYA
HANAKAWADO
Asakusa
NISHI-ASAKUSA
ASAKUSA
Narihirabashi
Tawaramachi
KAMINARIMON
Honjoazumabashi
Oshiage
KOMAGATA
KOTOBUKI
SUMIDA-KU
Kuramae
KURAMAE
Asakusa Line
YANAGIBASHI
Ryogoku
JR Sobu Line

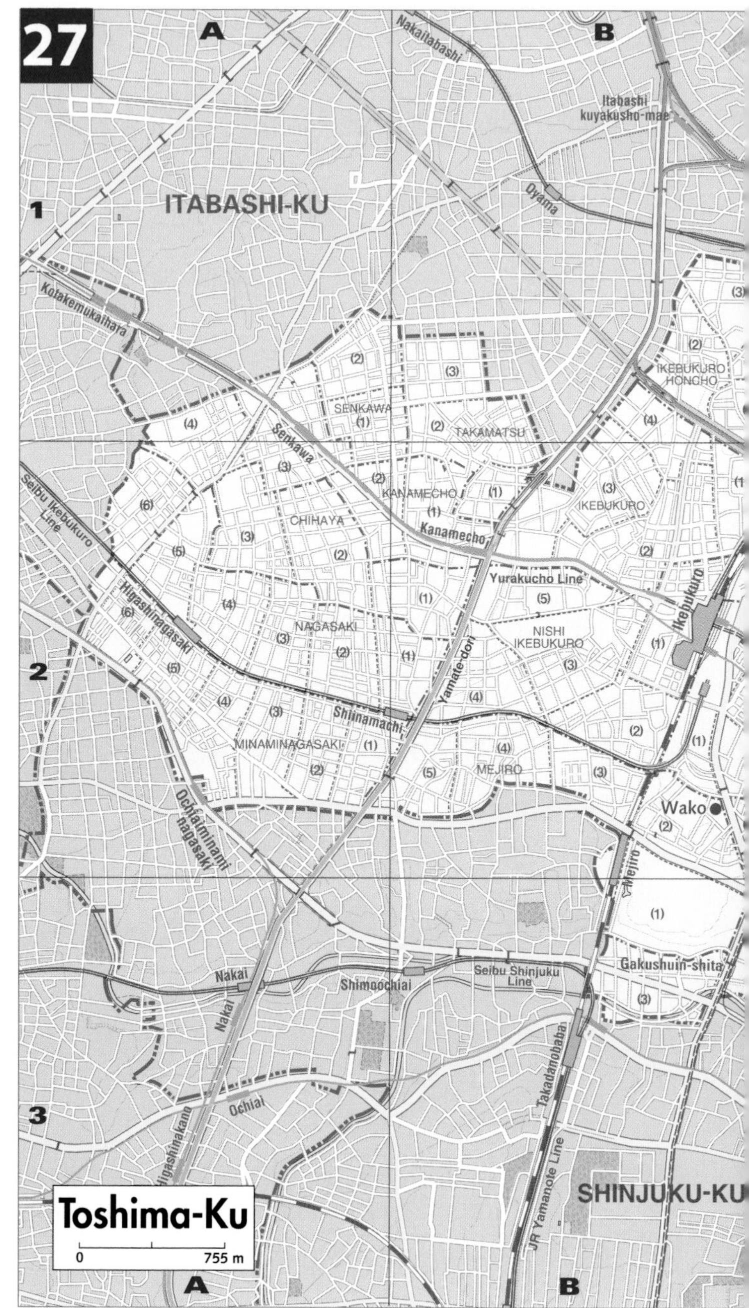
27
A
B
1
2
3
ITABASHI-KU
Nakaitabashi
Itabashi kuyakusho-mae
Oyama
Kotakemukaihara
SENKAWA
TAKAMATSU
Senkawa
KANAMECHO
Kanamecho
CHIHAYA
IKEBUKURO HONCHO
IKEBUKURO
Seibu Ikebukuro Line
Yurakucho Line
Ikebukuro
Higashinagasaki
NAGASAKI
NISHI IKEBUKURO
Yamate-dori
Shiinamachi
MINAMINAGASAKI
MEJIRO
Wako
Ochiaiminami nagasaki
Mejiro
Gakushuin-shita
Nakai
Shimoochiai
Seibu Shinjuku Line
Takadanobaba
Ochiai
Higashinakano
JR Yamanote Line
SHINJUKU-KU
Toshima-Ku
0
755 m

28
C
D
KITA-KU
BUNKYO-KU
Ojiekimae
Oji
Sakaecho
Kajiwara
Toden Arakawa Line
JR Takasaki Line
Asukayama
Asukayama-koen Park
Kaminakazato
Tohoku Shinkansen
JR Keihin-Tohoku Line
Nishigahara
Toden Arakawa Line
Takinogawaitchome
Nishigaharayonchome
JR Saikyo Line
Shin-itabashi
Itabashi
Shimoitabashi
Mita Line
Nishisugamo
Shin-koshinzuka
Koshinzuka
NISHISUGAMO
Hakusan-dori
Namboku Line
JR Yamanote Line
Komagome
KOMAGOME
Tobu Tojo Line
Kitaikebukuro
KAMIIKEBUKURO
Sugamoshinden
JR Yamanote Line
SUGAMO
Sugamo
Sugamo
Rikugi-en
KITAOTSUKA
Otsuka
Otsukaekimae
HIGASHIIKEBUKURO
Mukohara
Higashi-ikebukuro-yonchome
MINAMIOTSUKA
Shin-otsuka
Sengoku
MINAMI-IKEBUKURO
Zoshigaya
Higashiikebukuro
Toden Arakawa Line
Gokokuji
Koishikawa Botanical Garden
Hakusan
Kishibojinmae
ZOSHIGAYA
Gokokuji
Myogadani
TAKADA
Omokagebashi
Waseda
Marunouchi Line
Edogawabashi
Korakuen
Waseda
Kagurazaka
Tozai Line
1
2
3
C
D

# PICTURE COPYRIGHT

Abe, 52 - Aimée Vibert, 54 - Michelin, 56 - Michelin, Aragawa, 58 - Argento Aso, Michelin, 60 - Michelin, 62 - Michelin, 64 - Michelin, 66 - Michelin, 68 - Michelin, Banrekiryukodo, 70 - Michelin, 72 - Bice, 74 - Michelin, 76 - Chez Matsuo, Michelin, 78 - Michelin, 80 - Michelin, 82 - China Blue, Conrad, 84 - Chugoku Hanten Fureika, 86 - Michelin, 88 - Coucagno, Cerulean Tower Tokyu, 90 - Michelin, 92 - Cuisine[s] Michel Troisgros, Hyatt Regency, 94 - Daigo, 96 - Michelin, Dons de la Nature, 98 - Édition Koji Shimomura, Michelin, 100 - Michelin, 102 - Faro, 104 - Michelin, 106 - Michelin, 108 - Michelin, Fukudaya, 110 - Michelin, 112 - Gordon Ramsay, Conrad, 114 - Hamadaya, 116 - Michelin, 118 - Michelin, 120 - Hei Fung Terrace, The Peninsula, 122 - Michelin, 124 - Hinokizaka, The Ritz-Carlton, 126 - Hiramatsu, 128 - Michelin, 130 - Michelin, 132 - Michelin, 134 - Michelin, 136 - Michelin, 138 - Michelin, 140 - Joël Robuchon, 142 - Michelin, 144 - Kamiya Nogizaka, 146 - Michelin, 148 - Keyakizaka, Grand Hyatt, 150 - Michelin, 152 - Michelin, 154 - Kikunoi, Michelin, 156 - Michelin, 158 - Michelin, 160 - Michelin, 162 - Michelin, 164 - Michelin, 166 - Michelin, 168 - Michelin, 170 - L'Alliance, 172 - Michelin, 174 - La Table de Joël Robuchon, 176 - L'Atelier de Joël Robuchon, 178 - Michelin, 180 - La Tour d'Argent, New Otani, 182 - L'Auberge de l'Ill, 184 - Michelin, 186 - Michelin, 188 - Michelin, 190 - Michelin, 192 - Les Créations de Narisawa, 194 - Les Enfants Gâtés, Michelin, 196 - Le 6eme Sens, 198 - Les Saisons, Imperial, 200 - L'Osier, 202 - Michelin, 204 - Maison Paul Bocuse, 206 - Michelin, 208 - Michelin, 210 - Michelin, 212 - Michelin, 214 - Michelin, 216 - Monnalisa Ebisu, Michelin, 218 - Monnalisa Marunouchi, 220 - Morimoto XEX, 222 - Michelin, 224 - Nadaman Honten Sazanka-so, Michelin, 226 - Michelin, Nakajima, 228 - Michelin, 230 - Michelin, Nasubi-tei, 232 - Ogasawara Hakushaku-tei, 234 - Michelin, 236 - Michelin, 238 - Michelin, 240 - Michelin, 242 - Michelin, 244 - Pierre Gagnaire, Michelin, 246 - Michelin, 248 - Michelin, 250 - Reikasai, 252 - Ristorante Aso, 254 - Michelin, 256 - Michelin, 258 - Michelin, 260 -

Sakuragaoka, Michelin, 262 - Michelin, 264 - Michelin, 266 - Sant Pau, 268 - Michelin, 270 - Michelin, 272 - Michelin, 274 - Sense, Mandarin Oriental, 276 - Michelin, 278 - Michelin, 280 - Michelin, 282 - Signature, Mandarin Oriental, 284 - Michelin, 286 - Michelin, 288 - Michelin, 290 - Michelin, 292 - Michelin, 294 - Michelin, 296 - Michelin, 298 - Michelin, 300 - Michelin, 302 - Michelin, 304 - Michelin, 306 - Michelin, 308 - Michelin, 310 - Michelin, 312 - Michelin, 314 - Michelin, 316 - Michelin, 318 - Michelin, 320 - Michelin, 322 - Tamao, 324 - Tapas Molecular Bar, Mandarin Oriental, 326 - Tateru Yoshino Shiba, Michelin, 328 - Tateru Yoshino Shiodome, 330 - Michelin, 332 - Tensei, 334 - Michelin, 336 - Tofuya Ukai Shiba, 338 - Michelin, 340 - Michelin, 342 - Michelin, 344 - Michelin, 346 - Michelin, 348 - Michelin, 350 - Ukai-tei Ginza, 352 - Ukai-tei Omotesando, 354 - Michelin, 356 - Michelin, 358 - Michelin, 360 - Waketokuyama, 362 - Michelin, 364 - Michelin, 366 - Yamamoto, 368 - Yamane, Michelin, 370 - Michelin, 372 - Michelin, 374 - Yebisu, Westin, 376 - Michelin, 378 - Michelin, 380 - Michelin, 382 - Michelin, 384 - Michelin, 386 - Yotaro, Michelin, 388 - Michelin, 390 - Yukicho, 392 - Michelin, 394 - Michelin, 396 ANA Intercontinental, 402 - Century Southern Tower, 404 - Cerulean Tower Tokyu, 406 - Conrad, 408 - Four Seasons Chinzan-so, 410 - Four Seasons Marunouchi, 412 - Grand Hyatt, 414 - Grand Pacific Le Daiba, 416 - Hilton, 418 - Hyatt Regency, 420 - Imperial, 422 - Intercontinental Tokyo Bay, 424 - Keio Plaza, 426 - Mandarin Oriental, 428 - Marunouchi, 430 - Meguro Gajoen, 432 - Mitsui Garden Ginza, 434 - New Otani, 436 - Nikko, 438 - Okura, 440 - Park Hyatt, 442 - Royal Park, 444 - Royal Park Shiodome Tower, 446 - Seiyo Ginza, 448 - The Agnes, 450 - The Peninsula, 452 - The Prince Park Tower, 454 - The Ritz-Carlton, 456 - The Strings by Intercontinental, 458 - Westin, 460

**Manufacture française des pneumatiques Micheli**
**Société en commandite par actions au capital de 304 000 000 EUR**
**Place des Carmes-Déchaux – 63000 Clermont-Ferrand (France)**
**R.C.S. Clermont-Fd B 855 200 507**


Dépot légal Novembre 2008

Made in Japan

Published in 2008



E-mail: nmt.michelinguide@jp.michelin.com
Maps: 2008 Cartographic data Shobunsha / Michelin
Publication design: Akita Design Kan Inc.

Pre-Press: Nord Compo, Villeneuve-d'Ascq, France
Printing and Binding: Toppan, Tokyo (Japan)